KFO
508
.H46

Hensley, Thomas R.

The Kent State
incident

The Kent State Incident

Recent Titles in
Contributions in Political Science
Series Editor: Bernard K. Johnpoll

The New Red Legions
Richard A. Gabriel

Contemporary Perspectives on European Integration: Attitudes, Non-governmental Behavior, and Collective Decision Making
Leon Hurwitz, editor

The Italian Communist Party: Yesterday, Today, and Tomorrow
Simon Serfaty and Lawrence Gray, editors

The Fiscal Congress: Legislative Control of the Budget
Lance T. Leloup

Iran, Saudi Arabia, and the Law of the Sea: Political Interaction and Legal Development in the Persian Gulf
Charles G. MacDonald

Improving Prosecution? The Inducement and Implementation of Innovations for Prosecution Management
David Leo Weimer

Creating the Entangling Alliance: The Origins of the North Atlantic Treaty Organization
Timothy P. Ireland

The State as Defendant: Governmental Accountability and the Redress of Individual Grievances
Leon Hurwitz

Ethnic Identities in a Transnational World
John F. Stack, Jr., editor

Reasoned Argument in Social Science: Linking Research to Policy
Eugene J. Meehan

The Right Opposition: The Lovestoneites and the International Communist Opposition of the 1930s
Robert J. Alexander

Quantification in the History of Political Thought: Toward a Qualitative Approach
Robert Schware

The Kent State Incident
IMPACT OF JUDICIAL PROCESS ON PUBLIC ATTITUDES

Thomas R. Hensley

WITH JAMES J. BEST,
JAMES L. KOTSCHWAR,
MARLYN G. HELLER,
AND JUDITH W. REID

CONTRIBUTIONS IN POLITICAL SCIENCE,
NUMBER 56

GREENWOOD PRESS
WESTPORT, CONNECTICUT · LONDON, ENGLAND

Library of Congress Cataloging in Publication Data

Hensley, Thomas R.
    The Kent State incident.

    (Contributions in political science; no. 56
ISSN 0147-1066)
    Bibliography: p.
    Includes index.
    1. Justice, Administration of—Ohio—Public opinion.
2. Judicial process—Ohio—Public opinion. 3. Ohio.
State University, Kent—Students—Attitudes. 4. Ohio.
State University, Kent—Riot, May 4, 1970. 5. Public
opinion—Ohio. I. Title. II. Series.
KFO508.H46   347.771'077   80-1712
ISBN 0-313-21220-1 (lib. bdg.)

Library of Congress Catalog Card Number: 80-1712
ISBN: 0-313-21220-1
ISSN: 0147-1066

First published in 1981

Greenwood Press
A division of Congressional Information Service, Inc.
88 Post Road West, Westport, Connecticut 06881

Printed in the United States of America

10 9 8 7 6 5 4 3 2 1

Contents

Figures

Tables

Acknowledgments

The genesis of this book can be traced to a conversation between myself and a graduate student, James Kotschwar, in the late fall of 1973, when Mr. Kotschwar expressed interest in undertaking an individualized research project in the field of judicial politics. Shortly after this conversation, the U.S. Attorney General's Office announced that it would be convening a federal grand jury investigation into the May 4, 1970 shootings at Kent State University. I suggested to Mr. Kotschwar that it would be interesting to study the impact of the grand jury's decision on the attitudes of Kent State students. A faculty colleague, James Best, joined us in creating the research design and the questionnaires for the project as well as in gathering the data. Mr. Kotschwar subsequently produced a master's thesis on the subject. In 1975 another major judicial activity related to the May 4 shootings occurred when a federal civil trial was held. Another master's degree student, Marlyn Heller, became involved in analyzing the impact of this trial on Kent State students' attitudes and subsequently wrote her thesis on an aspect of this issue. The final episode in the May 4 trials occurred in late 1978 and early 1979 when a retrial of the 1975 federal civil trial occurred. A third master's degree candidate, Judith Reid, became involved at this stage and is currently completing her thesis. Each individual shares authorship in this book, for without their efforts it could not have been completed. Professor Best's contributions deserve special mention. He had primary responsibility for questionnaire construction and authored the chapter on the May 4 shootings.

Many other individuals need to be recognized for their contributions to the book. Steven Brown, a colleague in the Political Science Department, has been exceptionally helpful. He introduced me to the experimental design/analysis of variance approach used in the book, and he provided me with many helpful insights during the data analysis stage of the research. Another colleague, Jerry M. Lewis of the Sociology Department, worked with me for several years, making our joint teaching and research both challenging and fun. Two members of the Psychology Department, Donald Elman and Lawrence Melamed, provided helpful comments on portions of the manuscript. Richard Taylor, Chairman of the Political Science Department, provided many types of support for the project. Stephen Wasby of the State University of New York at Albany made important contributions to the book, both because his research provided the early theoretical foundations for the study and because he read early portions of the manuscript. Janice Toth helped me master some of the mysteries of the computer programming required by the data analysis. Two of my graduate assistants, Lisa Handley and Barb Poole, did a substantial amount of work in preparing the data for the study. Much of the manuscript was typed by Sherry Scullin. Another graduate assistant, Lynn Plannick, prepared the index.

A special note of appreciation must be given to the Kendall/Hunt Publishing Company of Dubuque, Iowa for granting permission to use portions of *Kent State and May 4th: A Social Science Perspective*, edited by Thomas R. Hensley and Jerry M. Lewis, published in 1978. Portions of chapter 4 have also been published in "The Impact of Judicial Decisions on Attitudes of an Attentive Public: The Kent State Trials," by Thomas Hensley in *Sociological Focus* 13, 3 (August 1980): 273–92 and are used with the permission of the editors.

Finally, my wife Janie and sons Paul and Bradley have my deep appreciation and love, not only for tolerating long periods of my absence but also for making my life so pleasant during the writing of this book—and every day.

The Kent State Incident

1
Introduction

What impact do judicial decisions have upon attitudes? The norms of American society maintain that courts are legitimate, authoritative institutions for conflict resolution in American society, and therefore citizens should accept the decisions of the courts and adjust their behavior to these decisions. This does not always seem to occur, however. Strong criticism is frequently aroused by controversial court decisions. This criticism can involve not only opposition to the substance of a court's decision but also attacks on the court itself. Does this mean that courts cannot change deeply held attitudes, and that they risk the loss of substantial support in controversial cases? Unfortunately we do not know a great deal about these types of questions. "Does law change attitudes? Are attitudes the necessary catalyst for behavioral compliance? These are questions that have only recently been the subject of systematic inquiry and the results are far from in."[1]

The legal aftermath of the May 4, 1970 shootings at Kent State University has provided us with a unique opportunity to examine the question of the impact of the decisions of legal structures upon attitudes. Focusing upon the 1974 federal grand jury investigation, the 1975 federal civil trial and the 1978–1979 retrial of the 1975 civil case, we will examine attitudes of Kent State University students both before and after each legal decision to determine their effects on student attitudes. Utilizing cognitive consistency theory from the field of social psychology, our primary focus will be upon the impact of the decisions from the respective legal structures on attitudes regarding responsibility for the shootings, support for the relevant legal structures, and support for the American legal system.

3

THE AFTERMATH OF MAY FOURTH

The words "Kent State" hold a singular meaning in the minds of most Americans. A large but relatively unknown university in northeast Ohio gained instant worldwide attention during a thirteen second span on May 4, 1970 when Ohio National Guardsmen killed four Kent State University students and wounded nine others. From that moment in history Kent State was to be thought of not only as an institution of higher education but also as the place where the agony of a country divided over the Vietnam War crystallized in a manner that left the entire country shocked and embittered.

The tragedy of May 4 gave rise to a plethora of questions ranging from broad philosophical inquiries about the nature of American society to specific questions about the events of May 4 on the Kent State campus. It is these latter, more specific questions which aroused the greatest passions in the immediate aftermath of the shootings, and it is these questions which continue to command attention, despite years of exhaustive investigation. Should the National Guard have been sent to the campus? Were revolutionary elements behind the disturbances in the city of Kent and on the Kent State campus? Did federal agent provocateurs contribute to these disturbances? Why did university officials have so little control over events on the campus? Did the guardsmen conspire to shoot the students? Were the protesters threatening the lives of the guardsmen? The overreaching question, however, has been: who was responsible for the shootings? A brief survey of the long aftermath of the shootings can provide not only an overview of the attempts to answer these questions but also the background for setting forth the specific research concerns of this study.

Reaction to the tragedy was immediate and widespread, and the vitriolic public response revealed clearly the intensity of the generational and ideological polarization over the shootings. It was not uncommon to hear or read the opinion that the students got just what they deserved and that it was too bad that more of them didn't get it too. At a polar extreme, students issued warnings that next time the guardsmen wouldn't be the only ones with guns. Systematic public opinion polls taken shortly after the shootings provided further evidence of the sharp divisions of opinion over responsibility for the shootings, reflective of the deep cleavages among generational and ideological groupings in American society.

In light of the enormous public attention given to the shootings and the sharp divisions among the American people, governmental investigations were instituted in the immediate aftermath of the shootings to determine exactly what had happened on the Kent State campus and why. The most significant investigations were conducted by the Federal Bureau of Investigation, the President's Commission on Campus Unrest (Scranton Commission), and the Ohio Highway Patrol.[2] While only the Scranton Commission report has been made fully available to the public, it is clear that the governmental investigatory bodies reached remarkably different conclusions concerning responsibility for the killings. While the Scranton Commission concluded that the killings were "unnecessary, unwarranted, and inexcusable,"[3] and the FBI report led the Justice Department to consider the prosecution of at least six guardsmen,[4] the Ohio Highway Patrol's investigation was reported to have identified several hundred protesters as possible grand jury indictees.[5] The conflicting nature of these official reports reduced the credibility of each report, and people could simply choose the interpretation which coincided most closely with their personal assessment of the events.

Answers to the questions of what happened and why were next taken up by a host of authors, some of whom had done a great deal of research and some of whom had little more than a desire to express their views.[6] These efforts proved no more successful than earlier attempts to find a definitive accounting of the shootings. It is unquestionably true that James Michener's book *Kent State: What Happened and Why* received the widest attention and circulation,[7] but Michener's book was sharply criticized by many,[8] and his position of basic support for the established authorities was directly challenged by Peter Davies' *The Truth About Kent State: A Challenge to the American Conscience*[9] and I. F. Stone's *The Killings at Kent State University: How Murder Went Unpunished.*[10] Once again, attempts to unravel the complexities of May 4 and to assess responsibility for the shootings resulted in dramatically divergent accountings, and it seems likely that these conflicting interpretations served to reinforce existing attitudes, for a person could choose the author whose views most closely coincided with his own.

This series of developments made it clear that hope for achieving definitive answers to the Kent State tragedy resided in only one source—the judicial system. Indeed, this avenue of inquiry and redress was considered in the immediate aftermath of the shootings by all sides, and the litigative activities were initiated within a few months of the tragedy in an attempt to establish the facts surrounding the shootings, to assess responsibility, to impose punishment on those responsible, and, more generally, to see justice realized. From the outset, however, polarization dominated the litigative maneuverings. Local and state officials, responding to demands by the general public, sought to activate the Ohio court system, seemingly confident that Ohio courts would find radical youths and perhaps radical professors responsible for the events of May 4. In sharp contrast, most students and those older adults sympathetic to the students' causes believed that the Ohio courts would make a mockery of justice, and they began to focus their attention on the federal judiciary where they felt an impartial search for justice was much more likely to occur.

The litigative activities in the Ohio courts, stretching over a period of eighteen months, seemed to have had the primary effect of confirming peoples' previous viewpoints, for nothing was resolved and all sides could claim some measure of satisfaction. The initial judicial body to consider evidence was the Special State Grand Jury convened in Portage County, Ohio, the location of Kent State University. The grand jury on October 16, 1970 issued indictments against twenty-five persons, primarily Kent State students, and also issued a blistering report placing responsibility on students, faculty, and especially the university's administration. The report was ordered expunged by a federal district court judge several months later, however, on the grounds that it was prejudicial to the defendants' rights, and in the subsequent trial in September of 1971 the state's case broke down almost immediately, resulting in the state dropping charges against nearly all the defendants for lack of evidence.

These developments gave strong impetus to the supporters of the wounded students and the parents of the dead students, for the failure of the state of Ohio to press successfully a criminal case provided added stimulus to the efforts already underway to mount both criminal and civil cases at the federal level. These efforts were, however, to meet with years of futility.

At the criminal level, a sustained drive was launched to pressure the federal government to initiate a grand jury investigation. Despite enormous pressures, Attorney General John Mitchell announced on August 13, 1971 that there would be no federal grand jury convened. This announcement did not end the pressures on the Justice Department, and finally in August of 1973, recently-appointed Attorney General Elliot Richardson ordered the Kent State case reopened. A four month review by the Justice Department resulted, in December of 1973, in the convening of a federal grand jury, whose investigation was one of the most complicated and widely publicized in American history. On March 29, 1974 the grand jury returned indictments against eight persons who were members of the Ohio National Guard in May of 1970. As with the state grand jury, the federal indictments did not lead to convictions, for on November 9, 1974 Federal District Court Judge Frank Battisti dismissed the charges against all the guardsmen on the grounds that the government had failed to prove its case beyond a reasonable doubt.

With the possibility of criminal prosecution being foreclosed, the focus of attention then shifted to federal civil litigation where four years of struggle had led to a U.S. Supreme Court decision on April 17, 1974 stating that the doctrine of sovereign immunity was not absolute and that the parents and students could sue Ohio officials in their individual capacities. This cleared the way for a federal civil trial, which began in May of 1975. The trial was viewed with great hope by the students and parents, who had struggled for five years to get their "day in court," but these hopes were shattered when on August 27, 1975 the jury returned its verdict against the plaintiffs, deciding that none of the defendants were liable for damages.

An appeal was filed by lawyers for the students and parents in the U.S. Sixth Circuit Court of Appeals in Cincinnati, and in September of 1977 the three judge panel ruled that a new trial had to be held because of the 1975 trial judge's improper handling of a threat to a juror. The retrial began in December of 1978, but on January 4 an out-of-court settlement was reached. The parents and students received $675,000 from the state of Ohio, and each of the defendants signed a statement of regret about the shootings.

THE RESEARCH QUESTIONS

The decisions resulting from the 1974 federal grand jury investigation, the 1975 federal district court trial, and the 1979 retrial provide the setting for the basic research thrust of this study: do authoritative judicial outputs affect attitudes?[11] Focusing upon an attentive public[12]—Kent State University students—we seek through the use of mailed, panel questionnaires[13] to analyze if the judicial decisions produced attitude changes in regard to perceptions of responsibility for the shootings, support for the respective legal structures, and support for the American legal system. The common sense foundation for these questions stems from a juxtaposition between, on the one hand, the authoritative position of the federal grand jury and federal district court in the American legal system and, on the other hand, the deeply held views of so many concerning the shootings. What is the reaction of those persons whose views concerning responsibility for the shootings are rejected by authoritative decisions coming from the legal system? Will they alter their views to conform to the decisions, or will they reject the decisions and maintain their previous views? This leads to a second line of questioning. What effect will the judicial decisions and individual's reactions to the decisions have upon attitudes toward the respective legal institutions? For example, if the decision goes against the individual's previous view, will his attitude toward the legal structure become less favorable? The final concern is what effect there will be upon an individual's support for the entire legal system. Are these attitudes firmly based, or can they be affected by decisions in particular cases; for example, if a person disagrees with a decision of the federal court will he/she not only have less favorable opinions about the federal court, but also have less faith in the judicial system?

THEORETICAL FOUNDATIONS: THE JUDICIAL IMPACT LITERATURE

The theoretical foundations of the study are closely tied to the existing body of literature on judicial impact,[14] and hence a review of this literature is necessary not only to establish the theoretical bases of the research but also to specify precisely the original contributions of the study. The study of judicial impact has become a major research area in the field of judicial politics, paralleling the general emphasis upon policy analysis in other fields of political science. The attention which the impact of judicial output has received is of relatively recent vintage, for the effects of judicial decisions were largely neglected until the famous *Brown* decision of 1954.[15] Prior to *Brown,* political scientists seem to have generally assumed that compliance with court decisions was fairly automatic, but the aftermath of *Brown* revealed quite clearly that the Supreme Court's decisions could be met with evasion and even outright defiance. Considerable attention was given to the *Brown* case and closely related civil rights cases during the 1950s and 1960s, and two other large and important series of studies arose during the 1960s as a result of Supreme Court decisions in the areas of school prayer and criminal procedures.[16] The growth of this area of research coalesced with a broader movement within the discipline of political science toward focusing upon policy analysis.[17] The result was the production of three major books by Theodore Becker, Stephen Wasby, and Samuel Krislov and associates[18] that cumulatively served to define this major new area of judicial research, to bring together in various organizational frameworks the wide variety of heretofore disparate studies, to specify both the achievements and shortcomings of the state of knowledge in this field, and to set forth the research frontiers which most needed exploration. These studies have in turn been at least partially responsible for an impressive amount of research in the 1970s.[19]

Despite the substantial number of impact studies, it is widely recognized that many important limitations characterize this body of literature. One commonly cited limitation is the focus on the United States Supreme Court and its activities, an emphasis which is necessary but is not sufficient if a broad understanding of judicial impact is to be achieved.[20] A second problem involves the limited range of cases and issues which have been studied, for primary focus has been given to racial equality, criminal procedure, and school prayer cases in which noncompliance has tended to be more pronounced.[21] A third criticism heard frequently is methodological in nature, involving the overwhelming preponderance of "after-the-fact" studies in which effect is very difficult to determine because of the absence of comparative assessments of conditions both before and after the judicial decision.[22] The shortcoming which has been cited most frequently, however, is the paucity of theory, for most studies have been basically descriptive and the explanatory research has generally not been based upon any well-developed conceptual framework.[23]

While this study addresses each of these limitations in the literature, the primary thrust is directed toward theoretical concerns. The paucity of theoretical development in the judicial impact field was noted by Wasby in 1970, who attempted to address the problem by developing and categorizing a wide variety of hypotheses from his extensive survey of the impact literature.[24] While these hypotheses certainly did not constitute a theory, Wasby hoped that they might provide a starting point from which a broad theory of judicial impact might emerge. Developments since the publication of Wasby's book have taken a variety of directions. Some scholars have followed Wasby's lead by identifying specific variables which seem to be of significance in describing and explaining judicial impact.[25] At a somewhat more general level, several scholars have borrowed theoretical formulations from other disciplines or other fields of political science to provide middle range conceptual frameworks. Predating Wasby's work, Richard Johnson utilized concepts from communications theory in his 1967 book on reactions to the *Schempp* case,[26] and William Muir employed cognitive dissonance theory in his study of the impact of *Schempp*.[27] More recently, Robert Stover and Don Brown have applied utility theory,[28] Lawrence Baum has advanced an implementation model for studying judicial impact,[29] and Wasby has further developed communications theory.[30] Finally, others have suggested broad conceptual frameworks for organizing impact studies and suggesting avenues of inquiry which could lead to comparable research activities that could have a cummulative effect over time. Sheldon Goldman and the late Thomas Jahnige have placed impact studies within the broad framework of systems analysis,[31] and Charles Johnson has developed a broad conceptual framework which is also based upon systems analysis and which provides specificity by identifying four populations which can be affected by judicial decisions while also identifying concepts which tap the various forms of impact upon these populations.[32]

Although scholars differ with regard to which theoretical thrust holds the most promise, it is widely acknowledged that efforts are needed to test each of these frameworks because of the paucity of existing empirical studies which do so. Several scholars have identified cognitive consistency theory[33] as an especially promising theoretical area,[34] and it is this theoretical perspective which we will utilize in this study. Certainly the outstanding work utilizing this approach is Muir's 1967 study of the effect of the 1963 *Schempp* decision on twenty-eight educators who were interviewed before and after the decision concerning their attitudes on schoolhouse religion. Despite the warm reception which this book received and calls for further utilization of cognitive consistency theory, only a few additional judicial impact studies have utilized consistency theory and these have not examined attitude change based upon before-and-after data.[35] The lack of testing of consistency theory is all the more surprising in light of its substantial applications in other areas of political science. [36]

THEORETICAL FOUNDATIONS: THE COGNITIVE CONSISTENCY APPROACH TO ATTITUDE CHANGE[37]

The consistency approach to attitude change,[38] which has received the overwhelming amount of research attention from social psychologists,[39] is based upon an assumption that when a person's attitude toward some object, subject, or event comes into conflict with some other attitude or attitudes that he holds, a condition of dissonance emerges which must somehow be reduced because of the psychologically uncomfortable feeling which exists. The reduction of this dissonance and restoration of balance or consistency may come about through the changing of one's attitudes.

Cognitive consistency theory is built around two basic stages: dissonance arousal and dissonance reduction. It is easiest to understand the dissonance arousal stage through the use of some simple diagrams, which are represented in Figure 4.1, page 137. Although the diagrams are oversimplified, they nonetheless represent the basic situation in which an individual could find himself during the dissonance arousal stage, that is, immediately following the decision by a legal structure concerning a matter of significance to the individual. The first diagram shows a situation in which no dissonance should be created; the individual views the legal structure positively, and the legal structure has issued a decision which is similar to his own viewpoint. For the person, then, his attitudes are in balance or consistent because the legal structure has decided as he wished. The fourth diagram is also one of consistency or balance because the individual feels negatively toward the legal structure and holds a belief at variance with the decision of the legal institution; no conflict in attitudes is raised by the legal structure's decision because the individual would not expect the structure to make the "correct" decision. In the second situation, however, a condition of dissonance is created because the individual has a negative view of the legal structure yet it has made a decision consistent with his attitude toward the legal issue. The third situation is the opposite of the second and also represents a condition of dissonance, for the individual has a positive view of the judicial structure but finds that the decision of the structure conflicts with his attitude concerning the issue. By comparing individual attitudes toward the legal structures and toward the respective legal issues involved before the authoritative decisions are made, we can thus determine who would presumably experience dissonance.

The second stage in consistency theory involves dissonance reduction, for the assumption is that it is psychologically unpleasant to hold conflicting attitudes and that somehow the condition of conflict or dissonance must be eliminated or at least reduced. Dissonance reduction can be achieved through a variety of processes: changing the importance of relevant cognitions or an entire set of cognitions, selective recall of dissonant information, denial of commitment, perceptual distortion, selective exposure to dissonant information, changing behaviors that produce dissonant cognitions, and changing the dissonance-producing attitude.[40] It is the last alternative—the change of a dissonant producing attitude—which is of primary interest in this study. In terms of Figure 4.1, we postulate that Kent State students will engage in dissonance reduction through changing either their attitude about responsibility for the shootings or their attitude toward the particular legal structure. Which attitude seems most likely to change? The cognitive consistency approach cannot provide us with a definitive answer to this question, but the literature does provide a basis for setting forth a working hypothesis: "the general rule for determining the mode of dissonance reduction is that of least effort; that is, the cognition least resistent to change will be changed."[41]

To this point in our discussion of cognitive consistency theory, we have been focusing upon individual's attitudes toward specific legal structures. People also have attitudes toward the entire legal system, however, and consistency theory also allows us to examine attitude change by Kent State students in regard to the American legal system. In terms of the diagrams in Figure 4.1, it is simply a matter of substituting "American legal system" for "legal structure." The basic research question we pose is this: if individuals experience dissonance because of conflicting attitudes regarding responsibility for the shootings and support for the American legal system, do they resolve this dissonance by changing either their attitude about responsibility for the shootings or their attitude about the American legal system? It will be especially fascinating to examine attitude change toward the specific legal structures as compared with attitude change regarding the legal system.

It should be obvious that this study will contribute to the theoretical literature on judicial politics in one additional area which we have not yet identified, research on the concept of support. Support for specific courts and the American legal system has been a subject which has attracted considerable scholarly attention.[42] Despite the rather abundant literature, however, research on the impact of authoritative output on support is limited indeed,[43] and several scholars have identified this as an important research concern.[44] This study makes unique contributions to the support literature in two major ways: it is based upon before-and-after data, assessing directly change in support levels related to specific legal decisions,[45] and it allows for direct comparison of the effects of legal decisions upon two types of support, specific support for particular legal structures and diffuse support for the American legal system.

POLICY IMPLICATIONS

The primary thrust of this study is in the theoretical directions which have just been identified. The results of the analysis should also have some interesting policy implications, however. The most obvious of these involves jury selection in well-publicized, controversial cases. If our findings reveal that authoritative decisions by legal structures do not change people's attitudes regarding the substantive issues of a case, then serious questions are raised about selecting an impartial jury in such cases. It was this very concern which led Sanford Rosen, chief attorney for the wounded students and parents of the slain students in the 1978–1979 civil retrial, to ask us to submit to Judge William K. Thomas an affidavit based upon the results of our earlier analyses of the 1974 federal grand jury decision and the 1975 federal civil trial jury decision.[46] While we do not know what effect our affidavit had upon Judge Thomas, he did accept the plaintiffs' lawyers arguments that selecting an impartial jury would be very difficult, and a novel method of jury selection was utilized in the 1978–1979 case.[47] Another policy-relevant aspect of our analysis deals with the question of public acceptance of out-of-court settlements as opposed to decisions reached after a full trial. Our data are unique in the history of judicial process research, for circumstances presented us with the opportunity to gather before-and-after data in a quasi-experimental situation where the same case was resolved in two entirely different manners. Is public acceptance of a court's decision higher in an out-of-court settlement? Common sense suggests that acceptance and support should be higher because the ambiguity of a compromise solution of a dispute allows everyone to claim victory. If this is true, then an important argument is raised for seeking the out-of-court settlement of civil cases. A final policy concern which needs to be mentioned is the link between attitudes and behavior as they relate to compliance with court decisions. It is widely accepted that attitudes are an important determinant of behavior.[48] Frequently a judicial decision will conflict with the attitudes of persons directly or indirectly affected by the decision. Because the behavior of these persons may be important in terms of compliance with the decision, it is therefore important to understand how judicial decisions affect attitudes.[49] This study cannot, of course, make any direct links between attitudes and behavior, for no behavioral responses are involved for the students we are studying. The results of the data analysis will, however, provide insights into the first part of this attitude/behavior relationship.

ORGANIZATION OF THE BOOK

Having set forth the research questions of the study, the theoretical framework, and the policy implications, we conclude the introductory chapter by presenting an overview of the remaining chapters. Chapters two and three provide the setting for the book. Chapter two focuses upon the background to the disturbances on the Kent State campus and the events of May 1–4, while chapter three examines the litigative activities which arose in the aftermath of the shootings. While these chapters are presented primarily to give the necessary context for analyzing the data, they constitute the first comprehensive analysis of this major American drama.[50] Chapter four analyzes our data to determine if the attitudes of Kent State University students seem to have been affected by the outcomes of judicial decisions regarding responsibility for the May 4 shootings. This chapter sets forth a series of hypotheses based upon cognitive consistency theory as well as the literature on judicial support, and then uses analysis of variance to test these hypotheses. The fifth and concluding chapter offers a comparative analysis of the findings of the study, evaluates the utility of the theoretical framework, and discusses the policy implications of the research.

NOTES

1. Sheldon Goldman and Thomas P. Jahnige, *The Federal Courts as a Political System*, 2nd ed. (New York: Harper & Row, 1976), p. 263.

2. Many nongovernmental organizations also carried out investigations of the tragedy.

3. The President's Commission on Campus Unrest, *The Kent State Tragedy* (Washington, D.C.: U.S. Government Printing Office, 1970), p. 90.

4. *Akron Beacon Journal,* 20 May 1975, p. A1.

5. *Akron Beacon Journal,* 22 July 1970, p. A1.

6. Listed alphabetically, the books are: Ottavio Casale and Louis Paskoff, eds., *The Kent State Affair: Documents and Interpretations* (Boston: Houghton Mifflin, 1971); Peter Davies, *The Truth About Kent State: A Challenge to the American Conscience* (New York: Farrar, Straus & Giroux, 1973); Joe Eszterhas and Michael Roberts, *Thirteen Seconds: Confrontation at Kent State* (New York: Dodd, Mead, 1970); Edward Grant, *I Was There: What Really Went on at Kent State* (Lima, Oh.: C. S. S. Publishing Company, 1974); James Michener, *Kent State: What Happened and Why* (New York: Random House, 1971); Richard E. Peterson and John A. Bilorusky, *May*

1970: The Campus Aftermath of Cambodia and Kent State (Berkeley, Cal.: Carnegie Commission on Higher Education, 1971); Isidor F. Stone, *The Killings at Kent State University: How Murder Went Unpunished* (New York: A New York Review Book, 1971); Stuart Taylor et al., *Violence at Kent State, May 1 to 4, 1970: The Student's Perspective* (New York: College Notes and Texts, 1971); Phillip K. Tompkins and Elaine Vanden Bout Anderson, *Communication Crisis at Kent State: A Case Study* (New York: Gordon and Breach, 1971); and Bill Warren, *The Middle of the Country: The Events of May 4th as Seen by Students and Faculty at Kent State University* (New York: Avon, 1970). A recent book on the shootings draws together social science analyses of the events of May 4 and their aftermath: Thomas R. Hensley and Jerry M. Lewis, eds., *Kent State and May 4th: A Social Science Perspective* (Dubuque, Ia.: Kendall/Hunt, 1978). The latest book on the shootings is by Joseph Kelner and James Munves, *The Kent State Coverup* (New York: Harper and Row, 1980). Kelner was chief counsel for the wounded students and parents of the slain students in the 1975 federal civil trial.

   7. Michener, *Kent State: What Happened and Why.*

   8. For example, Joe Eszterhas and Michael Roberts, "James Michener's Kent State: A Study in Distortion," *The Progressive* 35 (September 1971): 35–40.

   9. Davies, *The Truth About Kent State.*

   10. Stone, *The Killings at Kent State University.*

   11. An attitude may be defined as "a relatively enduring way of thinking, feeling, and behaving toward an object, person, group, or idea." James V. McConnell, *Understanding Human Behavior* (New York: Holt, Rinehart & Winston, Inc.: 1974), p. 803.

   12. An attentive public refers to those people who have interest in and knowledge of the phenomena under study and therefore hold meaningful opinions but lack direct access to those who make the decisions. Cf. James Rosenau, *Public Opinion and Foreign Policy* (New York: Random House, 1961).

   13. The term panel is used here to indicate that questionnaires were sent to a random sample of the population before the respective decisions were reached, and then each person who responded to the before questionnaire was sent a second questionnaire after the decision.

   14. It is important to recognize that a grand jury decision is different than a regular judicial decision as the latter term is commonly used, for grand juries only determine if there is sufficient evidence to bring a person or persons to trial. The decisions of both grand juries and courts are authoritative outputs of a political system, however, and both types of legal structures can have significant impacts on the system's environment. Given these fundamental similarities, it seems appropriate to include the impact of grand juries' decisions within the rubric of judicial impact, recognizing the unique characteristics of this legal structure.

   15. It should be noted that political scientists had given close attention to the effects of judicial decisions in subsequent cases, frequently tracing the "lines" of particular areas of the law.

   16. A useful overview of these studies can be found in Stephen Wasby, *The Impact*

of the United States Supreme Court (Homewood, Ill.: Dorsey Press, 1970), pp. 169–85, 126–35, and 147–68, respectively.

17. See David Easton, "The New Revolution in Political Science," American Political Science Review 63 (December 1969): 1051–61.

18. Theodore Becker, ed., The Impact of Supreme Court Decisions (New York: Oxford University Press, 1969); Wasby, The Impact of the United States Supreme Court; and Samuel Krislov et al., eds., Compliance and the Law: A Multidisciplinary Approach (Beverly Hills: Sage Publishing Co., 1972).

19. Useful overviews of the field of judicial impact in addition to the three books mentioned in note 18 include: Theodore Becker and Malcolm Feeley, eds., The Impact of Supreme Court Decisions, 2nd ed. (New York: Oxford University Press, 1972); Stephen Wasby, "The Study of Supreme Court Impacts: A Round-up," Policy Studies Journal 2,2 (Winter 1973): 136–40; Charles H. Sheldon, The American Judicial Process: Models and Approaches (New York: Dodd, Mead and Co., 1974), chap. 5; Charles Johnson, "The Implementation and Impact of Judicial Policies: A Heuristic Model," in John A. Gardiner, ed.. Public Law and Public Policy (New York: Praeger, 1977), pp. 107–26; Stephen Wasby, The Supreme Court in the Federal Judicial System (New York: Holt, Rinehart & Winston, 1978), pp. 215–41; Sheldon Goldman and Austin Sarat, eds., American Court Systems (San Francisco: W. H. Freeman and Co., 1978), pp. 523–648; and Walter F. Murphy and C. Herman Pritchett, eds., Courts, Judges, and Politics, 3rd ed. (New York: Random House, 1979), pp. 397–440.

20. See Sheldon, The American Judicial Process, p. 139 and William P. McLauchlan, American Legal Processes (New York: John Wiley and Sons, 1977), p. 186.

21. See Sheldon, The American Judicial Process, p. 140 and McLauchlan, American Legal Processes, pp. 185–86.

22. See Sheldon, The American Judicial Process, p. 139. Much more elaborate discussions are presented in Richard Lempert, "Strategies of Research Design in the Legal Impact Study: The Control of Plausible Rival Hypotheses," Law and Society Review 1 (November 1966): 111–32 and James P. Levine, "Methodological Concerns in Studying Judicial Efficacy," Law and Society Review 4 (1970): 583–611.

23. See the studies cited in note 19 above.

24. Wasby, The Impact of the United States Supreme Court, chap. 8.

25. For example, Harrell Rodgers, "Law as an Instrument of Public Policy," American Journal of Political Science 17, 3 (August 1973): 638–47; Sheldon, The American Judicial Process, pp. 201–02.

26. Richard Johnson, The Dynamics of Compliance: Supreme Court Decision-Making from a New Perspective (Evanston, Ill.: Northwestern University Press, 1967).

27. William Muir, Prayer in the Public Schools: Law and Attitude Change (Chicago: University of Chicago Press, 1967).

28. Robert V. Stover and Don Brown, "Understanding Compliance and Noncompliance with Law: The Contributions of Utility Theory," Social Science Quarterly 56 (1975): 363–75. See also Charles S. Bullock and Harrell Rodgers, Jr. "Coercion

to Compliance: Southern School Districts and School Desegregation Guidelines,"
Journal of Politics 38, 4 (November 1976): 987–1011; and Douglas S. Gatlin,
Michael W. Giles, and Everett F. Cataldo, "Policy Support Within a Target Group:
The Case of School Desegregation," *American Political Science Review* 72, 3 (September 1978): 985–95.

29. Lawrence Baum, "Implementation of Judicial Decisions: An Organizational
Analysis," *American Politics Quarterly* 4 (1976): 86–114.

30. Stephen Wasby, *Small Town Police and the Supreme Court: Hearing the
Word* (Lexington, Mass.: Lexington Books, 1976). See also Wasby, *The Supreme
Court in the Federal Judicial System*, pp. 217–26.

31. Goldman and Jahnige, *The Federal Courts as a Political System*, chap. 7; See
also Rodgers, "Law as an Instrument of Public Policy."

32. Johnson, "The Implementation and Impact of Judicial Policies."

33. Social psychologists speak of cognitive consistency as an "approach" to attitude change which encompasses several more specific theories, including Fritz
Heider's balance theory, Charles Osgood and Percy Tannenbaum's congruity theory,
and Leon Festinger's theory of cognitive dissonance. Despite differences among these
theories, there are strong commonalities among them, and we will be focusing upon
elements common to all of them. Useful overviews of these concepts and theories can
be found in Robert Zajonc, "The Concepts of Balance, Congruity, and Dissonance,"
Public Opinion Quarterly 24 (Summer 1960): 280–96 and John Sherwood, James
Barron, and H. Gordon Fitch, "Cognitive Dissonance: Theory and Research," in
Richard Wagner and John Sherwood, eds., *The Study of Attitude Change* (Belmont,
Cal.: Wadsworth Publishing Co., 1969), pp. 56–86. Cf. also Robert Abelson et al.,
eds., *Theories of Cognitive Consistency: A Sourcebook* (Chicago: Rand McNally,
1968) and Shel Feldman, *Cognitive Consistency* (New York: Academic Press, 1966).

34. Cf. Stephen Wasby, "The U.S. Supreme Court's Impact: Broadening Our
Focus," paper presented at the 1973 Annual Meeting of the International Political
Science Association; Johnson, "The Implementation and Impact of Judicial Policies,"
pp. 133–34; Sheldon, *The American Judicial Process*, pp. 160–63; and Krislow et
al., eds., *Compliance and the Law*, pp. 18–30.

35. Gregory Casey, "Popular Perceptions of Supreme Court Rulings," *American
Politics Quarterly* 4, 1 (January 1976): 3–46; Harrell Rodgers and Roger Hanson,
"The Rule of Law and Legal Efficacy: Private Values vs. General Standards," *Western
Political Quarterly* 27 (1974): 387–94; and Gatlin, Giles, and Cataldo, "Policy Support Within a Target Group."

36. An application of cognitive consistency theory which contains a good review of
earlier literature is Stephen Bennett, "Consistency Among the Public's Social Welfare
Policy Attitudes in the 1960's," *American Journal of Political Science* 17, 3 (August
1973): 544–70. An application of this theory in the field of international politics is
Randolph Siverson, "A Research Note on Cognitive Balance and International Conflict: Egypt and Israel in the Suez Crisis," *Western Political Quarterly*, 27, 2 (1974):
387–94. Cognitive consistency theory is discussed in detail in Jarol B. Manheim, *The
Politics Within: A Primer in Political Attitudes and Behavior* (Englewood Cliffs, N.J.:
Prentice-Hall, 1975), and a useful discussion of cognitive theory within the broader

context of the utility of social psychology for political science research is in Richard Merelman, "On Social Psychological Handy Work: An Interpretive Review of *The Handbook of Social Psychology,* Second Edition," *American Political Science Review* 71, 3 (September 1977): 1109–20. A recent use of consistency theory is found in David Sears, Carl P. Hensler, and Leslie K. Spear, "Whites' Opposition to 'Busing': Self-Interest or Symbolic Politics?" *American Political Science Review* 73, 2 (June 1979): 369–84.

37. The material presented in this section is drawn primarily from two sources: Manheim, *The Politics Within* and Wagner and Sherwood, eds., *The Study of Attitude Change.*

38. Social psychologists generally identify four distinctive approaches to attitude change: functional, learning, consistency, and social judgment/involvement. Discussions of the four general approaches can be found in Manheim, *The Politics Within,* pp. 72–90 and Wagner, "The Study of Attitude Change: An Introduction," in Wagner and Sherwood, eds., *The Study of Attitude Change,* pp. 1–18.

39. H. G. Fitch did a systematic search of the literature in 1967 and found nearly 400 studies dealing with dissonance theory: Fitch, "Dissonance Theory and Research: A Complete Bibliography," unpublished manuscript, Purdue University, 1967.

40. See Sherwood, Barron, and Fitch, "Cognitive Dissonance: Theory and Research," p. 70.

41. Ibid., p. 59.

42. The literature on judicial support is too extensive to cite in a single footnote. Some useful general sources include Goldman and Jahnige, *The Federal Courts as a Political System,* pp. 136–54 and Goldman and Sarat, eds., *American Court Systems,* pp. 155–201.

43. Several studies address this issue at least indirectly. See Muir, *Prayer in the Public Schools;* A. S. Miller and A. W. Scheflin, "The Power of the Supreme Court in the Age of the Positive State: A Preliminary Excursus," *Duke Law Journal* (April 1967): 273–320; R. Engstrom and M. Giles, "Expectations and Images: A Note on Diffuse Support for Legal Institutions," *Law and Society Review* 6, 4 (May 1972): 631–36; Walter Murphy, Joseph Tanenhaus, and Daniel Kastner, *Public Evaluations of Constitutional Courts: Alternative Explanations* (Beverley Hills: Sage Publications, 1973); Rodgers and Hanson, "The Rule of Law and Legal Efficacy: Private Values vs. General Standards," pp. 387–94; Harrell Rodgers and Edward Lewis, "Political Support and Compliance Attitudes," *American Politics Quarterly* 2 (1974): 61–77; Austin Sarat, "Support for the Legal System: An Analysis of Knowledge, Attitudes, and Behavior," *American Politics Quarterly,* 3 (1975): 3–24; Casey, "Popular Perceptions of Supreme Court Rulings," pp. 3–45; and Richard Lehne and John Reynolds, "The Impact of Judicial Activism on Public Opinion," *American Journal of Political Science* 22, 4 (November 1978): 896–904.

44. For example, Goldman and Jahnige, *The Federal Courts as a Political System,* p. 283 and Sheldon, *The American Judicial Process,* p. 191.

45. For an attempt at this in a hypothetical case, see Murphy, Tanenhaus, and Kastner, *Public Evaluations of Constitutional Courts,* p. 54.

46. "Causes and Consequences of Student Perceptions of Responsibility for the

1970 Kent State Shootings," *Heuristics* 8, 1 (Spring 1978): 30–52; "The Impact of the 1974 'Kent State Grand Jury' on Student Attitudes Toward Guard Responsibility and Judicial Support: An Application of Dissonance Theory," presented at the 1977 meeting of the Midwest Political Science Association (with Marlyn Heller); and "The Impact of the 1975 Kent State Civil Trial on Student Attitudes: An Application of Dissonance Theory," presented at the 1978 meeting of the Midwest Association for Public Opinion Research (with Marlyn Heller).

47. Judge William K. Thomas, "Jury Selection in the Highly Publicized Case," *Columbus Bar Association Journal* 35, 5 (May 1979): 3–4 ff.

48. This point is emphasized throughout Manheim's *The Politics Within: A Primer in Political Attitudes and Behavior*, especially pp. 4–7, 22–24, and 134. It is important to recognize, however, that people do not always act consistently with the attitudes they express or hold. The relationship between attitudes and behavior has generated an extensive literature, beginning at least as early as R. T. LaPiere's article on "Attitudes Versus Actions," *Social Forces* 13 (1934): 230–37. Recent scholarly debate on this issue has been summarized by Steven J. Gross and C. Michael Niman, "Attitude-Behavior Consistency: A Review," *Public Opinion Quarterly* 39, 3 (Fall 1975): 358–68.

49. While the judicial impact literature is very sparse on the relationships between attitudes and behavior, Austin Sarat has found a significant relationship between supportive attitudes and compliant behavior. See Sarat, "Support for the Legal System: An Analysis of Knowledge, Attitudes, and Behavior," pp. 3–24. No such relationship was found, however, by Rodgers and Lewis, "Political Support and Compliance Attitudes," pp. 61–77.

50. Earlier versions of chapters two and three appeared in Hensley and Lewis, eds., *Kent State and May 4th: A Social Science Perspective*. Several important developments have occurred since the Hensley and Lewis book has been published, especially the 1979 civil trial, and all of these new developments have been incorporated into the present work.

2

The Tragic Weekend of May 1 to 4, 1970*

In this chapter we present an historical narrative of the events of May 1–4, 1970 and an analysis of the context within which those events took place, a narrative which serves a number of purposes. For those unfamiliar with what happened in Kent, Ohio, during the period of May 1 to 4 the narrative provides a time-ordered description of the major actors and activities, making use of all the major published as well as many unpublished descriptions and analyses of the events, as well as testimony given by the participants during the 1975 civil suit trial. From these sources we reconstruct in sufficient detail the fateful events of those four days.

Since no action occurs in a vacuum it is important for us to present and analyze the social, historical, and political context within which the shootings took place. We concentrate our efforts on several factors which we consider important: the social context provided by the city of Kent, the historical context of demonstrations on the campus of Kent State University, and the political context provided by the statements and actions of President Nixon and Vice-President Agnew, as well as the Republican primary campaign of Governor James Rhodes.

*An earlier version of this chapter appeared in Thomas R. Hensley and Jerry M. Lewis, eds., *Kent State and May 4th: A Social Science Perspective* (Dubuque, Ia.: Kendall/Hunt Publishing Co., 1978), pp. 3–30. We gratefully acknowledge Kendall/Hunt's permission to use portions of the previous work. This chapter was written by James J. Best.

We have also asked a number of questions during the narrative: What factors led to the fatal confrontation between National Guardsmen and demonstrators on Monday, May 4? Why did Mayor Satrom call for the Ohio National Guard after only one night's disturbances? Why did city and university officials think that the National Guard had complete control of the campus on May 4? Why did Governor Rhodes make a speech on Sunday morning, May 3, which served to inflame the emotions of many who heard or read about it? Were radicals involved in the events of May 1–4? How did townspeople and students react to the shootings? What impact did the shootings have on the larger society in which they occurred?

In reconstructing these events we have had to choose which sources to use and, when sources conflicted, which sources to believe. Extensive use has been made of two major works—Michener's *Kent State: What Happened and Why*[1] and *The Report of the President's Commission on Campus Unrest*[2] (the Scranton Commission Report)—although each work has its defects. Michener's book suffers from his research methods and his political and educational biases; he selectively interviewed participants in the weekend's events and uncritically accepted what he was told. Politically, Michener believes in the democratic process and, while he understood the frustrations students felt when they learned of the U.S. invasion of Cambodia, he could not condone the damage to downtown businesses on May 1 or the burning of the ROTC building on May 2. Educationally, he has an obvious affection for Kent State University and its administration, particularly President Robert White, which colored his evaluation of White's role in the weekend's events. These criticisms notwithstanding, Michener has the uncanny ability to recreate the ambience of a situation, particularly Blanket Hill on the morning of May 4: you can almost smell the tear gas and see the tear gas-masked guardsmen striding up the hill.

The Scranton Commission Report is concerned with establishing for the public record what "really" happened. The quest to describe what happened is both the strength and weakness of this book; it stands as the most authoritative statement of what happened but it rarely explores inconsistencies between various participant's testimony, leaves unanswered a number of questions regarding the motivation of many participants, and is relatively unconcerned with the impact of the shootings on subsequent events.

A number of other reports were useful as well. The Knight newspaper report,[3] published less than three weeks after the shootings, is important because the reporters interviewed many of the participants, particularly guardsmen, shortly after the shootings. The decision to focus on the events of May 4, however, leaves unanswered a number of questions regarding events earlier in the weekend. Nonetheless, "The fact that the *Journal* got this report out so rapidly and with relatively few serious errors set the tone for facts that govern the remainder of the studies."[4] The report subsequently won a Pulitzer Prize.

The Joe Eszterhas and Michael Roberts' book on Kent State[5] is a journalistic quickie, published after the Knight newspaper report but before the Scranton Commission report and the Michener book. It is replete with inaccuracies, and the authors rarely cite the sources of their information.

Peter Davies' *The Truth About Kent State*[6] argues, primarily through an analysis of photographs of the shootings and testimony before the Scranton Commission, that the shootings were the result of a conspiracy on the part of certain guardsmen. Readers of this work should remember that it was written in an attempt to convince the Justice Department to convene a federal grand jury to investigate the shootings.

Another conspiracy theory is advanced by Charles Thomas in "The Kent State Massacre: Blood on Whose Hands?"[7] For Thomas the guardsmen and students were merely pawns in a larger game being played by the Nixon administration; Kent State was a demonstration of Nixon's get-tough policy toward student dissent, and after the shootings President Nixon and John Mitchell consciously attempted to cover-up the administration's role in the fateful events. Thomas's allegations are at variance with other research on the subject and many are unsubstantiated: he reconstructs conspiratorial conversation by guardsmen on May 4 which have never been verified by anyone else. His research is based, however, on materials to which he had access as an archivist working in the National Archives, material generally not available to other researchers. As a result his analysis and conclusions may be correct but are impossible to corroborate independently.

The Phillip Tompkins and Elaine Anderson,[8] and Stuart Taylor et al.[9] books are based on research conducted by Kent State faculty and students shortly after the shootings. The former focuses on communication failures within the administration and between administrators and students as they contribute to the events of May 1 to 4. Taylor and his colleagues focus on KSU student perceptions of the events, and their survey research data represent our best knowledge of the phenomenon.

Only two works have been written which present the perspective of the guardsmen. Ed Grant and Mike Hill's book,[10] although factually incorrect on occasion and leaving time gaps, does provide some insight as to what guardsmen were thinking on Saturday and Sunday night. William Furlong's piece in the *New York Times Magazine*[11] also provides some insight as to why guardsmen turned and fired on the demonstrators.

Three unpublished sources have been useful as well. The Justice Department Summary of the FBI Report was entered by Congressman John Seiberling in the Congressional Record.[12] Volume IV of the *Report of the Commission on KSU Violence*[13] (the Minority Report) represents an attempt by a group of KSU faculty and students to write a history of the events; division within the committee is reflected in the fact that the volume is called the "Minority Report," although a "majority" report has never been published. The Minority Report's principal weakness stems from its attempt to prove that radicals and outside agitators were responsible for the shootings. The report is valuable because it includes a great deal of information from people who did not testify before the Scranton Commission or talk to Michener and his researchers. The third source has been the transcript of the 1975 civil suit trial,[14] in which the major participants testified. Unfortunately, the plaintiff's case was poorly handled (for reasons which will be discussed in the next chapter) and potentially illuminating questions were rarely asked.

These materials constitute the primary data sources for our description of the events of the period. They have been supplemented by a body of research by social scientists at Kent State who have focused on one or more aspects of the events and which have been brought together in *Kent State and May 4th: A Social Science Perspective,*[15] edited by Thomas R. Hensley and Jerry M. Lewis. This volume contains an analysis of the events of May 1 to 4, 1970 and its legal aftermath, empirical and theoretical research by Lewis (several pieces in conjunction with various colleagues) and Steven Brown, and analyses of the 1977 controversy over a gym annex which impinged on the site of the shootings.

Our primary job in this chapter will be to compare and contrast these sources so that we might construct as accurately as possible an historical narrative of events. From this narrative we have asked and sought answers to a number of questions which we feel are of primary importance. We have not asked all the questions possible nor have we answered all the questions we have asked.

THE SOCIAL, POLITICAL, AND HISTORICAL CONTEXT

Kent, Ohio is a small city located approximately thirty miles south of Cleveland and ten miles east of Akron, an intrinsic part of the industrial heartland of northeastern Ohio which is so heavily dependent on the steel of Youngstown, the rubber of Akron, and the manufacturing and commerce of Cleveland. Kent was first settled in 1805 and the water power of the Cuyahoga River made industrial development attractive and inevitable. Later, the construction of the railroad through Kent insured that local manufacturers would have access to markets and that freight trains would daily tie up traffic in the center of the town. In 1910, after substantial lobbying, the state legislature agreed to create a state normal school in Kent on fifty-four acres of land donated by W. S. Kent; the purpose of the school was to train elementary school teachers but its early leaders had greater ambitions. The first students were admitted in 1913, and the school achieved the status of a four year college in 1929 and university status in 1938.[16]

As the university grew so did the town. In 1913 the normal school enrolled forty-seven students, while the town had a population of approximately 5,000; by 1970 the university had grown in enrollment to over 21,000 while the town (now a city) had a population of 28,000. Much of the growth for both the city and university had occurred in the twenty-five years between the end of World War II and 1970. By 1970 the city had developed into the largest population center in Portage County and the university had become the second largest in the state and one of the twenty-five largest in the United States. The size of the university insured that it would be the dominant industry in the city as well as the county. In the early 1970s KSU employed over 2,500 people and had an annual payroll in excess of $20 million and a budget of over $50 million.

There are three Kents—the downtown area, the residential areas, and the university. Downtown Kent, centered around the intersection of state routes 43 and 59, is unlike the center of most college towns. Aside from the two banks, two drug stores, two movie theaters, the post office, and a grocery store that you expect in a college town, there are no art galleries, boutiques, men's specialty shops, or good restaurants. Michener describes downtown Kent in these terms:

Route 59, which runs east and west, is a tacky, grubby thoroughfare onto which all the ugliest enterprises of Kent have been piled. . . .

But the apex of this ugliness comes on North Water Street in the center of town, for here are collected all the sleazy bars frequented by the university students.[17]

The downtown area is a continual point of friction between university students and merchants. Students dislike shopping in an area where they have little choice and where they feel prices are inflated, while the merchants feel that students don't provide enough business to compensate for the trouble involved—checks that bounce and beer bottles littering the streets after a long weekend. After 9:00 P.M. the only lights in downtown Kent are those in the movie theater marquee and the bars on North Water.

If you travel a block or two from routes 43 and 59, you find another more attractive Kent. The residential areas are spacious, tree-lined, and generally middle-class. Neighborhoods are mixed. Clusters of modern, tract-built houses, as well as older, restored or restorable frame homes share maple and oak-shaded streets, highlighting Kent's reputation as "the Tree City." The residential areas provide homes for many of the university faculty and staff, people who work in nearby cities and towns but prefer the amenities of a university locale, and those who provide services for the university.

Students who live in Kent tend to live in apartments on the edge of the city or in subdivided older homes close to the campus. The people who live in Kent are predominately white (96.7 percent) and native-born (88.8 percent), well-educated (30.4 percent have at least a college education), and most work in Kent. The median family income for 1970 was $10,886, with only 5.7 percent of the families having incomes below the poverty level.[18] Behind the tacky facade of the downtown area live middle and upper-middle class people, proud of themselves and their homes.

Kent State University is the third Kent—a city within a city, located in, but not part of, the city which surrounds it. The yellow stone buildings which initially composed the normal school, college, and then the fledgling university, are clustered on Hilltop Drive, where they formed the heart of the early campus. More recently, the university has had to build new dormitories and classrooms to house, feed, and teach the thousands of new students who swelled the university during the late 1950s and 1960s. From its original fifty-four acre grant the university had grown by 1970 to more than 600 acres. President White, KSU's president during the 1960s, viewed the period in these terms: "With the tremendous growth after World War II and the results of this baby boom hitting us in the 1960's, we had to find buildings to put the students in and professors to teach them. Our primary obligation was to keep the place running."[19]

Because of its rapid growth Kent State in the late 1960s was described by students and faculty as "the largest unknown university in the United States."[20] Students tended to be first generation college students, the sons and daughters of working class parents who saw college as a way for their children to advance themselves. But on weekends and during vacations those same parents began to realize that their children were changing, were different, were no longer the same. Robert O'Neill, John Morris, and Raymond Mack suggest that, as a result, parents began to see Kent State "as the institution that takes their children away, changes their values, expands their horizons, and thus drastically realigns family and social relationships. Kent graduates will probably never join their fathers and uncles making tires in Akron, steel in Cleveland, or heavy machinery in Elyria."[21]

Although Kent State may have broadened the lives and minds of

its students it did not make many of them radicals, or even very
liberal.[22] According to Michener the first Vietnam war protest on
campus took place in 1965 and drew thirteen people.[23]

In the late 1960s, however, student activism began to increase at
Kent State as it did at other universities. On November 13, 1968 the
Black United Students (BUS) and the Kent Students for a Democratic Society (SDS) staged a protest against the appearance on
campus of recruiters from the Oakland, California police department.
When the university announced that it planned disciplinary action
under the student code against the protestors, the black community
threatened to withdraw from school unless all protestors were given
amnesty. Two days later, President White, citing a procedural techni-
cality, decided not to press charges and the blacks returned to campus.

In the spring of 1969 the SDS chapter at Kent State began to press
the university to meet four demands: abolition of the ROTC program
on campus, removal of the Liquid Crystals Institute (whose research
was funded in part by the U.S. Department of Defense), removal of a
state criminal investigation laboratory from campus, and abolition of
the university's program in law enforcement. On April 8, 1969 a
group of students, including SDS leaders, marched to the Administration Building to post a list of demands. They were met at the doors
to the building by campus police. Fights broke out between campus
police and demonstrators and six demonstrators (four of them students) were arrested for assault and battery. The four students (subsequently known as the "Kent State Four") were summarily suspended from school and were later tried in county court, found guilty
of assault, and sentenced to six months in the county jail. In addition
the SDS chapter lost its campus charter, thereby depriving it of a
share of student fees and access to university facilities.[24]

Eight days after the demonstration a disciplinary hearing was held
in the Music and Speech Building for two of the suspended students.
Campus police chained and locked the doors of the building, preventing a large crowd from entering the building and attending the
hearing. Fights broke out between supporters and opponents of the
suspended students. Somehow—no one is quite clear how[25]—
supporters of the suspended students found their way into the build-

ing and gained access to the third floor where the hearing was being held. The clamor in the hallway was loud enough to disrupt the hearing and the noise rose even louder when the demonstrators discovered that the campus police had locked all doors leading down from the third floor. A stalemate resulted: the demonstrators could not get through the locked doors (although some did get out of the building by using an unwatched elevator) and the campus police lacked the personnel to deal effectively with them. The Ohio State Highway Patrol was called, and they arrested fifty-eight people for inciting to riot or criminal trespass.

The arrested demonstrators felt they had been entrapped by the campus police—allowed into the building by the campus police and then locked in so they could be arrested for trespassing. The day after the Music and Speech arrests a new organization was formed, the Concerned Citizens of the Kent Community (CCC or 3-C or Tri-C); it was a coalition of moderates, liberals, and radicals united in their concern for procedural due process and student rights. Tri-C demanded:

1. all charges and suspensions be dropped since they were not in accordance with the Student Conduct Code.
2. the university follow the November, 1968 Student Conduct Code.
3. the SDS charter be reinstated since the revocation did not follow the regulations in the Student Conduct Code.

The CCC demands struck a responsive chord in the student body. Those concerned with procedural due process joined in the protest with those supporting SDS. The focus of their activities was a campus-wide referendum on the CCC demands to be held in late April. A counter-group, quickly formed by student leaders and with the tacit support of the university administration, attacked the CCC and tried to link it with SDS and other radical organizations. Leaflets appeared warning students that 400 radicals from other schools had descended on KSU. An "extra" edition of the *Daily Kent Stater* featured a front page editorial showing an alleged link between CCC and SDS.[26] These tactics made many CCC supporters resentful and forced CCC to shift its strategy to one of arguing it was not dominated by radicals nor linked to radical organizations. Many liberal faculty members became alienated from the university administration because of their role in the campaign.[27]

The election results were ambiguous. The Tri-C position lost but the referendum, which drew the largest campus vote in university history, demonstrated substantial support for their position. Shortly after the referendum CCC folded as an organization and their final statement reflects the frustration and bitterness which many moderates and liberals on campus must have felt:

In 3-C's short, three week existence, many sincere and dedicated members of the steering committee have learned that moderate tactics are meaningless here.

. . . .

To conclude: we played the administration's game in good faith. We hoped to win a larger measure of justice at KSU, and we hoped to move the university in a democratic direction. But we find ourselves ineffective and powerless. Needless to say, an impotent organization, one which has lost credibility with its student supporters, cannot long survive. Consequently, 3-C, a coalition of moderate students, hereby disbands.[28]

A subsequent investigation and report by the Kent chapter of the American Association of University Professors is generally critical of the administration's handling of the Music and Speech demonstration, arguing that academic due process had been infringed upon and the university had not operated within the letter and spirit of the student code.[29] By the time the report was issued it was too late. Tompkins and Anderson argue that

although the administration received applause from elements outside the university for its handling of the April (1969) incidents, it also succeeded in alienating a large part of the faculty and students—overwhelmingly unsympathetic to the SDS—for acting in a way perceived to be inconsistent with the Student Conduct Code, for overreacting, for discrediting the CCC and for failing to listen.[30]

Much of the criticism of the administration was aimed at President White and the difficulty of people in gaining access to and communicating with him. Decision making in the university was centralized in his office and he rarely delegated that authority to others; vice-presidents and deans were rarely involved in university-wide policy making and occasionally found the president making policy in their areas of competence. Ordinarily this administrative style worked well enough, but in crises it placed the burden of decision making on White and left other administrators without direction. This unwillingness to delegate authority was to cause difficulties on May 1 and 2 when White was out of town.

The Music and Speech incident seemed to establish a pattern for the university's handling of demonstrations. Campus police would serve as the first line of defense, with the Ohio State Highway Patrol serving as back-up, making arrests after criminal acts had been committed. What would happen if the campus police could not effectively cope with a demonstration and the Highway Patrol were not available were questions left unasked.

While the fall quarter 1969 began quietly at KSU, the situation was tense and potentially explosive at a number of other universities. The war in Vietnam was unpopular with many university students and in October the New Mobilization Committee to End the War in Vietnam organized nationwide antiwar demonstrations. In November 250,000 people gathered in Washington, D.C. to protest the war. The Nixon administration's response to these demonstrations was indifference—Nixon and his staff watched the Purdue-Ohio State football game during the November demonstration—or hostility— Vice-President Agnew told a New Orleans meeting that the October demonstrations were "encouraged by an effete corps of impudent snobs who characterize themselves as intellectuals."[31]

In Ohio, a group of black university students at Akron University took over the administration building for four hours on December 10, before they were evicted by the National Guard, called by Governor James Rhodes. Early in February, 1970 demonstrations at Ohio University resulted in a bomb explosion outside the campus police building. Protests over the war in Vietnam and ROTC on campus took place at Dennison University in March and at Ohio University, Dayton University, Miami University and Ohio State in April. At Ohio State several hundred guardsmen were called out on April 30 to break up a demonstration and in the process several hundred people were injured. The situation at Ohio State remained unstable, and it was almost four weeks before the National Guard began to withdraw from the campus.

Thus, by the first week in May, 1970, violence on Ohio's state-supported campuses was an old story. Few institutions had been spared. Governor Rhodes had already acquired a reputation for prompt and firm response; he had called out the National Guard forty times during the preceding two years. In fact, Ohio's expenditure for National Guard duty is said to have exceeded the total for all other forty-nine states during 1968–70.[32]

Antagonism on campus toward the Nixon administration escalated when, on April 30, President Nixon ordered U.S. and South Vietnamese troops to invade Cambodia, further widening the scope of the conflict. On Friday, May 1, President Nixon added to student dissatisfaction by contrasting the "bums" on campus with the "kids" fighting in Vietnam:

You see these bums, you know, blowing up the campuses. Listen, the boys that are on the college campuses today are the luckiest people in the world, going to the greatest universities, and here they are burning up the books, storming around about this issue. You name it. Get rid of the war there will be another one. Then out there (in Vietnam) we have kids who are just doing their duty. They stand tall and they are proud. . . . They are going to do fine and we have to stand in back of them.[33]

President Nixon's decision to invade Cambodia must have been a mixed blessing to Ohio Governor Rhodes, coming during the last week of his long and intense Republican primary campaign against Robert A. Taft, Jr. for the U.S. Senate nomination. The family name' had given Robert Taft an enormous advantage initially, but Rhodes seemed to be closing the gap between the two men during the last few weeks of the campaign. As a result the race was a close one, and the last weekend of the campaign, May 1–4, promised to be crucial for Rhodes's political future (he was prohibited from serving more than two consecutive terms as governor).

Another group of actors important in the events of May 1 to 4 were also busy during the last week in April. The 107th Armored Cavalry and the 145th Infantry (National Guard units based in northeastern Ohio) had been called to active duty in Akron on April 29 as a result of a truckers' strike which had been violent periodically. These were the guardsmen ordered to Kent on May 2, after four days of hard, grueling, and potentially dangerous duty in Akron.

The factors which we have discussed in this section did not "cause" the events of May 1—4, but they did serve as the context within which those events took place and within which those events must be understood. As we shall see in the following pages it is important to know how President White's administrative style shaped the way he responded to the demonstrations and the presence of the National Guard on his campus. It is also important to understand why students reacted as they did to President Nixon's announcement of the Cambodian invasion and why city and university officials reacted as they did to the resultant demonstrations.

Although the announcement of the Cambodian invasion had sparked a large and violent demonstration at Ohio State on Thursday, April 30, the scene in Kent had been relatively calm. The Cambodian invasion was a source of conversation and many students were upset and frustrated over the turn of events in southeast Asia. But the first demonstration did not occur until Friday, May 1.

FRIDAY, MAY FIRST

In response to the invasion of Cambodia a group of history graduate students—World Historians Opposed to Racism and Exploitation (WHORE)—quickly organized a protest demonstration for noon at the Victory Bell on the Commons. The Commons provided a natural amphitheater setting and was a convenient meeting ground for students moving between dormitories and classes; the Victory Bell, located near one corner of the Commons, had traditionally served as a center for student speeches and rallies.

Approximately five hundred people attended the rally, listening with quiet attention to a variety of student speakers. "The general theme of the speeches was that the President had disregarded the limits of his office imposed by the Constitution of the United States and that, as a consequence, the Constitution had become a lifeless document, murdered by the President."[34] To symbolize its "murder" a copy of the Constitution was buried; several students volunteered their draft cards and discharge papers to be burned as well. The speeches ended with a call for another rally to be held in the same spot at 12:00 noon on May 4, to protest further the war in Vietnam, the U.S. invasion of Cambodia, and other students demands, including the abolition of the ROTC program on campus.[35] All in all, it was a quiet, peaceful rally, certainly not the start of what would be a long and violent weekend. The most important event during the rally was the call for another meeting at noon on Monday, a rally which would precede the killing of four students.

Later that afternoon the Black United Students (BUS) held a rally to hear blacks speak about disturbances that were taking place at Ohio State. This rally, which also took place on the Commons and attracted 200-400 people, ended peacefully at 3:45 P.M. The BUS rally was to be the last black political activity on campus that quarter. Michener suggests that black student leaders anticipated trouble on campus and had warned blacks to stay out of it,[36] which they did.[37] The desire of blacks to "cool it" contradicts one report of the BUS rally which states that one of the speakers had invited his listeners to "come down to the street affair in Kent tonight at 9:00 P.M."[38]

President White waited until he had received reports on both rallies before leaving for a weekend in Iowa with his sister-in-law and a Sunday meeting of the American College Testing Program, of which he was chairman of the Board of Trustees. The reports convinced him there was little cause for concern; at the BUS rally "only 47 blacks appeared," he said, "no more than 20 radicals."[39] His decision to leave campus was a fateful one. By the time he returned to Kent on Sunday at noon the town and campus had experienced two nights of confrontation and conflict, the ROTC building had been burned to the ground, and the Ohio National Guard had effectively taken command of White's university.

Friday night started like many other spring nights. The first warm weather of the spring made those on campus anxious to avoid the drudgery of studying for mid-term exams. A Lab Band concert was scheduled for Friday night as were films from the recent Ann Arbor film festival. The All-University Spring Ball, scheduled for Saturday night, had been cancelled due to lack of interest—only seven tickets were sold. At the local movies students could see *Midnight Cowboy*, *Alice's Restaurant*, or *Zabriskie Point*. For those with autos the Route 59 Drive-In offered *Destroy All Monsters* and *Scream and Scream Again*.

For many students Friday night meant beer drinking on North Water Street, whose bars and rock music were well known to college and high school students throughout northeastern Ohio. This Friday, with warm weather and impending exams, the bars were even more crowded than usual. Two topics dominated conversation in the bars—the playoff series between the New York Knicks and the Los Angeles Lakers and the invasion of Cambodia. Many students that night were angry and frustrated over President Nixon's decision to invade Cambodia, which seemed to stifle any hope that the war in Vietnam would be winding down soon.

Throughout the early evening people spilled from the bars onto the sidewalks and into the streets. Between 10:00 and 11:00 P.M. petty vandalism occurred when firecrackers were lit, beer bottles were thrown at passing cars, and the rare city police car driving down Water Street was booed. Soon the excitement was on the streets rather than in the bars. Shortly after 11:00 people formed a human chain in the middle of Water Street, doing a snake dance and forcing cars and trucks to back up toward the center of the city. The atmosphere was lighthearted, if frantic.

From 11:20 P.M. on the mood of the crowd on North Water changed. City police cars patrolling North Water were bombarded with bottles. A trash fire was started in the center of the street. "Soon the crowd blocked the street and began to stop motorists to ask their opinion about Cambodia."[40] Shortly before midnight the crowd turned its attention toward the center of the city; a group moved en masse down Water Street, breaking windows in local business establishments and causing an estimated $10,000 damage.[41] Kent City Police Chief Roy Thompson, initially hopeful that the crowd would "simmer down,"[42] finally decided that the situation was getting out of hand and all twenty-one members of the Kent police force were summoned to duty.[43] In addition, a request for assistance was sent to the Portage County Sheriff and law enforcement agencies in surrounding communities. The first clash between "rioters" and police occurred near the intersection of Main and Water, where fifteen policemen in riot gear dispersed the crowd which had been breaking windows on North Water Street.[44]

Mayor Leroy Satrom, who had been in Aurora, Ohio at a Law Day celebration and a subsequent poker game, returned to Kent at 12:20 A.M. to find a chaotic scene.[45] The remains of the trash fire burned on

North Water, broken glass littered the streets and sidewalks on Water and Main streets, and the police were moving in full riot gear through the center of the city. After conferring with Chief Thompson, the mayor made a strategic mistake—he declared a state of emergency, ordered all bars in the city closed, and established an 11:00 P.M. curfew for the city and a 1:00 A.M. curfew for the campus. Police informants had warned that SDS Weathermen were on campus and when the disturbances began downtown, Chief Thompson and Mayor Satrom assumed that it was part of a radical plot.[46] A few minutes later Mayor Satrom telephoned Governor Rhodes' office in Columbus and reported to the governor's administrative assistant "that SDS students had taken over a portion of Kent."[47] Within minutes of Satrom's call the governor's office telephoned the commander of the Ohio National Guard, Major General Sylvester T. Del Corso, who immediately dispatched a National Guard liaison officer, Lt. Charles J. Barnette, to Kent to keep him informed about the situation.

The declaration of a state of emergency was a mistake not only because it was based on incomplete evidence (there was no evidence that Weathermen were in Kent or on campus that night) but in closing all the bars the police forced hundreds of people who were primarily interested in drinking beer, listening to rock music, or watching the end of the Knicks-Laker basketball game, into the streets. "This arbitrary action threw a new mass of young people into the streets and infuriated many who up to now had done nothing wrong."[48] On the streets they found themselves being herded by city police and sheriff's deputies using tear gas away from the center of the city and toward the campus. Those who refused to disperse were arrested.

By 2:00 A.M. the downtown area had been cleared of people, although people were still visible through clouds of tear gas on East Main Street. The warm weather, the uphill walk toward campus, the tear gas, and constant prodding from riot-geared police frayed tempers. Finally, at the intersection of East Main and Lincoln—next to the university entrance at Prentice Gate—the crowd stopped and faced the pursuing police. Standing on one side of the street and on campus property, the crowd seemed to challenge the local police to violate the campus sanctuary. Local police stopped and waited for assistance from the university police, but the assistance never came. Michener reports that this annoyed city police who were unaware that University Police Chief Donald L. Schwartzmiller had felt it necessary to utilize his men to protect buildings on campus.[49]

A potentially violent confrontation was avoided when a car collided with a Tree City Electric truck repairing the traffic light in the center of the intersection, leaving one of the electricians hanging from the light. Police and "rioters" cooperated to form a rescue team, and the dangling repairman was the center of attraction until he was rescued. By that time the tension had dissipated, and the crowd quickly and quietly melted away.[50]

By 2:27 A.M. both the campus and town were reported quiet once more, and shortly thereafter Lt. Barnette of the National Guard reported to Mayor Satrom at City Hall to get a status report. The first National Guard presence had arrived in Kent.

Looking back on Friday night one must ask, "Why did it happen?" Michener, in his interviews with participants and bystanders, finds a lack of agreement on motivation—the invasion of Cambodia, the weather, a need to let off steam, or the premeditated plans of radicals were all given as reasons. Michener leans toward a theory of radical involvement, based on the presence of one of the Kent State Four on Water Street early in the evening and a number of demonstrators wearing red armbands.[51] Chief Thompson felt that the disturbance was "instigated by a bunch of agitators and subversive groups."[52] Based on responses from over 7,000 students to a survey conducted soon after May 4, Stuart Taylor concluded:

According to these results and the many letters written by the students who witnessed the events, one might conjecture that the "style" and actions of the Nixon Administration "primed" or increased the "readiness" of students for action. The disturbance, however, appears to have been instigated or "triggered" by a few persons, possibly "radical KSU students."[53]

The Minority Report of the Commission on KSU violence perhaps best summarizes the feeling of many. "The participation of outsiders in the events of May 1−4 ought not to be summarily dismissed as fantasy. The kind of participation is what cannot be established."[54]

Although many people feel that the Friday night disturbances were part of a radical plot, there is little concrete evidence to support that conclusion. The Justice Department Summary of the FBI Report makes no mention of radicals in the Friday night activity, noting that fifteen people were arrested, all of them Ohio residents. The Scranton Commission, which had access to the full FBI Report, notes, "The FBI uncovered no evidence that the Kent State Four were involved in planning or directing any of the events of the May 1–4 weekend."[55] In addition, the activities engaged in—a trash fire, throwing bottles, and breaking windows—are not normally ones which revolutionaries choose. The FBI findings and the Scranton Commission report did not stop Michener from concluding that Friday night's activities were led by "a hard core of radical activists— abetted by a few real revolutionaries, not necessarily from the university—who grasped at the disturbance as a means of advancing their own well-defined aims."[56]

Without the invasion of Cambodia, the violence at Ohio State the preceding night, President Nixon's speech earlier in the day about "bums" on campus, and city officials' fears of SDS activities, it is possible that Friday night's action might have been treated merely as students celebrating the first good weather of spring. Traffic had been disrupted and windows broken on North Water in the past, a price which businessmen seemed willing to pay. But May 1, 1970 was unlike any spring day in the past. Frustration over the Cambodian invasion, anger because they were turned out of bars, and the sting of tear gas turned what might have otherwise been a relatively harmless release of emotion into an ugly incident. The local officials were inept in their handling of the event:

The pattern established on Friday night was to recur throughout the weekend. There were disorderly incidents; authorities could not or did not respond in time to apprehend those responsible or to stop the incidents in their early stages; the disorder grew; the police action, when it came, involved bystanders as well as participants; and, finally, the students drew together in the conviction that they were being arbitrarily harassed.[57]

While resentment against the authorities grew among those involved, directly or indirectly, in the Friday disturbances, many other people—townspeople, students, university officials, and city officials—were disturbed at the magnitude of the damage done on Friday night. For many the glass shards on Main and Water streets were concrete evidence that "student radicals" or "outside agitators" were out to destroy their city and they became convinced that the community was under siege.

SATURDAY, MAY SECOND

Saturday morning witnessed one of those cruel ironies that were to permeate the weekend; while rumors spread through the city that radicals were planning to burn down the city, a number of students were downtown helping to clean up the debris from the preceding night. Store owners, fearful of being burned out or having their windows smashed, posted antiwar signs in the windows of their businesses.

City and university officials also began to prepare for what they feared would happen Saturday night. At the first of many meetings that day, university officials decided to seek an injunction against 500 "John Does," barring them from doing further property damage on campus. According to the Justice Department Summary, "it is not known . . . if the injunction was served upon any person or disseminated in any way."[58] As we shall soon see, notice of the injunction was contained in leaflets distributed to students on campus that afternoon.

When Mayor Satrom returned to his office on Saturday morning he formalized the proclamation of civil emergency which he had promulgated eight hours earlier. He banned the sale of liquor, beer, firearms, and gasoline (except for that pumped directly into an automobile), and established an 8:00 P.M. to 6:00 A.M. curfew for the entire city (including the campus).

At 11:00 A.M. Mayor Satrom held the first of four meetings with university officials and Lt. Barnette, the National Guard liaison officer.

Although the university officials regarded the action as unnecessary, in that they felt that local law enforcement personnel could cope with any situation that might arise, the Mayor, other city officials and the National Guard representative decided at that time to put a company of 110 National Guardsmen on standby.[59]

Apparently in response to pressure from university officials Satrom exempted the campus from the 8:00 P.M. curfew and established a 1:00 A.M. curfew instead.[60] The change in curfew was recognition that if students could not go beer drinking downtown after 8:00 P.M. and were confined to their rooms on campus after that time, the situation would become even more tense. University officials, particularly Vice-President for Student Affairs Robert Matson, began arrangements for social activities on campus for the period after 8:00 P.M.

At a 1:00 P.M. meeting Lt. Barnette and Vice-President Matson discussed how to handle disturbances which might occur on campus. Matson explained that the campus police would be used first; if they failed, the Sheriff's Department would be called in, and then, as a last resort, reliance would be placed on the Ohio State Highway Patrol which, in riot situations where state laws had been violated, could make arrests. Lt. Barnette replied that if the National Guard were called, they would make no distinction between city and campus and would take jurisdictional control of the entire area.[61] Barnette's description of the National Guard mission is very different from that of General Del Corso, Barnette's immediate superior officer in the National Guard, whose concept of the guard's mission was that it would be used to *assist* rather than *replace* local law enforcement agencies.[62] Barnette's concept of the National Guard mission, however, was the only authoritative source that city and university officials had, and it shaped their perceptions all weekend of what would happen if the Guard were called to Kent—they would assume total control of the city and the university.

Sometime during the morning or early afternoon Lt. Barnette told Mayor Satrom that he would have until 5:00 P.M. to ask for National Guard help, since it would take some time to move them from their strike duty in Akron to take up positions in Kent. This deadline meant that Satrom would have to make a decision on using the National Guard before knowing whether there would be any disturbances in the city or on campus Saturday night.

He was not without information, however incorrect or distorted it may have been. Businessmen told of receiving threatening phone calls. Throughout the day Police Chief Thompson heard rumors of guns, Weathermen, burning down the city, and putting LSD in the city water supply.[63] "False fire alarms, bomb threats and violent rumors kept the day ugly, and always at the mayor's elbow stood Lieutenant Barnette of the National Guard, warning him, 'If you're going to call the Guard, you have to do it before 5:00 this afternoon.' "[64]

While Satrom was trying to decide whether to call for the National Guard, Vice-President Matson and student leaders were making plans on campus. Recognizing that university students would not be allowed in the city after 8:00 P.M., the dormitory cafeterias were ordered to stay open late, and live entertainment and dancing were arranged for several dormitory complexes. In addition, a leaflet was printed and distributed to dormitory residents informing them of the injunction and the 8:00 P.M. curfew in the city. However, the leaflet failed to mention the 1:00 A.M. curfew on campus. The leaflet also stated that peaceful campus assemblies were not banned (such a prohibition would have made much of the evening's planned entertainment illegal).[65]

Anticipating that there might be some disturbances on campus that night—there were rumors that a rally would take place—university officials established a rumor control center and activated an emergency operations center in the Administration Building. This windowless room would be the administration's command post for the remainder of the weekend. Vice-President Matson also asked Glenn Frank, Harold Kitner, and Jerry Lewis to organize a faculty group to serve as faculty marshals for the time being, wearing armbands to identify themselves. Many faculty marshals were unsure of their role in case of a disturbance. "Ultimately, most marshals decided that they would not physically intervene in case of disturbances but would confine their activities to discussion and persuasion, fact-finding, and reporting events to the university emergency operations center."[66]

Mayor Satrom's final meeting of the day took place in City Hall at 5:00 P.M., the deadline for telling Lt. Barnette whether or not the Guard would be needed. There were a number of factors that influenced Satrom's decision. Rumors had been circulating that plans were afoot to destroy the ROTC building on campus and the local Army recruiting office and post office downtown.[67] In addition, Mayor Satrom had received two disturbing reports of "Weathermen observed on campus and positively identified, and evidence of weapons on campus."[68] Neither of these reports was substantiated,

but they did fit Satrom's sharpening perceptions of Kent as a city
under siege by radicals. Threats to downtown businesses, if they
didn't show overt signs of opposition to the Cambodian invasion,
and memories of the destruction of the preceding night undoubtedly
played a role in his decision.[69]

In view of these rumors and threats Mayor Satrom felt he needed
help. He hoped for assistance from the county sheriff while university
officials hoped for assistance from the highway patrol; Satrom
learned that the sheriff's deputies would not be available and that the
Highway Patrol would be available only to make arrests for law
violations. There would be a time lag while they were mobilized. The
unavailability of law enforcement back-up assistance highlighted a
problem of coordination between the city police and the campus
police which had surfaced the night before—neither wanted to coor-
dinate operations. Campus police would make no commitment to
help city police control disturbances off-campus, just as city police
were unwilling to move on-campus.

As the meeting broke up, Mayor Satrom felt he had no option
except to call on the National Guard for help. Unfortunately, when
the university representatives left the meeting, "they were under the
impression that the National Guard was being requested for duty
only in Kent, not on the Kent State campus."[70] University officials
assumed that their strategy of relying on campus police, backed up
by the highway patrol, would be sufficient to handle problems on
campus. Earlier in the day, however, Lt. Barnette had told university
officials that if called, the National Guard would not differentiate
between the city and the campus.

Mayor Satrom then called the governor's administrative assistant
(the governor was campaigning in Cleveland) to order up the National Guard, and the assistant both called Governor Rhodes to au-
thorize the commitment of the Guard to duty in Kent and called
General Del Corso to mobilize the Guard for duty in Kent. Del Corso,
in turn, ordered guardsmen bivouacked in Akron on strike duty to be
ready to move in one hour.[71] Shortly after 6:00 P.M., the National
Guard was on alert and ready to move into Kent, although there had
been no disturbances on campus or in the city yet that day.

Around 7:00 P.M. a crowd began to gather at the Victory Bell for
the rumored rally, a crowd which by 7:30 had grown to around

600.[72] According to the Scranton Commission, the group was "an idle collection of students whom the curfew had prevented from going downtown."[73] According to Michener, however, "there was also a substantial cadre of hard-core radical leaders and perhaps one or two revolutionaries who had their eyes on much more than the rickety old ROTC building; among them, too, were many who had no connection with the university."[74]

The crowd soon moved off the Commons toward the dormitories where students were attending dances. A number of students were "liberated" from the dorms so that by the time the crowd returned to the Commons it had grown substantially—to approximately 1,000 or 2,000.[75] Once back on the Commons the crowd, some chanting antiwar slogans, moved purposely toward the ROTC building on one edge of the Commons.

As the crowd surrounded the old, wooden two-story structure, some shouted, "Get it" and "Burn it." Initially rocks were thrown at the building; then a trash can was thrown through a first floor window. Railroad flares were lit, and people threw them at the building or through the broken windows, hoping to start a fire. Their only success was a curtain which flamed briefly but soon sputtered out. Most of the crowd took little part in the efforts to destroy the ROTC building; some watched quietly while others cheered and chanted antiwar slogans. The lack of success in starting a fire was not a deterrent. A rag dipped in gasoline from the tank of a nearby motorcycle was lit and at 8:45 P.M. the ROTC building was aflame at last.[76]

The mood and intent of the people who participated in the fire Saturday night has been the subject of some debate. The Minority Report describes them as a "mob" with leaders,[77] which seems to fit Michener's view of the crowd as being led by radical leaders and revolutionaries, who sought to burn down the ROTC building and then to extend the rioting to the rest of the campus and the city.[78] For a leadership cadre who supposedly knew what they were doing and how to do it, they were remarkably inept. It took approximately thirty minutes of diligent effort to set the ROTC building afire, and then the fire went out. In addition, the bulk of the participants at the fire were hardly "riotous."

The Scranton Commission differentiates between three groups of people involved on Saturday night: those who actively tried to set the

building on fire and whose mood was one of anger, another group
who cheered and shouted as if the fire were part of a carnival, and a
third group who merely watched.[79] These three groups, called the
"active core," "cheerleaders," and "spectators," respectively, by
Lewis[80] were not equal in numbers. Most of the crowd were "cheerleaders" or "spectators," although the "active core" did the physical
damage to the building. Taylor's student survey data show that
people's perceptions of the mood of the crowd depended on one's
role. There was disagreement as to whether the mood of the crowd
was "angry," "unconcerned," "lighthearted," or "fearful," depend-
ing on whether one participated or merely observed the events on
Saturday night.[81] There is also a discrepancy between observers and
participants and their perceptions of the role of "outside agitators."
Of the observers, 54 percent as opposed to 16 percent of the participants, thought that outside agitators were "very" or "moderately"
responsible for the Saturday night disturbance.[82] But one student
noted:

> Those who claim to have recognized "outside agitators" must be praised
> for the remarkable feat of memorizing the faces of 20,000 KSU students to
> know that there were in fact outsiders in the crowd. Only an FBI agent who is
> looking for someone in particular could know for certain who caused the
> mob action.[83]

At 8:35 P.M., Mayor Satrom, informed of the trouble on campus
and without consulting university officials, called for the National
Guard, and they were ordered to Kent immediately, arriving between 9:30 and 10:30 P.M.

Shortly after the ROTC building began to blaze in earnest the fire
was reported to the Kent Fire Department and within fifteen minutes
a city fire truck arrived at the scene. The firemen soon found themselves battling the crowd as well as the fire; hoses were wrestled away
from the firemen and others were punctured and chopped with ice
picks and machetes. Rocks were also thrown at the firemen and,
since they had no police protection, they withdrew from the campus.
Shortly thereafter (approximately 9:15), the fire went out by itself. It
began again a short time later, this time detonating live ammunition
stored inside the building.

With the renewed fire at the ROTC building and the explosion of live ammunition, the campus police finally arrived at the scene. As Michener notes caustically, "They were two hours and twelve minutes late."[84] Where had the campus police been while the crowd was trying to burn down the ROTC building? According to the Minority Report, Chief Schwartzmiller's logic was that until the destruction started he didn't want to start a riot by having his men appear on the scene, but after the destruction had begun he felt it was too dangerous for his men to intervene.[85] When the ROTC building was initially threatened the campus police had called the city police for help, but the Kent police said they were busy protecting the downtown area. "Schwartzmiller said later he received the impression that the Kent police department was 'getting even' with him for his failure to dispatch his men to Prentice Gate to disperse the crowd there on Friday night."[86]

While the campus police were trying to decide when and how to intervene, twenty state highway patrolmen entered campus and took positions near the residence of President White, with the intent of protecting his home from destruction.[87] Whether the campus police knew that the highway patrol was on campus is not known, but the highway patrol, law enforcement officials of the state of Ohio, did nothing to prevent the destruction of the nearby ROTC building.

Ten county sheriff's deputies arrived on the Commons at about the same time as the campus police, and, together, using tear gas, they cleared the demonstrators from the Commons with some demonstrators heading back toward the dorms. While the campus police and sheriff's deputies were clearing the Commons, the National Guard was entering Kent, and the ROTC building was burning more brightly than ever. As one guardsmen described the scene, "The sky was all lit up. It was something out of 'Gone With the Wind' with Atlanta burning."[88] In response to the renewed fire in the ROTC building another Kent fire truck was dispatched to campus.

General Del Corso, who had accompanied Brigadier General Robert H. Canterbury and his men to Kent, after conferring with Mayor Satrom, ordered one detachment downtown to prevent destruction of businesses and another detachment to campus to protect the firemen who were answering the second alarm. "Neither Del Corso nor Canterbury requested permission of any university official before sending troops onto campus. General Canterbury said later that because the building was located on state property, the Guard needed no specific invitation to enter the campus."[89] While Del Corso was ordering the Guard to protect the firemen on campus, an unidentified guardsman called Vice-President Matson at the emergency operation center, and, after conferring with university officials and campus police, Matson agreed that the National Guard was needed.[90]

By 10:10 P.M., when the firemen arrived back on campus with National Guard protection and were met by the contingent of campus police and sheriff's deputies, the fire had completely gutted the ROTC building. The detachment of guardsmen ordered downtown intercepted a group of demonstrators who had moved from the campus, and the guardsmen, using tear gas, drove them back toward the campus. For approximately two hours (from 10:00 to midnight) the Guard cleared the campus, using tear gas to force people into the dorms, some of whom were not KSU students and had no rooms in the dorms, and others who were KSU students but were forced to spend the night in other dorms on campus. By midnight the situation on campus and in the city was "secure."

A number of questions remain regarding Saturday night. Who burned the ROTC building? Michener and others see the fire as part of a radical conspiracy, led by radicals and revolutionaries.[91] The Scranton Commission regards the presence of machetes, ice-picks, and flares as evidence of preplanning, perhaps by radicals.[92] Charles Thomas believes Saturday night's events were orchestrated by agents of the federal government, thereby creating an opportunity and rationale for Governor Rhodes and President Nixon to "get tough" with radical protestors.[93] Although a number of authors see the burning of the ROTC building as a radical plot, there is little direct evidence that radicals were directly involved in Saturday night's events. Certainly the bulk of the crowd at the fire were neither radical nor revolutionary.

The presence of the National Guard in Kent on Saturday night was a mixed blessing at best. Michener argues that "if the Guard had not been present, it seems clear that several more university buildings, and perhaps some downtown, would have been burned."[94] If the Guard was instrumental in preventing further destruction on Saturday night, its role in clearing the campus with the use of tear gas created resentment on the part of many students. "Students who had nothing to do with burning the building—who were not even in the area at the time of the fire—resented being gassed and ordered about by armed men."[95] After reviewing the Guard's activities on Saturday night the Minority Report suggests, "The Guard . . . was perceived by a large number of the student body as 'outsiders.' . . . They possessed 'power' rather than 'authority.' "[96]

The delay in deploying the campus police raises an interesting question: if the bulk of the crowd by the ROTC building consisted of "cheerleaders" and "spectators," would Schwartzmiller's men have faced any major danger in trying to stop the burning of the ROTC building? Schwartzmiller assumes that they would have been in danger, but was that a valid assumption? Rapid deployment of the campus police might have prevented the complete destruction of the ROTC building and negated the need for the National Guard to appear on campus, thereby altering the events of the next two days.

Although students may have seen the guardsmen as "outsiders" who possessed "power" rather than "authority," townspeople reacted differently. Grant and Hill describe the reactions of some townspeople as the National Guard entered the city:

People from some of the neighborhoods on our route ran out to our jeep. They said things like, 'Kill those S.O.B.'s if they cause any more trouble.' 'Get tough with them.' Maybe we agreed with some of these statements when we were entering a riot situation in a city, but now we were facing white young people like us and we thought that these remarks were stupid.[97]

Kent residents were clearly unhappy with what was happening to their city and its university. They saw the damage of Friday night and listened to rumors of what was happening on campus Saturday night, and the town-gown split, hidden below the surface under normal circumstances, emerged. Lewis argues:

In Kent, middle-American townspeople and their officials tended to equate anti-war sentiment with unpatriotic, subversive activity. Moreover, equally important, they regarded the violent outbursts, from the breaking of storewindows to the burning of the ROTC as illegitimate ways of resolving domestic conflict.[98]

Not only were the demonstrators illegitimate and unpatriotic, but the National Guard represented "authority" which could and would reimpose "order" on the campus. For many Kent residents, taking sides with the students was an act of disloyalty, an endorsement of lawlessness, and a threat to the established social and political order.

SUNDAY, MAY THIRD

Governor Rhodes helicoptered into the KSU airport at 9:00 A.M. from Cleveland where he had been campaigning. He was met at the airport by Mayor Satrom and National Guard officials who showed him the damage on campus and in the city. After his tour Rhodes met with representatives of the highway patrol, the county sheriff, the county prosecutor, General Del Corso and three university vice-presidents to determine what should be done. Rhodes was described as angry[99] but not intemperate.[100] The discussion, which took place in the City Fire Station, centered on whether to keep the university open, which Rhodes favored, and on how to do so. The university officials who were present played virtually no role in the discussion, even though it was their institution whose future was being discussed. This curious lack of effort to keep control of the campus in their own hands, which surfaced again on Monday morning in the same fire station, may have been the result of a reluctance to question or challenge the governor of the state, or it may have reflected a recognition that with the Guard now on campus, control had passed from their hands. Governor Rhodes did not ask their opinions.

The meeting had not been in session long when it was decided to admit the press; what had been a policy-making session quickly degenerated into a press conference. According to one of the participants, "At that moment Jim Rhodes changed completely. He became a candidate for United States Senate."[101] After the press entered the room and pictures were taken, Rhodes launched into a fifteen-minute statement whose impact has been the subject of substantial debate.

Rhodes began by describing disturbances at Ohio State and Miami universities and argued that Kent State was merely one more in a coordinated series of attacks on authority, the National Guard, and the Ohio State Highway Patrol, using the state universities as sanctuaries. He called the disturbances at KSU "probably the most vicious form of campus-oriented violence yet perpetrated by dissident groups and their allies in the state of Ohio," and he vowed to use "every force of the law" to control them.[102] The troublemakers, who moved from campus to campus fomenting trouble, were described as

worse than the brown shirts and the communist element, and also the night riders and the vigilantes. They are the worst type of people that we harbor in America. And I want to say this—they are not going to take over the campus and the campus now is going to be part of the county and the state of Ohio. It is no sanctuary for these people to burn buildings down of private citizens, of businesses (sic), in the community, then run into a sanctuary. It is over with in the state of Ohio.[103]

Rhodes went on to state that the vast majority of students at Kent State weren't interested in violence and destruction but were on campus for an education.[104]

What was Governor Rhodes trying to do by making this statement? As the Knight newspaper investigating team discovered, "It was impossible to learn what was going on in Governor Rhodes' mind at this time."[105] After analyzing Rhodes's statements, the Minority Report concluded that they were consistent with his statements in the past; they were not inflamatory and were not incendiary.[106] In essence, Governor Rhodes was merely repeating what he had said so often in the past. Michener argues that the statements were inflammatory because they were reported out of context and that if there was any difficulty it stemmed from the fact that "they were uttered in the hortatory style of a politician seeking votes rather than the persuasive style of a leader trying to defuse a perilous situation."[107] Unfortunately, the situation called for leadership rather than horation, and during those fifteen minutes when James Rhodes was a candidate for the Republican nomination to the Senate, rather than Governor of the state of Ohio, his words served to inflame rather than heal the wounds of the community.

Five years later Governor Rhodes offered his evaluation of his remarks.:

Question: Sir, by those pronouncements about Brown Shirts, Communist
           elements, Night Riders and vigilantes, did you consider that you
           were, perhaps, inflaming a volatile potentially explosive situa-
           tion?
Answer: It was not inflamatory, no, sir.[108]

Peter Davies offers an alternative explanation for Rhodes' statements: they were to be a symbolic warning to the National Guard.

You men are up against the scum of America, but be careful. They are
vicious, organized, and dangerous. Your job is to protect the citizens of Kent
and Portage County, where no one will be safe if we fail, and remember,
your commanding officer has said, we can stop them with gunfire if necessary.[109]

One important result of Rhodes' statement was that they
"changed the mission of the Guard from one of protecting lives and
property to one of breaking up any assembly on campus, peaceful or
otherwise."[110] This change in mission lends some credence to Davis'
interpretation of Rhodes' statement and is reflected in the Governor's
promise at the end of his press conference to have the courts declare
a "state of emergency" in Kent. This promise was repeated shortly
after noon when Governor Rhodes met briefly with President White,
who had just returned from Iowa. (He had tried to return Saturday
night but had been unable to arrange air transportation). Rhodes
reaffirmed his pledge to keep the university open and told White that
he was going to the courts to seek a state of emergency. After
Rhodes's pledge on Sunday morning, many people thought Kent
was operating under a state of emergency, which would have prohibited any public gathering, but Governor Rhodes never sought such
relief from the courts. "After the governor departed, widespread
uncertainty regarding rules, prohibitions, and proclamations remained. Many people were unsure about what was to be legal and
what not, particularly with regard to rallies."[111]

University officials, who were part of, but never participants in, the
meeting with Governor Rhodes, were unsure of what was permitted
under a state of emergency. Were rallies legal? If so, under what
circumstances? Equally important, did a state of emergency relieve
university officials of control of the campus? Did the National Guard

now officially control the campus? There were more questions than answers.

Conversations between university administrators and Guard officers convinced university officials that Governor Rhodes's proposed state of emergency order gave the Guard complete legal authority on campus. Based on this information Vice-President Matson and student body president Frank Frisina printed and distributed on campus 12,000 leaflets, which stated that the National Guard had assumed control of the campus, that all rallies were banned, that a curfew was in effect (and curfew hours were listed), and that the Guard had the authority to make arrests. With the publication and dissemination of this leaflet the mission of the Guard changed from *assisting* local law enforcement officials to *replacing* them. The leaflet was based on the assumption that the state of emergency was in effect (which was not true) and, as a result, "the only accurate information in this document are the curfew hours."[112]

Sunday afternoon a group of twenty-three faculty members drafted and published a statement deploring the appearance of the National Guard on campus, the burning of the ROTC building, violence, the war in Vietnam, the police vendetta against the Black Panthers, President Nixon's policies and Governor Rhodes' statements at the morning press conference. It read, in part:

We call upon our public authorities to use their high offices to bring about greater understanding of the issues involved in and contributing to the burning of the ROTC building at Kent State University on Saturday, rather than to exploit this incident in a manner that can only inflame the public and increase the confusion among the members of the university community.[113]

Sunday newspaper headlines in Akron and Cleveland announced to northeastern Ohio the details of the Saturday night fire. *Akron Beacon Journal* readers discovered that "rioters" had burned down the ROTC building,[114] while *Cleveland Plain Dealer* readers learned that those "rioters" were "student radicals."[115] The *Beacon Journal* readers were aware that the National Guard was on campus,[116] while *Plain Dealer* readers were not.[117]

Intrigued by the headlines and spurred by clear and mild spring weather, crowds of sightseers descended on Kent. Traffic became so thick that by 1:00 P.M. no more traffic was permitted on campus, and traffic in the city and on approach roads put a severe strain on local law enforcement agencies already tired from two nights of disturbances. Tourists found the campus deceptively calm under the watchful eye of the National Guard. Guardsmen and sightseers talked quietly with one another, and an air of stability pervaded the campus. The charred remains of the ROTC building were a "must" attraction, as was the Guard helicopter parked on the university high school football field.

As darkness returned so did the tensions of the previous two nights. Shortly after 7:00 P.M. the Victory Bell began to toll and by 8:00 a crowd had begun to gather around the burned-out ROTC building. The crowd "was certainly less unified in temper and less dominated by a purpose that (sic) the crowd on Saturday night,"[118] although Taylor found that the majority of students who participated in Sunday's events did so to protest the presence of the National Guard on campus.[119] By 8:45 the crowd had grown so large that the campus curfew was moved from 1:00 A.M. to 9:00 P.M. At 9:00 the Ohio Riot Act was read to the crowd; they were given five minutes to disperse, being liable to arrest if they did not. When the crowd failed to disperse, tear gas was fired at them and the crowd broke in two— one group heading for President White's home and another for Prentice Gate at the corner of Main and Lincoln. Those who headed for White's house were tear-gassed by National Guardsmen, and the crowd retreated to the Commons. The group heading toward Prentice Gate sat down in the intersection of Main and Lincoln, effectively blocking traffic on both streets. Remnants of the group from President White's house, as well as a group of demonstrators from downtown, joined them. According to the FBI, "Law enforcement officers from the city and county faced the students while National Guardsmen took a position behind them. State police helicopters were overhead with searchlights being played on the crowd."[120]

An uneasy truce lasted until 10:10 when the demonstrators demanded to talk to Mayor Satrom and President White about six demands: abolition of ROTC on campus, removal of the Guard from campus by Monday night, lifting of the curfew, full amnesty for those arrested Saturday night, the granting of all demands made by BUS (Black United Students), and the reduction of student tuition. A young man was given access to a police car public address system, and he announced that Mayor Satrom would soon be there to talk with them and that efforts were being made to contact White.[121] Vice-Presidents Matson and Roskens decided that White should not go, since the Guard was in charge of the campus and "there was no point negotiating in the streets," a decision in which they say White concurred. White does not recall that he was personally contacted by Matson regarding the matter.[122] Mayor Satrom tried to get to the scene but by the time he arrived the crowd was being dispersed.

At 11:00 P.M., the Riot Act was read once again, and the demonstrators were ordered to clear the intersection. The demonstrators, who up to this point had behaved peacefully, became hostile and angry at what they felt was a betrayal by the authorities who had promised to talk with them. Rocks were thrown, obscenities shouted, while tear gas and a bayonet charge by the National Guard were used to clear people from the intersection and drive them back across campus. One group of people was driven into the Rockwell Library, where they were imprisoned by police and guardsmen until given a forty-five minute grace period to clear the building. Another group was chased across campus toward the Tri-Tower dormitories by guardsmen firing tear gas and wielding bayonets. A number of people were injured Sunday night—several guardsmen from rocks, and two or more people bayonetted by guardsmen.[123]

Sunday night witnessed an escalation in violence between demonstrators and authorities, indicating that both groups were losing patience with the other. Demonstrators were resentful of what they viewed as broken promises made by the police and the excessive force used to clear the intersection. Policemen and guardsmen seemed to be increasingly impatient with demonstrators who cursed them, threw stones, and refused to obey them. The National Guard seems to have become particularly resentful. During Sunday it became apparent to many guardsmen that demonstrators did not view them as citizen/soldiers—the view which many guardsmen had— "but as something like Nazi Storm Troopers who would delight in having an excuse to attack them."[124] The verbal abuse, the bombardment of rocks, their long duty, and fear were beginning to take a toll. The Sunday night confrontation resulted in " . . . the first rumblings of resentment toward the students. Even the Guardsmen who were students at Kent were mumbling about how insane they were."[125]

By early Monday morning the situation on campus had deteriorated badly. Thinking the city and university were operating under a state of emergency, the university officials had forfeited control of the university to the National Guard. The campus police would never again be a factor in the events that followed. Demonstrators were also becoming increasingly antagonistic toward the Guard; the National Guard represented the military, governmental authority, tear gas, and bayonets. The National Guard, in turn, began to see demonstrators as foul-mouthed, rock-throwing radicals, threatening the safety of the guardsmen as well as the security of the nation.

MONDAY, MAY FOURTH

Classes resumed on Monday morning and students who had been away over the weekend stared at the charred remains of the ROTC building and talked with classmates who had been part of the action. Many students were upset by the appearance of the National Guard on campus. The noon rally, originally scheduled to protest the Cambodian invasion, now took on a new focus: to protest the presence of the National Guard on campus.[126] Although a substantial proportion of the student body knew that the noon rally was prohibited, many felt strongly enough about the presence of the Guard to go to the rally, nonetheless.

At 10:00 A.M. the last meeting of the weekend, called by General Canterbury, was held at the Fire Station. President White, Vice-President Matson, Mayor Satrom, Police Chief Thompson, the Kent safety director, a representative from the highway patrol, and the Guard legal officer were also present.[127] There were several items which had to be settled. Confusion over curfew hours had to be cleared up; it was decided that the city curfew hours of 8:00 P.M. to 6:00 A.M. would apply to the campus as well.[128] General Canterbury also made known his desire to withdraw his troops from campus as soon as possible, even as early as Monday evening. Late in the meeting the noon rally scheduled for the Commons was discussed. Who said what has been the subject of some dispute—a dispute of some importance since the Guard's interpretation of what was decided governed their actions on campus at noon. The Justice Department concluded that the National Guard determined that the rally would not be held.[129] Canterbury stated to the Scranton Commission that he deferred to President White, who said, "No, it would be highly dangerous (to hold the rally)."[130] White testified that he played no role at all in banning the noon rally.[131] The contrast in perceptions between General Canterbury and President White is clearly seen in testimony given at the 1975 civil suit trial.

First, General Canterbury's description of the Monday morning meeting:

Question: What discussion was there concerning what, if anything, to do about the noon rally?
Answer: There was a discussion entered into by just about everyone there about that rally and all rallies and the decision was made by the Mayor, by the Sheriff, by the Chief of Police, by everyone including the University people, that the rallies should not be permitted.

. . . .

Question: Tell us what the conversation was between you and Dr. White on the subject of dispersals (of rallies)?
Answer: I asked Dr. White if the assembly was to be permitted, and his response was, that it would be highly dangerous.
Question: Did he say he wanted you or the Guard to disperse any and all assemblies?
Answer: I have given you the total of that conversation.[132]

From his conversation with White, Canterbury assumed that White agreed with everyone else at the meeting that all rallies would not be permitted. If rallies were not permitted, then the Guard's mission on Monday was clear—to disperse any assembly on the Commons.

White's description of the Monday morning meeting is at variance with that of General Canterbury.

Question: Was there anything discussed with respect to permitting assemblies on the Commons?
Answer: There was no general discussion that I recall concerning the status of assemblies in general.

. . . .

Question: Did you say anything at the meeting with respect to whether it would be dangerous to permit a rally on Monday, May 4th?
Answer: No, sir.

Question: Did General Canterbury ask you whether or not you wanted to
          have the assembly dispersed?
Answer: I don't recall such a question.
Question: Now, did General Canterbury suggest to you or say anything to
          you that there was going to be a rally?
Answer: No, I don't believe he said that.
Question: You knew there was going to be a rally, didn't you?
Answer: No, I didn't know that.[133]

Obviously, President White and General Canterbury had different
perceptions of what happened and what was said at the Monday
meeting. Testimony of other participants at the meeting tends to
support Canterbury's view that a "consensus" of the meeting
emerged, with none of the university officials voicing strong opposition to the proposal that rallies not be allowed on campus.

Why White and Matson didn't speak in favor of holding a rally is
not clear. With the deteriorating climate of opinion on campus it was
sure to be dangerous for the National Guard to ban a rally. In his
testimony before the Scranton Commission President White stated,
"From past history, all know that my response would have been
affirmative to a rally."[134] It is doubtful, however, that public officials
and Guard officers were aware of White's "past history" on holding
rallies, and his support for the noon rally was not apparent to those
attending the meeting. The acquiescence of university officials to the
rally ban fits into a pattern of behavior which emerged after the
National Guard's appearance on campus and Governor Rhodes'
statement that he would seek a state of emergency; the acquiescent
behavior was based on the assumption that the National Guard had
taken over effective control of the campus and, under the state of
emergency, could determine whether rallies were prohibited. The
assumption that a state of emergency existed, an assumption shared
by all of the participants in the Monday morning meeting, was er-
roneous. Because everyone assumed a state of emergency existed,
there was little need to debate whether to ban rallies; under the state
of emergency they were naturally banned. The meeting concluded
with the agreement that the noon rally should not be allowed.

At the conclusion of the meeting (11:15 A.M.) White and Matson
returned to campus for a brief meeting with other university officials

and then went to the Brown Derby restaurant for a luncheon meeting to discuss a Faculty Senate meeting scheduled for later that afternoon; they were eating when they heard news of the shooting.

After the meeting General Canterbury returned to Guard headquarters in the Administration Building on campus, informing those present that the noon rally had been banned.[135] Canterbury had at his command Companies A and C of the First Batallion, 145th Infantry Regiment and Troop G of the Second Squadron, 107th Armored Cavalry Regiment, all of whom had been on duty for much of Sunday night, getting three hours sleep at most before being summoned back to duty on Monday morning.

People began to gather on the Commons as early as 11:00 A.M. Some were aware of the proposed noon rally and wanted to take part. Many went out of curiosity, because they "wanted to see what was going on."[136] Both Michener and the Scranton Commission conclude that the rally was an anti-Guard rally rather than an antiwar rally (as originally planned) and that many people gathered on the campus to find out what could be done to get the Guard off campus.[137] Lewis also notes that some students "felt they had a right to be on the Commons and that the Guard was saying symbolically that they did not have this right."[138] If Lewis is correct, participation in the noon rally was viewed by some as a symbolic protest of and challenge to the authority of the Guard on campus. Taylor's student data indirectly support Lewis' argument—students felt the mood of the crowd was one of concern and anger rather than fear and few of them felt they were risking injury in appearing at the rally.[139]

By 11:45 A.M. ninety-nine guardsmen faced a crowd across the Commons estimated at 1,200 to 4,500.[140] Seventy percent of the students in Taylor's survey thought there were less than 2,000 people on the Commons at the time.[141] There is agreement that an active core of people around the Victory Bell, numbering 200 to 1,500,[142] shouted slogans at the Guard; on the surrounding hill there were 1,000 to 3,000[143] "cheerleaders" and "spectators." The total number of demonstrators was probably between 2,000 and 3,000.[144]

Enforcing the morning decision that no rally be allowed, a Kent State police officer, Harold Rice, standing near the ROTC ruins and using a bullhorn, ordered the crowd to disperse. When they didn't, the National Guard commander put Rice in a jeep with a driver and two riflemen, and the group drove across the Commons toward the crowd, who responded by chanting "Pigs off campus" and "One, two, three, four, we don't want your fucking war," as well as hurling rocks at the jeep. Officer Rice told the crowd through the bullhorn that their rally was prohibited and they would have to disperse. Those who heard him didn't move, and the jeep returned to the main body of the Guard.

Although Taylor found that many students knew the rally was prohibited,[145] there were still many, particularly those who commuted and did not hear the announcements on the local radio stations or read the Matson-Frisina flyer, who first learned the rally was prohibited when the campus police and the National Guard ordered them to disperse. Interestingly, there were no university officials involved in the attempt to stop the rally, and few writers fault university officials. Tompkins and Anderson, however, place much of the responsibility for what happened subsequently on the shoulders of President White. "That the President had failed to prepare them for this announcement, that he failed to appear at the rally, that he failed to 'legitimize' the Guard's orders, in our judgment, contributed to the metamorphosis of what had been a peaceful, almost playful rally into a fatal confrontation."[146] This criticism of White overlooks the point made earlier—White apparently assumed that the Guard was now in control of the campus and there was no need for him to be involved personally. In addition, appearing before the crowd to explain the Guard's presence on campus was not White's style.

When Officer Rice returned to the main body of troops, General Canterbury ordered his troops to load and lock their rifles, ready to fire if necessary. Use of weapons by the National Guard in civil disorder duty is governed by Section F of Annex F to OPLAN 2, which states:

f. Weapons. When all other means have failed or chemicals are not readily available, you are armed with the rifle and have been issued live ammunition. The following rules apply in the use of firearms:

   (1) Rifles will be carried with a round in the chamber in the safe position. Exercise care and be safety-minded at all times.

(2) Indiscriminate firing of weapons is forbidden. Only single aimed shots at confirmed targets will be employed. Potential targets are:
  (a) Sniper-(Determined by his firing upon, or in the direction of friendly forces or civilians) will be fired upon when clearly observed and it is determined that an attempt to apprehend would be hazardous or other means of neutralization are impractical. . . .
  (b) Other. In any instance where human life is endangered by the forcible, violent actions of a rioter, or when rioters to whom the Riot Act has been read cannot be dispersed by any other reasonable means, then shooting is justified.[147]

Unfortunately, as Taylor's data clearly show, students were unaware that the Guard had live ammunition in their weapons and did not think they would fire.[148]

As he stood by the ROTC building looking at the crowd across the Commons, General Canterbury saw his mission quite clearly; if the crowd would not disperse voluntarily he would be forced to use whatever means he had at his disposal. As he testified before the Scranton Commission: "The assemblies were not to be permitted because of the previous two days of rioting and to permit an assembly at this point would have been dangerous."[149] Many guardsmen must have agreed with Grant and Hill:

We were now, I believe, in an untenable situation from which there could be no turning back. For the first time in the many riots in which I participated, I believed there was a possibility that the demonstrators could attack us and be successful in overrunning our position, with little or no effort. This could have been accomplished in just a few seconds. I felt that we could have been killed with our own rifles if they got hold of them. This feeling was not mine alone. Most of the Guardsmen shared it.[150]

On orders from General Canterbury eight to ten Guard grenadiers used their grenade launchers to fire tear gas cannisters at the crowd. Two volleys of the pungent gas soon began to scatter some of the crowd, but a stiff cross-wind and poor aim by the grenadiers made the barrage largely ineffective. In addition, "the indiscriminate gassing of spectators had the effect of arousing anger among the crowd"[151] and led some spectators to become actively involved in harassing the Guard. Errant tear gas cannisters were lobbed back at the grenadiers who fired them.

Seeing that the tear gas had no effect in dispersing the crowd the men of Companies A and C and Troop G were ordered to advance against the crowd. Their rifles were loaded, safeties on, bayonets in place. Each guardsman wore a gas mask. Most carried M-1 rifles, a combat weapon, some carried .45 caliber pistols as sidearms, and there were several shotguns loaded with birdshot and buckshot, non-lethal except at very close range. According to the Justice Department Summary, but cited nowhere else, no firing instructions were issued except that Company C was told that the order to fire would come from one man, presumably the commanding officer, firing in the air.[152]

As the troops moved out from the ROTC building and across the Commons, Company A was on the right flank, Company C was on the left flank, and Troop G was in the center. General Canterbury, in a business suit, marched behind his men. The advance of the Guard and the tear gas forced the crowd to retreat—some of them going back up and over the hill behind the Victory Bell (Blanket Hill) and around Taylor Hall.

Canterbury's original plan was to march to the crest of Blanket Hill, a knoll beyond the bell, between the northern end of Johnson Hall and the southern end of Taylor Hall. When some of the students ran to the north end of Taylor Hall he sent a contingent of men around there to disperse them. He had hoped, after clearing the Commons, to withdraw his troops to the ROTC building.[153]

Tactically this plan made good sense. The crest of Blanket Hill gave Canterbury control of the immediate high ground and insured that the Commons had been cleared and the noon rally dispersed—his mission for the day. Company C, detached to the other side of Taylor Hall, provided protection for his flank and prevented people from end-running his position and returning to the Commons.

When Canterbury reached the crest of the hill, however, he decided that it would be necessary to push the demonstrators even further away from the Commons and toward the nearby dormitories.

His immediate target was a nearby athletic practice field. When the Guard contingent reached the practice field, they formed a skirmish line and patiently awaited further orders. Once on the practice field Canterbury discovered that he had not been very effective in dispersing the crowd; when his troops marched down the back side of Blanket Hill toward the practice field the crowd separated and let them through, closing ranks again after the Guard's passage. The practice field was also a poor site for his men to form a skirmish line—it was fenced on three sides, effectively preventing movement except back in the direction they had come, and it enabled the crowd, which had now split into two groups, to harass the guardsmen from the Prentice Hall parking lot and the walk at the bottom of Blanket Hill. As they stood on the practice field the Guard were under a heavy barrage of rocks and verbal abuse, and the tear gas vollies merely produced a "tennis match," with the demonstrators hurling the tear gas cannisters back at the guardsmen.[154]

While the National Guard was being barraged with rocks, their own tear gas cannisters, and verbal abuse, the mood of the students changed.

By this time, the crowd seemed more united in mood. The feeling had spread among students that they were being harassed as a group, that state and civic officials had united against them, and that the university had either cooperated or acquiesced in their suppression. They shouted "Pigs off campus" and called the guardsmen "green pigs" and "facist bastards."[155]

The Scranton Commission also suggests that many students felt that the Guard was violating the students' "turf," their traditional sanctuary, and interfering with their freedom of expression.[156] Taylor, for example, found that many students were aware that the rally had been banned but didn't think the ban was right.[157] The Guard charged across the Commons with rifles at the ready, and using tear gas merely reenforced their perceptions of the Guard as an alien entity on the campus.

The Guard contingent spent ten fruitless minutes on the practice field, with only stone bruises, frayed nerves, and growing discomfort to show for their time. The weather was warm, the situation was tense, and the gas masks which the guardsmen had been forced to wear as they crossed the Commons fogged up in the heat, making sight and breathing difficult.[158] With each passing minute in the practice field the guardsmen became increasingly uncomfortable.

At one point during their stay on the field some guardsmen kneeled and pointed their rifles at the crowd facing them, but did nothing further. According to the Scranton Commission a .45 caliber pistol was fired into the air by an officer on the practice field, but the only officer with such a weapon denies firing it.[159] The act of kneeling and pointing their weapons at the crowd without firing may have seemed to the crowd to be evidence that the guardsmen had no ammunition or they wouldn't use it.

Finally, General Canterbury decided that the guardsmen should retrace their steps to the top of Blanket Hill and back down into the Commons and across to the ROTC building. He defended his move in these words: "My purpose was to make it clear beyond any doubt to the mob that our posture was now defensive and that we were clearly returning to the Commons, thus reducing the possibility of injury to either soldiers or students."[160] To the watching crowd the Guard maneuver looked like a retreat, as though the demonstrators had "won," and this emboldened some of them, who marched in mock lock-step with the departing guardsmen and heaped a great deal of verbal abuse on them.[161] The crowd did not act en masse; some stayed at the foot of Blanket Hill watching the guardsmen march away; others ran around the end of the Taylor Hall toward the Commons. Individuals and small groups followed the guardsmen as they trudged up the hill, their backs to the people below.

At the crest of the hill, near a small pagoda, a group of guardsmen turned and fired. According to the Scranton Commission:

Twenty-eight guardsmen have acknowledged firing from Blanket Hill. Of these, 25 fired 55 shots from rifles, two fired five shots from .45 caliber pistols, and one fired a single blast from a shotgun. Sound tracks indicate that the firing of these 61 shots lasted approximately 13 seconds. The time of the shooting was approximately 12:25 P.M.[162]

Four students—Jeffrey Miller, Allison Krause, William Schroeder and Sandra Lee Scheuer—were killed and nine others wounded.

The closest casualty was twenty yards from the guardsmen, the farthest 245 to 250 yards away; Jeffrey Miller was 85–90 yards away, Allison Krause, 110 yards away, and William Schroeder and Sandra Lee Scheuer were both 130 yards away. The Scranton Commission found that Allison Krause, Jeffrey Miller, and William Schroeder had been on or near the Commons during the noon rally, although Miller is the only one of the three known to have been directly involved in harassing the Guard. Sandra Lee Scheuer was on her way to class when she was shot and killed.[163]

Why did the Guardsmen fire? A number of explanations have been advanced. At the 1975 civil suit trial several guardsmen argued that the crowd was within twenty feet of them and posed a serious threat to their lives.[164] Guardsman Barry Morris described his perceptions as he marched back up Blanket Hill:

Question: And what were the students doing as you were walking toward the Pagoda?

Answer: At first they were just walking kind of fast behind us, because we were walking at a quick pace.

As we quickened our pace, they started running, and at that point, it just, it seemed obvious that they were set on overtaking us.

The noise, you know, the noise level increased just to point that it, you know, that I was scared to death.[165]

Several other guardsmen testified that they felt their lives were in danger.

After interviewing a number of guardsmen, Eszterhas and Roberts concluded that while the guardsmen felt they were being threatened, and some were afraid, most realized that they were in no danger of being killed.[166] There was noise and some stones were thrown, but there was no evidence that the demonstrators had weapons. Michener suggests that the guardsmen shot because they feared for their lives and were tired of being harassed by people with whom they no longer had patience or sympathy.[167] In essence, the guardsmen had been pushed to the limit of their physical and psychological endurance—and they broke. The Scranton Commission, recognizing that some of the guardsmen were frightened and many were tired of being harassed, nonetheless, concluded: "The indiscriminate firing of rifles into a crowd of students and the deaths that followed were unnecessary, unwarranted, and inexcusable."[168] Peter Davies raises an interesting point:

If the guardsmen's claim that a crowd was charging them to within ten, fifteen, twenty, and thirty feet was true, then obviously most of the casualties would have been less than two hundred feet away. Why were they shooting at students two hundred, three hundred, and four hundred feet away from them, distances that remove any danger whatever to the soldiers?[169]

The Scranton Commission found that relatively few of the guardsmen were firing at people who were immediately threatening them—at least forty-one shots were fired into the air or the ground.[170] Those guardsmen who admit firing at specific people seem to have fired at people closest to them, although the closest casualty was sixty feet away, not the twenty or thirty feet claimed by some guardsmen.[171]

The answer to Davies' question may lie in the topography of the area of the shooting. The pagoda on Blanket Hill is the high point of the area and shots fired over the heads of people twenty or thirty yards away would carry in a downward trajectory and inflict mortal wounds hundreds of feet away to people at whom the guardsmen weren't aiming. Thus, the guardsmen who thought they were safely aiming over the heads of people near them may have inflicted wounds on others quite some distance away.

Several other explanations have been suggested. The Minority Report examines two alternatives—the "they followed orders" thesis and the "sniper" theory.[172] The "they followed orders" thesis stems from the statement of one guardsman that he heard the order to fire; the authors of the Minority Report wonder about the officer with a .45 caliber pistol aimed at the crowd before the shooting began and the single shot which preceded the barrage of rifle fire.[173] At the 1975 civil suit trial Harry Montgomery, a student standing by Taylor Hall, testified that he saw a guardsman with a .45 tap several guardsmen on the back as they walked up Blanket Hill, before he turned and fired his pistol.[174] The guardsman identified by Montgomery, First Sergeant Myron Pryor, testified that he did not tap his men on the back and did not turn and fire the first shot, since his .45 was empty at the time.[175] Since no check of ammunition was made by the Guard immediately after the shooting, it is difficult to know whether Pryor is telling the truth. However, Pryor did admit that he turned and aimed his empty pistol at the demonstrators but that he turned when his troops turned, which he assumed was because they had been ordered to take a stand.[176] Guardsman Richard K. Love also testified that he heard an order to halt and turn as the Guard neared the pagoda,[177] but there is no supporting testimony, and the Scranton Commission concluded, "The weight of the evidence indicates, however, that no command to fire was given, either by word or by gesture."[178]

The "sniper" theory—that the first shot was fired by a sniper and the guardsmen fired in retaliation—was initially proposed by Generals Canterbury and Del Corso, but there has been little supporting evidence. The Scranton Commission, noting that neither the FBI nor the Ohio State Highway Patrol—after extensive investigations—found evidence of a sniper, suggests that what appears to be a sniper's gun in the photographs is nothing more than the telephoto lens of a camera on a tripod atop a nearby building.[179] Perhaps the most telling criticism of the "sniper" theory is found in the Minority Report, which concludes, "What chiefly weakens the hypothesis that the Guardsmen shot thinking themselves endangered by student snipers is that they did not fire in any direction where snipers might be presumed to have been."[180]

Peter Davies suggests still another explanation for the shooting: while the guardsmen stood on the practice field, an agreement was reached to take action against those harassing them.[181] This theory, of course, assumes premeditation on the part of the guardsmen and/or their commanders. Based on the evidence available to him at the time Davies is forced to accept that

We still do not know whether or not a few guardsmen had conspired during those few minutes when they were immobile on the football practice field, compelled, by the folly of their commanders, to endure harassment by a handful of students in the parking lot and the particularly vocal abuse from many among the large crowd spread out in front of Taylor Hall.[182]

Davies' theory was one of the factors which subsequently led the
Justice Department to open a grand jury investigation of the shooting
in 1973, an investigation which resulted in the indictment of eight
guardsmen for violating the civil rights of the wounded and dead
students. In the subsequent criminal trial the case was dismissed for
lack of evidence. (This case will be discussed in greater detail in the
next chapter).

Charles Thomas argues that "Major Jones had informed his men
that if the students encroached on the Guard from behind on the
return march, the soldiers were to wheel around and fire a volley
over their heads, to brush them back."[183] Thomas presents no direct
evidence to substantiate these allegations nor is there any in the
public record. Following his logic Thomas argues that Major Jones, at
the top of the hill, shouted "Turn around and fire three rounds!"[184]
leading to the fatal fusillade. Nowhere in the public record, in films of
the events, or in the tape recordings made at the time, is Major Jones'
voice to be heard issuing that command.

The central question remains unanswered. Was the shooting a
conspiracy between officers and enlisted men to punish those who
had been harassing them? Or were the guardsmen pushed, by the
heat, the rocks, and the verbal abuse, beyond the breaking point?
These questions have not been completely answered, even after nine
years of litigation.

Upon hearing the gunfire, Majors Fassinger and Jones ran up and
down the line of guardsmen yelling, "Cease Fire!" Major Jones had
to hit several men on the helmet to stop their firing. Immediately after
the guardsmen at the top of Blanket Hill stopped firing, Captain
Snyder of Company C (stationed at the other end of Taylor Hall and
out of the action) took seven men to examine those students in the
Prentice Hall parking lot who had been shot. They found Miller and
Schroeder dead. The presence of a Guard contingent nearby in-
flamed those who slowly began to realize what had happened, and
Captain Snyder's contingent beat a retreat back to Taylor Hall and
later back across the Commons. General Canterbury, after the firing
had halted, ordered the men of Troop G and Company A back down
Blanket Hill and across the Commons.

The reaction of the crowd to the gunfire is well described by the
Scranton Commission:

As the shooting began, students scattered and ran. In the parking lot behind Prentice Hall, where two were killed and two wounded, students dove behind parked cars and attempted to flatten themselves on the pavement. On the slope east of Taylor Hall, where four were wounded, students scrambled behind a metal sculpture, rolled down the incline, or sought cover behind trees. The scene was one of pell-mell disorder and fright.

Many thought the guardsmen were firing blanks. When the shooting stopped and they rose and saw students bleeding, the first reaction of most was shock. Jeffrey Miller lay on the pavement of an access road, blood streaming from his mouth.

Then the crowd grew angry. They screamed and some called the guardsmen "murderers." Some tried to give first aid. One vainly tried mouth-to-mouth resuscitation on Sandra Lee Scheuer, one of the fatalities. Knots of students gathered around the fallen.[185]

In shocked and stunned silence people viewed the desolation created by the gunfire. Some stayed to try and help the living or weep for the dead, while others moved toward the Commons after the Guard.

Those who gathered on the Commons to face the National Guard once more had a strident, defiant, fatalistic mood. Michener describes the scene: "From the crowd rose many voices demanding that a frontal assault be made on the Guard. 'Let them spatter us if they want to,' was the defiant cry."[186] Guardsmen, some of whom had earlier feared that the crowd would take their weapons away and use them, now faced people who felt they had nothing to lose by doing just that. As the National Guard stood nervously in a circle on the Commons, rifles in position, surrounded by an ever-growing and increasingly hostile crowd, the bloodshed of a few minutes earlier looked as though it was merely a prelude.

Further bloodshed was averted by the intervention of faculty marshals, who worked to cool down the emotions of the crowd and prevent hostile and provocative actions by the Guard. Major Jones and General Canterbury seemed intent on dispersing the crowd through the use of force but they were convinced to give the marshals a chance to plead with the crowd to disperse before further violence occurred. A tense twenty minutes ensued, while the marshals—visible in their white armbands—talked with the crowd and the National Guard officers. By 1:30 P.M. the marshals were successful, leaving the Commons and Blanket Hill clear of demonstrators and the Guard standing at "parade rest" in a circle around the burned-out ROTC building.

Word of the shooting reached President White at the Brown Derby where he was eating lunch. He immediately returned to his office, and after conferring with his staff, decided to close the university for the rest of the week. Once again, however, effective control of the campus was taken from White's hands. Portage County Prosecutor Ronald Kane heard of the shooting over the radio, and after failing in his attempt to talk with Governor Rhodes he obtained an injunction from Common Pleas Court Judge Albert Caris closing the university indefinitely.

The injunction gave the National Guard complete control over the campus (the first specifically legal authorization granted them) and gave students until noon on May 5 to vacate the campus. Students packed what they could and left the rest in their dorms, using university buses and cars to get home as best they could. Worried parents also tried to call their children in Kent, putting such an overload on the city phone system that it had to close down, leading some students to think that the FBI was trying to isolate them and convincing many parents that a "revolution" was taking place in Kent.[187] Despite the enormous difficulties involved, the campus was virtually empty by evening, except for the police and National Guard, who patrolled its 660 barren and war-scarred acres.

During the afternoon and evening of May 4 city police and National Guardsmen closed down the city to outsiders. All traffic in and out of the city was halted and military vehicles patrolled the streets. A dusk-to-dawn curfew was in effect and everyone was off the streets; many spent the evening listening to the radio for news—much as they had when John F. Kennedy had been killed. "Rumors flew more swiftly than the military helicopters which circled the town incessantly, shining giant spotlights over houses and yards in an eerie treetop dance. Kent knew real fear."[188]

In retrospect, the events of Monday are more understandable if we realize that most of the participants in the drama believed that Governor Rhodes had ordered a state of emergency in Kent, which would have effectively placed legal control of the city and university in the hands of the National Guard. The Monday morning meeting in the fire station thus yields a different interpretation: General Canterbury and the officials at the meeting were not debating whether the Guard had the authority to disperse the noon rally (that was assumed) but where the rally was, or whether it should be prohibited. President White's oblique response that the rally "would be dangerous" provided Canterbury with the necessary rationale for his subsequent actions. The lack of overt opposition by university officials at the meeting can also be understood as tacit acceptance of the Guard's status on campus. White's decision to go to lunch with his staff at the Brown Derby at the time of the rally is still another indication that he regarded dispersal of the noon rally as the Guard's responsibility.

Although city, university, and National Guard officials were under the impression that Kent was under a state of emergency and that rallies were banned, many of the demonstrators were not. They were unaware of what Rhodes had planned to do, and those who knew that the rally was banned disagreed with the ban. Thus, the Guard's newly defined mission of dispersing the noon rally was regarded by many demonstrators as one more example of an illegitimate exercise of arbitrary military power.

Guardsmen and demonstrators thus viewed the legitimacy of the Guard's mission as it moved across the Commons and up Blanket Hill in quite different terms. Because the demonstrators felt the Guard's presence on campus was illegitimate, they felt no qualms about harassing them, physically and verbally. The guardsmen, who viewed their mission as a legitimate one, grew increasingly resentful of the physical and verbal abuse to which they were subjected. The consequence of these differing perceptions was the thirteen second fusillade which killed four people.

AFTERWARDS

Tuesday morning the mass media descended on Kent, insuring that KSU would no longer be the largest unknown university in the country. Some newsmen—from the *New York Times* and CBS— had been covering the story since the burning of the ROTC building on Saturday night. Along with the media came the FBI and the Ohio State Highway Patrol—each making a separate investigation of the shootings and neither making their complete report public.

The faculty, finding themselves barred from campus and wanting to take some form of collective action, held a mass meeting in the Akron Unitarian Church, attended by approximately half the faculty as well as many teaching fellows and graduate assistants. The resolution adopted by this assembly read, in part,

We hold the Guardsmen, acting under the orders and under severe psychological pressures, less responsible than are Governor Rhodes and Adjutant General Del Corso, whose inflammatory indoctrination produced those pressures. We deplore the prolonged and unduly provocative military presence on the campus not only because we regard the use of massive military force against unarmed students as inappropriate in itself, but because it symbolizes the rule of force in our society and international life.

We regard student protest against this rule of force as their moral prerogative. We profoundly regret the failure of the Governor and other civil officers to understand the complexity and variety of issues motivating our students, to comprehend the diversity of the students involved, and to adjust flexibly and humanely to their morally based unrest.[189]

Michener concludes that while the faculty manifesto contained some basic truths it showed "civic irresponsibility" because of the lack of appreciation for the difficult political situation in which the university was embroiled.[190] In essence, the charges—even though true—should not have been made public, or made public at that time. Michener, of course, fails to understand the sense of moral outrage which many faculty felt at the shootings, an outrage which demanded public expression.

Townspeople quickly took sides as well. The Knight news team investigating the shootings found:

By Wednesday, two days after the shooting, public opinion on the Kent State incident was clearly divided. There were those who felt that the student demonstrators had received exactly what they deserved and those who were quite ready to charge the national guardsmen involved with murder.[191]

Although there are no public opinion data from Kent for this period, letters to President White and the Kent-Ravenna *Record Courier* reflect this division of opinion, with the majority of letters sympathetic to the guardsmen.[192] The Republican primary, which took place the day after the shootings, resulted in Governor Rhodes' loss of the Senate nomination; Rhodes won 47.5 percent of the primary vote statewide and won 41.4 percent of the vote in Portage County. His vote in Portage county declined precipitously from 1966, when he had carried 86.4 percent of the Republican vote for governor against a weak opponent.

Student opinion was also divided. Taylor found that at least 45 percent of the students surveyed felt that Guard officers, Governor Rhodes, and radical KSU students were "very" responsible for the shootings.[193] There was a reluctance to place responsibility on the guardsmen who fired, many students feeling that the commanding officers had primary responsibility. Many students felt Governor Rhodes was more responsible than the Guard officers or the enlisted men. Many accused him of using the occasion to win votes in the primary. "Governor Rhodes had to show his power for the political scene and the up-coming primary by bringing in the troops. I put the entire blame on him. . . ."[194] Those who viewed student radicals as being very responsible seemed to focus on two dimensions of the Monday demonstration: students who defied the ban on rallies deserved whatever happened to them, and what happened at KSU was part of a broader conspiracy. "I believe that outside agitators were totally responsible because through a plan they accomplished their purpose of closing KSU. . . . KSU was a mission for the group and they accomplished their 'mission impossible.'"[195] Perceptions of responsibility were colored by the extent to which students were involved in Monday's events. Participants were far more likely than observers and nonparticipants to say that Governor Rhodes, National Guard officers, President Nixon, and Vice-President Agnew were "very" responsible for the shootings, and they were far less likely to perceive radicals, student and nonstudent, as being "very" responsible.[196] It is interesting to note that the participants hold the most visible symbols of civil and military authority, National Guard officers, governor, president, and vice-president responsible, rather than the enlisted men who fired the shots. For these people the context of events within which the shootings took place was an important determinant of responsibility.

The split between those who held radicals responsible and those who perceived the symbols of civil and military authority responsible is mirrored in a Q-sort by Steven Brown,[197] which found two major groupings—radicalized students, who were alienated from the established order, and intolerant townspeople, who were totally committed to the established order and intolerant of those who threatened it. A third group, the "reasonables," felt that the way to resolve conflict was by discussion and negotiation. The Brown data indicate that very shortly after the shootings student and townspeople's perceptions had differentiated.

A nationwide Gallup telephone poll, taken on May 13 and 14, found that 11 percent of the people thought that the National Guard was primarily responsible for the deaths, 58 percent that the demonstrating students were responsible, and 31 percent had no opinion.[198] The Gallup organization noted:

The question on the Kent State killing produced an unusually high number of "no opinion," suggesting that the no opinion column might harbor some people with qualms about the guard's behavior who were reluctant to say so outright. It also seems likely that some of those polled were suspending judgment about who was most to blame until the conflicting accounts of the shooting could be cleared up.[199]

The willingness to suspend judgment, which the Gallup pollsters found in the national sample, was not evident in Kent. In characterizing the mood of the city after the shootings the Knight newspaper team found, "Often it seemed to reporters that there was a plenitude of spite in Kent and a sad shortage of sympathy."[200]

The shock waves from the shootings at Kent State, and the subsequent shootings at Jackson State in Mississippi, were felt on college campuses across the nation. A study by Peterson and Bilowsky found that 57 percent, or almost 1350 colleges and universities, experienced some "significant" impact on campus operations as a result of the Cambodian invasion, the Kent State and Jackson State shootings.[201] The campus response varied by type of school; public and private universities were more likely to experience strikes or demonstrations than colleges which, in turn, were more likely to experience disruptions than sectarian institutions. The authors

suggest that the number of students attending the school was a critical factor in a school's response to the events of early May; they
reasoned that the larger schools contained a "critical mass" of
protest-prone students who could and would take advantage of
events such as Kent State to mobilize students at their institutions.[202]

The presidents of colleges and universities were concerned with
their students' reactions to the shootings at Kent State and Jackson
State, since many of the presidents, particularly those heading public
institutions, were concerned about the possible loss of public confidence in higher education and the reaction of state officials to demonstrations on their campuses. These fears were reflected in the
presidents' perceptions of which constituents would be critical of
happenings on campus; local area residents were viewed as being
most critical, followed in turn by state legislators, and alumni—three
very important clientele support for higher education in America.[203]

The fears of these presidents proved largely unrealistic. The campus demonstrations following Kent State, while large and frequently
militant, were also peaceful. In analyzing the largely peaceful nature
of the protest demonstrations the Scranton Commission concluded:

The main reason for the general nonviolence is again to be found in the
paradox of tactics: the massive number of moderates who had joined the
protest, partly because of violent acts against students, then guaranteed by
their involvement that the protests would be largely nonviolent. In part,
moderates were able to do this because they outnumbered extremists. But
more important were their decisions: on campus after campus, students,
faculty, and administrators set up programs of action designed to provide
politically viable alternatives to violent action.[204]

On campus after campus moderates took over control of the protest
movement from campus radicals. There were speeches, there was
rhetoric, there were marches, and there were demonstrations—
frequently larger than during the Student Mobilization days—but
they were more somber and thoughtful than before, and they attracted a broader cross-section of the campus community, some of
whom supported U.S. foreign policy in southeast Asia but could not
tolerate American students, like themselves, being shot and killed on
college campuses.

Although post-Kent State demonstrations proved attractive to substantial numbers of moderates, activating and involving many who had not been involved previously, research by Adamek and Lewis suggests that involvement in protest demonstrations, particularly where violence results, served to radicalize participants.[205] Interviews with Kent State students suggested that the violence of May 4 served to radicalize the students, "that is, they became more accepting of the use of violence, moved to the left in their political attitudes, and became more politically and protest active."[206] The Adamek and Lewis data show that the violence of May 4, rather than making students more quiescent, angered and made them more radical.

Two days after the shootings six Kent State students, visiting Congressman William Stanton (R-Ohio) in Washington, were able to spend more than an hour talking with President Nixon. The students explained to Nixon that they felt that campus unrest was caused by student opposition to the Vietnam War and by a lack of communication between students, campus administrators, and the federal government. The president expressed appreciation for their candor and promised them a full report on the killings. In the following days President Nixon also met with the heads of eight major universities and with state and territorial governors to hear their evaluations of his policies.

In the week following May 4, President White and the Faculty Senate sought ways to complete the spring quarter instruction, which still had five weeks remaining. At a faculty meeting on May 8, President White and the faculty decided to continue classes through whatever means possible. Classes met at nearby universities and colleges (Oberlin designated itself as "Kent State in Exile"), church halls, faculty homes, business and commercial facilities, and many courses were completed by mail and telephone.

May 8 also marked the withdrawal of the National Guard from campus and the departure of the Ohio State Highway Patrol and, due to a modification of the court injunction, the first day that faculty, staff, and administration were allowed back on campus (from 8:00 A.M. to 5:00 P.M., Monday through Friday).

When the faculty and staff returned to campus, they discovered the FBI and the Ohio State Highway Patrol busily gathering evidence in their investigations of the shootings. Neither report has ever been made public in its entirety, although the Portage County Grand Jury had access to the Highway Patrol report, and the Scranton Commission had access to the FBI report. On May 15, Portage County Prosecutor Ronald Kane revealed to the public "weapons" and "materials" confiscated in a search of empty dormitory rooms after the closing of the campus on May 4. The collection included a rifle, shotgun, several revolvers, baseball bats, knives, bows and arrows, and hypodermic syringes and needles. As Michener notes, however, these were the types of things one might expect to find in a college dormitory or in the homes of families with college-age students.[207]

In addition to these investigations by off-campus agencies, President White, on May 11, created the Commission on Kent State University Violence, chaired by Professor Harold K. Mayer. The Mayer Commission met with a large number of people and took documentary and tape-recorded evidence regarding the events of May 1−4. At the conclusion of their investigation the commission could not agree on a final report and a year after its establishment, published four volumes—three volumes represent subcommittee reports focusing on specific problems within the university and between the university and community, while the fourth volume, the Minority Report (so called because it was written by a minority of members of the commission), concluded that outside agitators played a predominant role in the events of the weekend.[208]

President White also created a forty-five member Commission to Implement a Commitment to Non-Violence, under the chairmanship of Professor Charles E. Kegley. The Kegley Commission had a two-fold task:

(1) to consider and recommend various control procedures including, but not restricted to, a marshalling program, group discussions and the development of an administrative policy in response to violence or threats of violence and (2) to attempt to prevent violence by identifying those conditions which might produce it and to suggest means by which to eliminate it.[209]

Unlike the Mayer Commission, the Kegley Commission was established to explore administrative problems within the university and to suggest solutions. As a result it issued no report. Instead it decided upon a series of administrative changes, which it submitted to the appropriate administrative officers for adoption or rejection. Naturally, not all of the recommendations were accepted but much of the administrative reorganization which occurred in the year following the shootings stemmed from the Kegley Commission recommendations.

Forty days after the shootings, on June 13, over twelve hundred graduate and undergraduate students returned to the campus—to receive their diplomas. They were the first students to be on campus since May. During his commencement address President White announced that President Nixon, responding to pleas from White and area congressmen, had named a special commission headed by former governor William Scranton, to investigate campus unrest, particularly the cases of Kent State and Jackson State.

On June 15 Judge Caris lifted the injunction under which the university had been operating and returned control to the trustees. A week later classes began for the first summer session of 1970. Security was tight: faculty, staff, and students had to carry valid and up-to-date ID cards and there were more law enforcement officers on campus than usual. The only visible reminders of the weekend were the fire-blackened plot of ground where the ROTC building once stood and bullet holes in the metal sculpture downhill from the pagoda where the guardsmen stood when they shot.

Although classes resumed their academic year schedule in September, 1970, the campus and community would never be the same. For people who live in Kent, who teach at or attend Kent State, or who were on or around the campus during this period, the events of May 1–4 will not be forgotten. Each year on May 3 and 4 there is an all-night vigil at the site of the killings, followed by a day of commemorative activities. Students attending KSU frequently must explain to their parents and friends what "really" happened on Blanket Hill that day and convince them that radicals no longer pose a threat on the campus. Finally, Kent State University is no longer "the largest unknown university" in the country—quite the reverse. KSU will not be known for the quality of its faculty (regardless of how talented they may be), nor the beauty of its now-quiet campus, but for what happened during thirteen fateful seconds on May 4.

Although the shootings brought notoriety to Kent State, they left a series of unresolved questions in their wake, the most important of which was: who was responsible? As we have seen in this chapter, responsibility can be assigned to any one or more of a number of actors—the National Guard officers; National Guard enlisted men; radicals, student and nonstudent; President White; Governor Rhodes; President Nixon; Vice-President Agnew; or, more generally, the students, faculty, and administration of the university. Answering the question of who was responsible has been the aim of several major investigations and an amazing number of judicial proceedings since 1970.

NOTES

1. James Michener, *Kent State: What Happened and Why* (New York: Random House, 1971).

2. *The Report of the President's Commission on Campus Unrest.* William Scranton, Chairman (Washington, D.C.: U. S. Government Printing Office, 1970), hereafter referred to as *Report of the President's Commission.* . . .

3. *Akron* (Ohio) *Beacon Journal,* "Kent State: The Search for Understanding," 24 May 1970.

4. Jerry M. Lewis, "Review Essay: The Telling of Kent State," *Social Problems* 19 (Fall 1971): 276.

5. Joe Eszterhas and Michael D. Roberts, *Thirteen Seconds* (New York: Dodd Mead, 1970).

6. Peter Davies, *The Truth About Kent State* (New York: Farrar, Straus & Giroux, 1973).

7. Charles Thomas, "The Kent State Massacre: Blood on Whose Hands?" *Gallery* 7,5 (April 1977): 39ff.

8. Phillip K. Tompkins and Elaine Vanden Bout Anderson, *Communication Crisis at Kent State* (New York: Gordon and Breach, 1971).

9. Stuart Taylor, Richard Shuntich, Patrick McGovern, and Robert Genther, *Violence at Kent State: May 1–4, 1970: The Student's Perspective* (New York: College Notes and Texts, 1971).

10. Ed Grant and Mike Hill, *I Was There: What Really Went On at Kent State* (Lima, Oh.: C. S. S. Publishing Co., 1974).

11. William Furlong, "The Guardsmen's View of the Tragedy at Kent State," *New York Times Magazine,* 21 June 1970, pp. 12–13, 64, 68–69, 71.

12. U.S. Congress, House, Representative John Sieberling's insertion of the Justice Department's Summary of the FBI Report, *Congressional Record,* 15 January 1973, pp. E207–E213, hereafter referred to as "Justice Department Summary."

13. Commission on Kent State University Violence, "Volume IV: Minority Report," Kent, Ohio, 1972 (mimeographed).

14. Trial Transcript, *Krause v. Rhodes,* 390 F. Supp. 1072 (N. D. Ohio, 1975).

15. Thomas R. Hensley and Jerry M. Lewis, eds., *Kent State and May 4th: A Social Science Perspective* (Dubuque, Ia.: Kendall/Hunt Publishing Co., 1978).

16. For an excellent history of Kent State University see Phillip R. Shriver, *The Years of Youth* (Kent, Oh.: Kent State University Press, 1960).

17. Michener, *Kent State,* pp. 42–43.

18. U.S. Department of Commerce, *County and City Data Book: 1972* (Washington: U.S. Government Printing Office, 1973), pp. 750–61.

19. Quoted in Michener, *Kent State,* pp. 104–05.

20. Jerry M. Lewis, "The Moods of May 4, 1970: The Student's View," *Political Science Discussion Papers,* Kent State University, Spring, 1971 (mimeographed).

21. Robert M. O'Neill, John P. Morris, and Raymond Mack, *No Heroes, No Villains* (Washington: Jossey-Bass, 1972), p. 6.

22. *Report of the President's Commission . . . ,* p. 234.

23. Michener, *Kent State,* p. 470.

24. A good description of the confrontation can be found in Michener, *Kent State,* pp. 96–98 and the *Report of the President's Commission . . . ,* pp. 235–36.

25. Michener, *Kent State,* pp. 99–100 and Kent Chapter of the American Association of University Professors, "Report of the Special Committee of Inquiry," Kent, Ohio, 1969 (mimeographed).

26. Kent Chapter of the American Association of University Professors, "Report . . .," p. 43.

27. *Report of the President's Commission . . . ,* p. 237.

28. Kent Chapter of the American Association of University Professors, "Report . . .," p. 43.

29. Ibid., pp. 14–15.

30. Tompkins and Anderson, *Communication Crisis at Kent State,* p. 8.

31. Quoted in Lester A. Sobel, ed., *News Dictionary: 1969* (New York: Facts on File, 1970), p. 138.

32. O'Neill, Morris, and Mack, *No Heroes, No Villains,* pp. 24–25.

33. Sobel, *News Dictionary: 1970* (New York: Facts on File, 1971), p. 300.

34. Justice Department Summary, p. E207.

35. *Report of the President's Commission . . . ,* p. 240.

36. Michener, Kent State, pp. 27–34.

37. *Report of the President's Commission . . . ,* p. 240.

38. Commission on Kent State University Violence, "Volume IV," p. 25.

39. *Akron Beacon Journal,* 24 May 1970, p. A18.

40. *Report of the President's Commission . . . ,* p. 241.

41. Ibid.

42. Eszterhas and Roberts, *Thirteen Seconds,* p. 39.

43. Justice Department Summary, p. E207.

44. Michener, *Kent State,* p. 51.

45. Ibid., p. 113.

46. Eszterhas and Roberts, *Thirteen Seconds,* p. 45 and Trial Transcript, *Kraus v. Rhodes,* vol. 10, p. 801.

47. *Report of the President's Commission . . . ,* p. 242.

48. Michener, *Kent State,* pp. 51–52.

49. Michener, *Kent State,* pp. 119–22.

50. *Report of the President's Commission . . .*, p. 242.

51. Michener, *Kent State,* pp. 56–63.

52. Kent-Ravenna (Ohio) *Record-Courier,* May 2, 1970, p. 3.

53. Taylor, Shuntich, McGovern, and Genther, *Violence at Kent State,* p. 13.

54. Commission on Kent State University Violence, "Volume IV," p. 17.

55. *Report of the President's Commission . . . ,* p. 243.

56. Michener, *Kent State,* p. 123.

57. *Report of the President's Commission . . . ,* p. 243.

58. Justice Department Summary, p. E208.

59. Ibid., E208.

60. *Report of the President's Commission . . . ,* p. 245.

61. Ibid., p. 245 and Davies, *The Truth About Kent State,* p. 15.

62. Trial Transcript, *Krause v. Rhodes,* vol. 32, p. 8038. Grant and Hill, *I Was There,* p. 15, use much the same language to describe the traditional role of the National Guard.

63. Eszterhas and Roberts, *Thirteen Seconds,* pp. 74–75.

64. Michener, *Kent State,* p. 170.

65. *Report of the President's Commission . . . ,* p. 245.

66. Ibid., p. 246.

67. Ibid.

68. *Akron Beacon Journal,* 24 May 1970, p. A18 and Trial Transcript, *Krause v. Rhodes,* vol. 43, p. 801.

69. *Akron Beacon Journal,* 24 May 1970, p. A18.

70. *Report of the President's Commission . . . ,* pp. 246–47.

71. Grant and Hill, *I Was There,* pp. 40–41 and *Report of the President's Commission . . . ,* p. 247.

72. Davies, *The Truth About Kent State,* p. 16.

73. *Report of the President's Commission . . . ,* p. 247.

74. Michener, *Kent State,* p. 174.

75. Estimates range from "more than 500" (Taylor, Shuntich, McGovern, and Genther, *Violence at Kent State,* p. 29) to "2000" (Michener, *Kent State,* p. 176). The higher estimates are probably more accurate according to people who were there.

76. *The Report of the President's Commission . . . ,* p. 248 and the Justice Department Summary, E208 agree on this point. Michener, *Kent State,* pp. 178–79 argues that the fire was started by flares and the gasoline soaked rags weren't used until after the firemen responded to the first alarm.

77. Commission on Kent State University Violence, "Volume IV," p. 51.

78. Michener, *Kent State,* p. 174.

79. *Report of the President's Commission . . . ,* pp. 248–49.

80. Lewis, "The Moods of May 4, 1970," pp. 2–3.

81. Taylor, Shuntich, McGovern, and Genther, *Violence at Kent State,* p. 31.

82. Ibid., Table 24, p. 43.

83. Ibid., pp. 33–34.

84. Michener, *Kent State,* p. 179.

85. Commission on Kent State University Violence, "Volume IV," p. 61.

86. *Report of the President's Commission* . . . , p. 249.
87. Michener, *Kent State*, p. 178 and Justice Department Summary, p. E208.
88. Furlong, "The Guardsmen's View . . . ," p. 250.
89. *Report of the President's Commission* . . . , p. 251.
90. Ibid., pp. 250–51.
91. Michener, *Kent State*, pp. 128–52 and Commission on Kent State University Violence, "Volume IV," p. 17.
92. *Report of the President's Commission* . . . , p. 251.
93. Charles Thomas, "The Kent State Massacre."
94. Michener, *Kent State*, p. 204.
95. *Report of the President's Commission* . . . , p. 253.
96. Commission on Kent State University Violence, "Volume IV," p. 80.
97. Grant and Hill, *I Was There*, p. 53.
98. Jerry M. Lewis, "A Study of the Kent State Incident Using Smelser's Theory of Collective Behavior," *Sociological Inquiry*, 42 (1971): 86.
99. *Akron Beacon Journal*, 24 May 1970, A18.
100. *Report of the President's Commission* . . . , p. 253.
101. Quoted in Michener, *Kent State*, p. 229.
102. *Report of the President's Commission* . . . , p. 253.
103. Ibid., p. 254.
104. Michener, *Kent State*, p. 104.
105. *Akron Beacon Journal*, 24 May 1970, p. A18.
106. Commission on Kent State University Violence, "Volume IV," pp. 84–92.
107. Michener, *Kent State*, p. 232.
108. Trial Transcript, *Krause v. Rhodes*, vol. 35, p. 8891.
109. Davies, *The Truth About Kent State*, p. 22.
110. *Akron Beacon Journal*, 24 May 1970, p. A18.
111. *Report of the President's Commission* . . . , p. 255.
112. Davies, *The Truth About Kent State*, p. 24.
113. Quoted in John Hubbell, "A Point of Clarification," *Left Review*, 4,2 (Spring 1980): 32.
114. *Akron Beacon Journal*, 3 May 1970, p. 1.
115. *Cleveland Plain Dealer*, 3 May 1970, p. 6.
116. *Akron Beacon Journal*, 3 May 1970, p. 1.
117. *Cleveland Plain Dealer* 3 May 1970, p. 6.
118. Commission on Kent State University Violence, "Volume IV," p. 94.
119. Taylor, Shuntich, McGovern, and Genther, *Violence at Kent State*, p. 48.
120. Justice Department Summary, p. E208.
121. *Report of the President's Commission* . . . , p. 257.
122. Ibid. and Michener, *Kent State*, p. 246.
123. The *Report of the President's Commission* . . . , p. 257 states that two people were bayonetted while Grant and Hill, *I Was There*, p. 57, state that there were ten.
124. Grant and Hill, *I Was There*, p. 52.
125. Ibid., p. 57.
126. Taylor, Shuntich, McGovern, and Genther, *Violence at Kent State*, pp. 55–56.

127. Michener's account in *Kent State*, pp. 520–24, does not place President White at this meeting, but all other accounts indicate that he was there.

128. *Report of the President's Commission* . . . , p. 260.

129. Justice Department Summary, p. E209.

130. *Report of the President's Commission* . . . , p. 260.

131. Ibid., p. 261.

132. Trial Transcript, *Krause v. Rhodes*, vol. 33, pp. 8317, 8324.

133. Ibid., vol. 34, p. 8748.

134. *Report of the President's Commission* . . . , p. 261.

135. Ibid.

136. Commission on Kent State University Violence, "Volume IV," p. 183.

137. *Report of the President's Commission* . . . , p. 267 and Michener, *Kent State*, p. 327.

138. Lewis, "A Study of the Kent State Incident . . . ," p. 91.

139. Taylor, Shuntich, McGovern, and Genther, *Violence at Kent State*, p. 76.

140. The *Report of the President's Commission* . . . , p. 265, estimates 2000 and that is probably the most accurate.

141. Taylor, Shuntich, McGovern, and Genther, *Violence at Kent State*, Table 42, p. 202.

142. The Justice Department Summary, p. E209 estimates the crowd at 200 while Eszterhas and Roberts, *Thirteen Seconds*, p. 150, estimate 1500. The latter estimate is too high.

143. The Justice Department Summary, p. E209, estimates 1000 while Eszterhas and Roberts, *Thirteen Seconds*, p. 150, suggests a crowd three times as large. The latter estimate is too high.

144. This figure agrees with the estimates of Grant and Hill, *I Was There*, p. 66, *Report of the President's Commission*, p. 265, and Lewis, "*Review Essay* . . . ," p. 270.

145. Taylor, Shuntich, McGovern, and Genther, *Violence at Kent State*, p. 76.

146. Tompkins and Anderson, *Communication Crisis at Kent State*, p. 41.

147. Quoted in the *Report of the President's Commission* . . . , p. 264.

148. Taylor, Shuntich, McGovern, and Genther, *Violence at Kent State*, p. 109.

149. *Report of the President's Commission* . . . , p. 264.

150. Grant and Hill, *I Was There*, p. 67.

151. Commission on Kent State University Violence, "Volume IV," p. 207.

152. Justice Department Summary, p. E209.

153. *Report of the President's Commission* . . . , p. 266.

154. Ibid., p. 267.

155. Ibid., p. 266.

156. Ibid., p. 267.

157. Taylor, Shuntich, McGovern, and Genther, *Violence at Kent State*, p. 56.

158. Grant and Hill, *I Was There*, p. 77, suggest this was a major reason for the shootings.

159. *Report of the President's Commission* . . . , p. 268.

160. Ibid., p. 268.

161. Michener's description of these events in *Kent State*, p. 304, is excellent.

162. *Report of the President's Commission* . . . , p. 273.
163. Ibid., p. 275.
164. Trial Transcript, *Krause v. Rhodes*, vol. 7, p. 1415; vol. 11, p. 2549; and vol. 14, p. 3308.
165. Ibid., vol. 11, p. 2605.
166. Eszterhas and Roberts, *Thirteen Seconds*, pp. 161–64.
167. Michener, *Kent State*, pp. 341, 371.
168. *Report of the President's Commission* . . . , p. 289.
169. Davies, *The Truth About Kent State*, p. 55.
170. *Report of the President's Commission* . . ., p. 274.
171. Trial Transcript, *Krause v. Rhodes*, vol. 7, p. 1415 and *Report of the President's Commission* . . ., p. 270.
172. Commission on Kent State University Violence, "Volume IV," pp. 242–49.
173. Ibid., p. 244.
174. Trial Transcript, *Krause v. Rhodes*, vol. 5, pp. 969–70.
175. Ibid., vol. 14, pp. 3281, 3292.
176. Ibid., vol. 14, pp. 3318–19.
177. Ibid., Vol. 12, p. 2857.
178. *Report of the President's Commission* . . . , p. 275.
179. Ibid., pp. 279–80.
180. Commission on Kent State University Violence, "Volume IV," p. 248.
181. Davies, *The Truth About Kent State*, p. 42.
182. Ibid.
183. Charles Thomas, "The Kent State Massacre," p. 101.
184. Ibid., p. 102.
185. *Report of the President's Commission* . . . , p. 275.
186. Michener, *Kent State*, p. 358.
187. Ibid., p. 376.
188. *Kent,* University alumni magazine, published by Kent State University, June, 1970, p. 3.
189. Ottavio Casale and Louis Paskoff (eds.), *The Kent Affair* (Boston: Houghton Mifflin, 1971), p. 26.
190. Michener, *Kent State*, p. 380.
191. American Newspaper Publishers Association, *Reporting the Kent State Incident* (New York: ANPA Foundation, 1971), p. 12.
192. See Casale and Paskoff, *The Kent Affair*, pp. 91–115 and Michener, *Kent State*, pp. 389–401.
193. Taylor, Shuntich, McGovern, and Genther, *Violence at Kent State*, p. 98.
194. Ibid., p. 94.
195. Ibid., p. 96.
196. Ibid., pp. 99–100.
197. Steven R. Brown, "The Resistance to Reason: Kent State University," *Political Science Discussion Papers*, Kent State University, 1971 (mimeographed).
198. *Newsweek*, 25 May 1970, p. 30.
199. Ibid., p. 25.

200. American Newspaper Publishers Association, *Reporting the Kent State Incident*, p. 17.

201. Richard E. Peterson and John A. Bilowsky, *May, 1970: The Campus Aftermath of Cambodia and Kent State* (Berkeley, Cal.: Carnegie Commission on Higher Education, 1971), p. 15.

202. Ibid., p. 50.

203. Ibid., pp. 36–37.

204. *Report of the President's Commission . . .* , p. 45.

205. Raymond J. Adamek, and Jerry M. Lewis, "Social Control Violence and Radicalization: The Kent State Case," *Social Forces* 51 (March 1973): 342–47.

206. Raymond J. Adamek and Jerry M. Lewis, "Social Control Violence and Radicalization: Behavioral Data," *Social Problems* 22 (June 1975): 670.

207. Michener, *Kent State*, p. 383.

208. Commission on Kent State University Violence, "Volume IV."

209. *Kent, June, 1970*, p. 5.

3

The May Fourth Trials*

Our analysis in the previous chapter of the events on Kent State's campus in May of 1970 makes it clear that widely varying attitudes existed concerning responsibility for the shootings. In the immediate aftermath of the shootings, judicial activities were initiated to determine this responsibility and to assess appropriate penalties against those responsible. These efforts resulted in one of the longest, costliest, and most complex set of courtroom struggles in American history. The litigative struggle stemming from the shootings spanned the decade of the 1970s, and the various cases involved the trial, appellate, and supreme courts of both Ohio and the United States.

These legal activities have provided us with the opportunity to analyze the impact of authoritative legal decisions on attitudes of Kent State University students concerning responsibility for the shootings, support for specific legal structures, and general support for the American judical system. Specifically, we will analyze the 1974 federal grand jury decision to indict eight Ohio National Guardsmen, the decision of the jury in the 1975 federal district court civil trial which found none of the guardsmen or officials liable for damages, and the 1979 federal district court retrial of the 1975 civil

*An earlier version of this chapter appeared in Thomas R. Hensley and Jerry M. Lewis, eds., *Kent State and May 4th: A Social Science Perspective* (Dubuque, Ia.: Kendall/Hunt Publishing Co., 1978), pp. 41–57. We gratefully acknowledge Kendall/Hunt's permission to use portions of the previous work.

case which resulted in an out-of-court settlement. While our focus is upon these three decisions, the entire litigative process resulting from the shootings must be analyzed to provide the necessary context for studying these specific decisions.

This chapter will therefore provide a detailed description of the activities associated with the seven major judicial investigations and trials which have focused upon the events of May 4: the 1970 Special State Grand Jury investigation, the 1971 state criminal trial resulting from the Special State Grand Jury investigation, the 1973–1974 federal grand jury investigation, the 1974 federal criminal trial resulting from the federal grand jury decision, the 1975 federal civil trial, the 1977 federal court of appeals decision ordering a retrial of the 1975 case, and the 1978–1979 federal civil retrial. These judicial investigations and trials have been the official, authoritative forums for seeking answers to the major questions arising from the shootings, but it will also be necessary to discuss some of the nonjudicial investigations which immediately followed the shootings, analyzing these in reference to their relationships to the grand jury investigations and the trials. Numerous other legal actions have stemmed from the events of May 4, but these will not be considered because they have not focused upon the question of who was responsible for the events which occurred on the Kent State campus on May 4.[1]

The analysis is based upon a variety of resources. One important source has been a thorough compilation of articles from the *Akron Beacon Journal* from May 4, 1970 through March of 1979. The *Beacon Journal* received a Pulitzer Prize for its reporting on the 1970 shootings, and its continuing coverage of the legal aftermath of the shootings has been excellent. A second important source involves legal documents, including briefs, trial transcripts, and court decisions. A variety of scholarly articles and papers dealing with various aspects of the Kent State trials have also been drawn upon heavily in the analysis.[2] Finally, both formal interviews and informal discussions with direct participants in the trials have provided useful insights.

NONJUDICIAL INVESTIGATIONS AND REPORTS

In the immediate aftermath of the shootings, a number of investigations were undertaken by both governmental and nongovernmental groups. The most important investigations were made by the Federal Bureau of Investigation, the President's Commission on Campus Unrest (commonly known as the Scranton Commission, named after its chairman, former Pennsylvania Governor William Scranton), and the Ohio Highway Patrol. Investigations were undertaken by a wide variety of other groups as well: the *Akron Beacon Journal,* the Inspector General's Office of the Ohio National Guard, the Special Kent State University Commission on Campus Violence, the Ohio Civil Liberties Union, the Ohio Council of Churches, the American Association of College and University Professors, and the Ohio Bureau of Investigation.

In this section, attention will focus upon the investigations and reports of the FBI, the Scranton Commission, and the Ohio Highway Patrol, for these have had the greatest impact on the subsequent judicial activities. The primary emphasis will be upon the most important findings of each of these reports and the significance of each report in the subsequent litigative proceedings.

Ohio State Highway Patrol

The first group to complete its investigation and file a report was the Ohio Highway Patrol. As reported in the *Akron Beacon Journal* on July 22, 1970, the Patrol's report, a 3,000 page document, was presented to Portage County Prosecutor Ronald Kane, who commented: "The patrol did a tremendous, thorough job. . . . It will be a terrible waste if this report can't be placed before a grand jury. . . ."[3] Little information has ever been revealed concerning the findings in this report, for it was labeled confidential for possible grand jury use. Although no conclusions were drawn in this report, it does seem apparent that it placed major responsibility for the shootings on the students. The *Beacon Journal* story stated that the report showed: "Between 2,500 and 3,000 students milling on the campus during the anti-war fracas. Remarkable photos marking several hundred as suspects and possible grand jury indictees."[4] The report was subsequently to become a major working document for the Special State Grand Jury which met in the fall of 1970 and issued indictments against twenty-five persons, mostly Kent State students.

Federal Bureau of Investigation

Within twenty-four hours of the shootings, FBI agents were on the Kent campus to gather evidence for a report to be submitted to the U.S. Department of Justice. It is estimated that more than 100 agents were in Kent to conduct the investigations, which resulted in the issuance by the Justice Department in late July of 1970 of a 7,500 page report, accompanied by a ten-page summary. The full report was not made public at the time, but highlights of the summary were reported by the *Akron Beacon Journal* on July 23, 1970,[5] and substantial excerpts were later published in the *New York Times* and the *Congressional Record*.[6]

It is important to list in some detail the most significant findings related to the events of May 4 which are contained in the Justice Department's Summary of the FBI Report, for these findings have played an important role in subsequent developments; they were utilized by the Scranton Commission in making its report on the May 4 shootings, they were cited continuously by those groups and individuals seeking a federal grand jury investigation, and they were utilized by the Justice Department in its decisions regarding the convening of a federal grand jury. It is therefore important to identify in detail the major conclusions of the Justice Department Summary.[7] The conclusions presented here are similar to those cited in several books and articles which have argued that National Guard members were responsible for the shootings.[8] It is important to note that the Summary does not specifically reach the conclusion that National Guard members were responsible for the shootings, and the Summary acknowledges that conflicting interpretations existed regarding the shootings.[9] Nonetheless, the clear thrust of the Summary points toward Guard responsibility.

Just prior to the time the Guard left its position on the practice field, members of Troop G were ordered to kneel and aim their weapons at the students in the parking lot south of Prentice Hall. They did so, but did not fire. One person, however, probably an officer, at this point did fire a pistol in the air. . . .

The Guard was then ordered to regroup and move back up the hill past Taylor Hall.

The crowd on top of the hill parted as the Guard advanced and allowed it to pass through, apparently without resistance. When the Guard reached the crest of Blanket Hill by the southeast corner of Taylor Hall at about 12:25 P.M., they faced the students following them and fired their weapons. Four students were killed and nine were wounded.

Six guardsmen, including two sergeants and Captain Srp of Troop G stated pointedly that the lives of the members of the Guard were not in danger and that it was not a shooting situation.

We have some reason to believe that the claim by the National Guard that their lives were endangered by the students was fabricated subsequent to the event. The apparent volunteering by some Guardsmen of the fact that their lives were not in danger gives rise to some suspicions.

(One guardsman) admitted that his life was not in danger and he fired indiscriminately into the crowd. He further stated that the Guardsmen had gotten together after the shooting and decided to fabricate the story that they were in danger of serious bodily harm or death from the students.

Also, a chaplain of Troop G spoke with many members of the National Guard and stated that they were unable to explain to him why they fired their weapons.

No verbal warning was given to the students immediately prior to the time the Guardsmen fired.

There was no request by any Guardsmen that tear gas be used.

There was no request from any Guardsman for permission to fire his weapon.

No Guardsman claims he was hit with rocks immediately prior to the firing.

The Guardsmen were not surrounded.

There was no sniper.

The FBI has conducted an extensive search and has found nothing to indicate that any person other than a Guardsman fired a weapon.

At the time of the shooting, the National Guard clearly did not believe that they were being fired upon.

Each person who admits firing into the crowd has some degree of experience in riot control. None are novices.

A minimum of 54 shots were fired by a minimum of 29 of the 78 members of the National Guard at Taylor Hall in the space of approximately 11 seconds.

Five persons interviewed in Troop G, the group of Guardsmen closest to Taylor Hall, admit firing a total of eight shots into the crowd or at a specific student.

Some Guardsmen (unknown as yet) had to be physically restrained from continuing to fire their weapons.

Four students were killed, nine others were wounded, three seriously. Of the students who were killed, Jeff Miller's body was found 85–90 yards from the Guard, Allison Krause fell about 110 yards away, William Schroeder and Sandy Scheuer were approximately 130 yards from the Guard when they were shot.

Although both Miller and Krause had probably been in the front ranks of the demonstrators initially, neither was in a position to pose even a remote danger to the National Guard at the time of the firing. Sandy Scheuer, as best as we can determine, was going to a speech therapy class. We do not know whether Schroeder participated in any way in the confrontation that day.

No person shot was closer than 20 yards from the guardsmen. One injured person was 37 yards away; another, 75 yards, another 95 or 100 yards; another 110 yards; another 125 or 130 yards; another 160 yards, and the other 245 or 250 yards.

Seven students were shot from the side and four were shot from the rear.

Of the 13 Kent State students shot, none, so far as we know, were associated with either the disruption in Kent on Friday night, May 1, 1970, or the burning of the ROTC building on Saturday, May 2, 1970.

As far as we have been able to determine, Schroeder, Scheuer, Cleary, MacKenzie, Russell and Wrentmore were merely spectators to the confrontation.[10]

President's Commission on Campus Unrest

On Sunday, May 24, 1970, Herbert G. Klein, White House communications director, announced that President Richard Nixon had decided to appoint "a high-level commission . . . to investigate the slaying of four students at Kent State University by National Guardsmen."[11] The Commission, under the direction of former Pennsylvania Governor William Scranton, was directed to study campus unrest throughout the United States, with specific focus upon Kent State University and Jackson State University, where two students were killed by police on May 15, 1970.

Nixon's decision to convene the commission remains a subject of speculation. Creating such a commission was hardly surprising. In the wake of national tragedies, commissions can serve as credible fact-finding agencies, can assure the general public that the government is "taking action," and can buy time while passions cool. The controversy which continues to surround the Scranton Commission's activities is the extent to which Nixon may have attempted to subvert the work of the commission, and, if he did, the motivations behind his actions. In December of 1978, Republican Senator Lowell Weicker of Connecticut called for a federal grand jury investigation of the Scranton Commission's report.[12] Weicker's action was based upon information supplied by Charles Thomas, a historian with the National Archives, and by the Military Audit Project, a Washington based group concerned with improper U.S. military activities. This information suggested that federal government agents may have been on Kent State's campus prior to the shootings and may even have served as agent provocateurs, thus contributing to the shootings on May 4.[13] According to this scenario, Nixon attempted to subvert the work of the commission through staff members who made certain that this information did not get to commission members.[14] No action has been taken by the Justice Department, and Weicker has not pressed his request. These questions thus remain unanswered.

The Scranton Report was made public on September 26, 1970, and it found both students and the National Guard at fault in the Kent State Shootings. Concerning student responsibility, the Commission concluded:

The conduct of many students and non-student protestors at Kent State on the first four days of May 1970 was plainly intolerable. We have said in our report, and we repeat: Violence by students on or off campus can never be justified by any grievance, philosophy, or political idea. There can be no sanctuary or immunity from prosecution on the campus. Criminal acts by students must be treated as such wherever they occur and whatever their purpose. Those who wreaked havoc on the town of Kent, those who burned the ROTC building, those who attacked and stoned National Guardsmen, and all those who urged them on and applauded their deeds share the responsibility for the deaths and injuries of May 4.[15]

. . . .

The actions of some students were violent and criminal and those of some others were dangerous, reckless, and irresponsible.[16]

Concerning National Guard responsibility for the tragedy, the Commission concluded:

The May 4th rally began as a peaceful assembly on the Commons—the traditional site of student assemblies. Even if the Guard had authority to prohibit a peaceful gathering—a question which is at least debatable—the decision to disperse the noon rally was a serious error. The timing and manner of the dispersal were disastrous. Many students were legitimately in the area as they went to and from class. The rally was held during the crowded noontime lunch period. The rally was peaceful, and there was no apparent impending violence. Only when the guard attempted to disperse the rally did some students react violently.[17]

. . . .

The indiscriminate firing of rifles into a crowd of students and the deaths that followed were unnecessary, unwarranted, and inexcusable.[18]

. . . .

The Guard fired amidst great turmoil and confusion engendered in part by their own activities. But the guardsmen should not have been able to kill so easily in the first place. The general issuance of loaded weapons to law enforcement officers engaged in controlling disorders is never justified except in the case of armed resistance that trained sniper teams are unable to handle. This was not the case at Kent State, yet each guardsman carried a loaded M-1 rifle.

The lesson is not new. The National Advisory Commission on Civil Disorders and the guidelines of the Department of the Army set it out explicitly.

No one would have died at Kent State if the lesson had been learned by the Ohio National Guard.

Even if the guardsmen faced danger, it was not a danger which called for lethal force. The 61 shots by 28 guardsmen certainly cannot be justified.[19]

In its final conclusions, the Commission offered no recommendations, but rather stated: "Our entire report attempts to define the lessons of Kent State, lessons that the Guard, police, students, faculty, university administrators, government at all levels, and the American people must learn—and begin at once, to act upon. We commend it to their attention."[20]

The true impact of the three major investigations on subsequent judicial processes is difficult to assess with a high degree of confidence. The secrecy surrounding both the Ohio Highway Patrol's report and the FBI report makes it impossible to determine their precise impact, although it seems clear that the Highway Patrol's report was an important resource for the Special State Grand Jury, and the FBI report was utilized by the Scranton Commission and by the Justice Department in determining whether to convene a federal grand jury. The Scranton Commission's report, on the other hand, appears to have had little impact on subsequent judicial proceedings, nor is there evidence that President Nixon gave serious attention to its plea to close the deep cleavages among generational groups in American society.

While these reports seem to have had varying impacts on the subsequent judicial proceedings, the reports certainly left unsettled the question of responsibility for the shootings. Fingers of guilt were pointed in many directions, but no individuals or groups emerged as being primarily responsible for the shootings. This judgment could only be made in the courts, and hence our attention shifts to an examination of the litigative proceedings stemming from the May 4 tragedy.

CRIMINAL TRIALS

The first set of litigative activities to be examined involves the 1970 Special State Grand Jury investigation; the 1971 state criminal trial, which stemmed from the State Grand Jury indictments; the 1973–1974 federal grand jury investigation; and the 1974 federal criminal trial, which resulted from the federal grand jury probe. These judicial activities are analyzed together because they involve criminal law rather than civil law; the judicial activities stemming from the May 4 shootings which involve civil law will be analyzed in the next section of this chapter. Given the centrality of this distinction, it is important to specify the basic differences between cases in civil and criminal law. A useful clarification of these differences is provided by Henry J. Abraham:

A case at *criminal law* is invariably brought by and in the name of the legally constituted government, no matter at what level—national, state, or local—it may arise. Chiefly statutory in the United States, criminal law defines crimes against the public order and provides for appropriate punishment. Prosecution brought under it by the proper governmental authority involves an accusation that the defendant has violated a specific provision of the law, an infraction for which a penalty has normally been provided by statute.[21] (emphasis in original)

In contrast, Abraham notes:

A case at civil law is normally one between private persons and/or private organizations, for civil law governs the relations between individuals and defines their legal rights. A party bringing suit under it seeks legal redress in a *personal interest* . . . yet while suits at civil law far more often than not are suits among private persons, the government, too, may conceivably be involved.[22] (emphasis in original)

Special State Grand Jury

Shortly after May 4, Portage County Prosecutor Ronald Kane announced that he would probably call a grand jury to investigate the shootings. According to an *Akron Beacon Journal* story of May 21, 1970, "the grand jury probe was recommended by County Coroner Robert Sybert to determine if the fatalities should be classified as 'accidental or homicidal.' "[23]

Kane was faced with enormous problems because of the scope and expense which such a grand jury probe would entail. The investigation would be "the most massive legal undertaking in Portage County's history,"[24] involving thousands of pages of information compiled by investigatory agencies and testimony from hundreds of witnesses. The cost of carrying out this investigation would go far beyond the county's financial capabilities. Kane, therefore, sought a grant for $100,000 from the state of Ohio to help finance the probe.

Ohio Attorney General Paul Brown ruled in July that the state could not legally approve the financial request, however, and on

August 3, 1970, Governor Rhodes announced that he had ordered Brown to head a Special State Grand Jury investigation of the May 4 shootings. The *Beacon Journal* story of August 3 reports that Rhodes wrote to Brown:

> "The people of Ohio are entitled to know what, if any, criminal acts took place at Kent State and who should be charged with perpetrating them.
> Only a grand jury can diminish the half-formed and mis-informed commentary on Kent State that still is heard. Only a grand jury could say who should face prosecution and for what."[25]

The *Beacon Journal* story also stated:

> Rhodes directed Brown to investigate acts leading to or inducing the illegal and criminal acts in any way associated with campus unrest that took place in Kent or on the Kent State campus between May 1 and 5.
> Such illegal or criminal acts themselves.
> The legality of official response to such acts and to the 'general temper and situation' prevailing in Kent and on the KSU campus during May 1–5. . . .[26]

A question which begs to be answered at this point is why Rhodes made the decision to convene the Special State Grand Jury. Insufficient evidence exists to provide answers to this question, but it is possible to examine some possible explanations. The governor, as quoted above, wrote that the people of Ohio were "entitled to know,"[27] and an aide of the governor stated: "'The Governor wants the facts come to light. . . .'"[28] A factor which may have been important in the decision was pressure from the U.S. Department of Justice. The *Beacon Journal* reported in the August 3 story that:

> Rhodes' announcement came just days after U.S. Attorney General John Mitchell said the federal government would step into the KSU prosecution and impanel a federal grand jury if Ohio officials failed to act.
> Mitchell's statement indicated the federal government might prosecute both students and Guardsmen.
> A Justice Department memorandum to Kane last month, signed by Jeris Leonard, head of the Justice Department civil rights division, said six Guardsmen could be prosecuted for their actions.
> Mitchell said last week there are "apparent violations of federal law."[29]

A different interpretation is offered by the Reverend John Adams, who has argued that Rhodes directed the Ohio Attorney General to

call the Special State Grand Jury as a response to the recently released "inculpatory reports of the FBI," seeking by this approach to
obfuscate the truth of May 4.[30]

The fifteen member jury was impaneled on September 14, 1970,
with testimony beginning on September 15 and concluding on October 8, with more than 300 witnesses being called. On October 16,
the grand jury issued secret indictments against twenty-five
persons—mostly Kent State students but including some nonstudents and one professor—on forty-three offenses. In addition, the
grand jury issued an eighteen-page report, which placed primary
responsibility for the events of May 2–4 on the university administration; found some students and faculty to share responsibility for the
events; criticized officers of the National Guard for their actions; and
declared that the guardsmen who fired their weapons were not subject to criminal prosecution. Concerning student and nonstudent activities, the report stated:

> The incidents originating on North Water Street in Kent, Ohio on Friday,
> May 1, 1970, and which spread to other parts of the downtown area and the
> University, constituted a riot.[31]

. . . .

> We find that the rally on the Commons on Saturday, May 2, 1970, which
> resulted in the burning of the R. O. T. C. Building, constituted a riot. There
> can never exist any justification or valid excuse for such an act. The burning
> of this building and destruction of its contents was a deliberate criminal act
> committed by students and non-students. Nor did the rioters stop with the
> burning of the R. O. T. C. building. They also set fire to the archery shed and
> moved from there to East Main Street on the front campus where they
> engaged in further acts of destruction and stoned the members of the Na-
> tional Guard as they entered Kent.
> Arson is arson, whether committed on a college campus, or elsewhere.
> The fact that some of the participants were college students changes nothing,
> except perhaps to further aggravate the seriousness of the offense.[32]

. . . .

> The Grand Jury finds that the events of Sunday, May 3, 1970, on campus
> and at the corner of Lincoln Street and East Main Street in Kent, Ohio,
> constituted a riot.[33]

. . . .

> The gathering on the Commons on May 4, 1970, was in violation of the
> directive of May 3rd issued by the University Vice President in charge of

Student Affairs. We find that all the persons assembled were ordered to disperse on numerous occasions, but failed to do so. These orders, given by a Kent State University policeman, caused a violent reaction and the gathering quickly degenerated into a riotous mob. It is obvious that if the order to disperse had been heeded, there would not have been the consequences of that fateful day. Those who acted as participants and agitators are guilty of deliberate, criminal conduct. Those who were present as cheerleaders and onlookers, while not liable for criminal acts, must morally assume a part of the responsibility for what occurred.[34]

Turning its attention to the guardsmen, the jury wrote:

It should be made clear that we do not condone all of the activities of the National Guard on the Kent State University campus on May 4, 1970. We find, however, that those members of the National Guard who were present on the hill adjacent to Taylor Hall on May 4, 1970, fired their weapons in the honest and sincere belief and under circumstances which would have logically caused them to believe that they would suffer serious bodily injury had they not done so. They are not, therefore, subject to criminal prosecution under the laws of this state for any death or injury resulting therefrom.[35]

. . . .

The circumstances present at that time indicated that 74 men surrounded by several hundred hostile rioters were forced to retreat back up the hill toward Taylor Hall under a constant barrage of rocks and other flying objects accompanied by a constant flow of obscenities and chants as "KILL, KILL, KILL." Photographic evidence has established, beyond any doubt, that as the National Guardsmen approached the top of the hill adjacent to Taylor Hall, a large segment of the crowd surged up the hill, led by smaller groups of agitators approaching to within short distances of the rear ranks of the Guardsmen.

The testimony of the students and Guardsmen is clear that several members of the Guard were knocked to the ground or to their knees by the force of the objects thrown at them. Although some rioters claim that only a few rocks were thrown, the testimony of construction workers in the area has established that 200 bricks were taken from a nearby construction site. Various students were observed carrying rocks in sacks to the "rally;" others brought gas masks and other equipment. . . . There was additional evidence that advance planning had occurred in connection with the 'rally' held at noon on May 4th.

It should be added, that although we understand and agree with the principle of law that words alone are never sufficient to justify the use of lethal force, the verbal abuse directed at the Guardsmen by students during the period in question represented a level of obscenity and vulgarity which we have never before witnessed.[36]

Concerning the National Guard officers, the report stated:

The fact that we have found those Guardsmen who fired their weapons acted in self-defense is not an endorsement by us of the manner in which those in command of the National Guard reacted. To the contrary, we have concluded that the group of Guardsmen who were ordered to disperse the crowd on the Commons were placed in an untenable and dangerous position.

The Grand Jury also concludes that the weapons issued to the National Guardsmen are not appropriate in quelling campus disorders.[37]

Primary responsibility for the shootings was attributed to the university administration by the jury, which wrote:

We find that the major responsibility for the incidents occurring on the Kent State University campus on May 2nd, 3rd, and 4th rests clearly with those persons who are charged with the administration of the University. To attempt to fix the sole blame for what happened during this period on the National Guard, the students or other participants would be inconceivable. The evidence presented to us has established that Kent State University was in such a state of disrepair, that it was totally incapable of reacting to the situation in any effective manner. We believe that it resulted from policies formulated and carried out by the University over a period of several years, the more obvious of which will be commented upon here.[38]

The administration at Kent State University has fostered an attitude of laxity, over-indulgence and permissiveness with its students and faculty to the extent that it can no longer regulate the activities of either and is particularly vulnerable to any pressure applied from radical elements within the student body or faculty.[39]

Finally, the faculty was also criticized by the report:

Among other persons sharing responsibility for the tragic consequences of May 4, 1970, there must be included the "23 concerned faculty of Kent State University. . . ."[40]

If the purpose of the authors was simply to express their resentment to the presence of the National Guard on campus, their timing could not have been worse. If their purpose was to further inflame an already tense situation, then it surely must have enjoyed some measure of success. In either case, their action exhibited an irresponsible act clearly not in the best interests of Kent State University.[41]

The indictments and report of the Special State Grand Jury stimulated intense and polarized reactions from the public and led to two major new chapters in the judicial history of the Kent State shootings. The most direct result was the state criminal trial, which was conducted more than a year later. The indictments and report also provided a major stimulus to efforts for convening a federal grand jury investigation of the shootings, for critics of the state grand jury saw glaring inconsistencies between the reports of the FBI and the Scranton Commission, on the one hand, and the conclusions of the state grand jury, on the other hand. It is the former of these results—the state criminal trial—to which attention will now turn; when the story of that trial is completed, the focus will shift to the efforts to convene a federal grand jury.

State Criminal Trials

The state criminal trials did not begin until November 22, 1971, because of a lengthy appeal process stemming directly from the indictments and report of the grand jury. Lawyers for the "Kent 25" filed suits in late October and early November of 1970 with the U.S. district court to have the grand jury's report destroyed and to overturn the indictments. Responding to these suits, Judge William K. Thomas on January 28, 1971, ordered that the report be expunged and destroyed, because "The Report irreparably injures, and as long as it remains in effect, the Report will continue to irreparably injure, as particularized, the rights of the indicted plaintiffs and of other persons similarly situated on whose behalf this action is brought,"[42] but he allowed the indictments to stand. Further appeal to the Sixth U.S. District Court of Appeals failed to alter Judge Thomas's decisions, for the court upheld his rulings on the report and indictments.[43] A final appeal to the United States Supreme Court also failed when the Court on November 19, 1971, refused to halt the start of the trials of the "Kent 25."

State prosecuting attorneys experienced difficulties from the very beginning of the trial. The first defendant was convicted by the jury of interfering with a fireman but was not convicted on three other charges of arson, assaulting a fireman at the ROTC fire on May 2, and first degree riot. The prosecution requested that charges be dismissed against the second defendant after four witnesses were called. The third and fourth defendants both pleaded guilty to first-degree riot, but the fifth defendant was ordered acquitted by Common Pleas Judge Edwin Jones on the basis of a lack of evidence and "a great possibility that some of the defendant's rights under the 14th Amendment were not necessarily observed."[44]

At this point, on December 7, 1971, sixteen days after the first defendant went on trial, special state prosecutor John Hayward issued a dramatic request for dismissal of charges against the remaining twenty defendants because of a lack of evidence. While the decision by the state surprised many, Ohio Attorney General William Brown revealed in an interview after the trial that he realized in June that many of the cases would have to be dropped: "the only evidence against (the fifth defendant) was her own statement to the grand jury, said Brown. 'And the cases were arranged according to their strength,' Brown added to illustrate how little evidence the state had in the remainder of the cases."[45] The reason the state pursued the cases as long as it did, Brown said, was that "we had an ethical and moral responsibility to go as far as we could . . . but if you don't have the evidence, you don't go to court."[46]

In the immediate aftermath of the state criminal trials, public reaction was once again both strong and divided, with students expressing support for the results and Kent townspeople generally opposing the outcome. Opponents of the state grand jury saw the results of the trials as vindicating their earlier criticism. This viewpoint was expressed clearly by former U.S. Senator from Ohio, Stephen Young:

I am pleased but not surprised. I have repeatedly stated that the indictments were a fakery and a fraud from the outset.

The purpose of the state grand jury in the first place was to whitewash Rhodes. . . .[47]

This view was also articulated by Benson Wolman, executive director of the Ohio chapter of the American Civil Liberties Union, who was quoted as saying that the dismissal request "exposes how outrageous the original action was. The flimsiness of the charges against the defendants . . . indicates, I think, what a fraud supposed Portage County justice really is."[48] It is interesting to note that in the front page news story on the request for the dismissals, the *Beacon Journal* writers stated that one of the major effects of the request was that it "further discredits the work of the special state grand jury that indicted 25 persons for 43 offenses."[49] Robert Balyeat and Perry Dickinson, two of the three special prosecutors for the grand jury investigation, defended their work and that of the grand jury, however. Balyeat said he was "'a little bit surprised,' explaining that he knew of no 'general problems as far as evidence was concerned.'"[50] Dickinson called the decision of the state prosecutors "surprising," stating that the grand jury

evidently had sufficient evidence to indict these people. I think we had good cases. From the information I had I thought the cases were worthy of prosecution. There was sufficient evidence to go forward.[51]

None of the members of the state grand jury who were contacted by the *Beacon Journal* had any comment on the developments.[52]

The contradiction between the grand jury's indictments and the results of the subsequent criminal trials made it clear that responsibility for the shootings would not be resolved through criminal proceedings in the Ohio court system. Criminal law remedies remained a possibility at the federal level, however, and it is to this facet of the litigative proceedings that we now turn our attention.

Federal Grand Jury

Of all the various stages of the litigative process which have developed from the May 4 shootings, the greatest amount of attention by scholars and journalists has been given to the quest for a federal grand jury investigation and the results of the grand jury's investigation.[53] During a four year period from 1970 to 1974, a number of major developments occurred: in early 1971 the U.S. Justice Department announced it would not convene a federal grand jury; in mid-1973 the Justice Department reopened its investigation of the shootings; in December of 1973 a federal grand jury was convened; and in March, 1974 indictments were issued against eight enlisted men of the Ohio National Guard. These events constitute a fascinating pattern of agonized decisions, conflicting opinions within the ranks of the Justice Department, extensive pressures on the department by the general public and by members of Congress, and reversals of earlier decisions.

Throughout the entire process, strong suspicions arose constantly of "political" motives behind "legal" decisions. On May 4, 1978, those suspicions were confirmed. On that day NBC-TV news revealed the existence of a 1970 memorandum from White House aide John Ehrlichman to Attorney General John Mitchell. The memo, marked "EYES ONLY," read:

The Tuesday, November 17, *Evening Star* at Page A-7, reporting Jerry Leonard's backgrounder today (the 17th) says:

"During the discussions with reporters today, the Justice Department official also said no decision has been made as to whether to seek a Federal grand jury to investigate the May killings of four students by National Guard troops at Kent State University."

In your office the other afternoon I showed you the President's memorandum on this subject and it was my understanding that you understood that the President had decided that no such grand jury would be sought. Will you please ask Mr. Leonard to advise the President by letter or memorandum that he fully understands the President's instruction in this regard?[54]

Why did Nixon issue this order?[55] Charles Thomas, the historian with the National Archives, believes it was because Nixon wanted to conceal the presence of federal agent provocateurs on the Kent State campus prior to the shootings.[56] A less sinister explanation is that Nixon did not want to give further publicity to this tragic result of his Vietnam war decisions. Nixon may have been especially concerned about a statement by Attorney General John Mitchell in July of 1970, indicating that FBI and Justice Department findings pointed to the apparent violations of federal law and the possibility of federal grand jury indictments against Ohio National Guard members.[57] Unfortunately we do not have a definitive answer to the question of why Nixon ordered no federal grand jury investigation. Our analysis of this aspect of the Kent State trials must therefore proceed with a recognition that an important piece of the puzzle is missing.

The issue of convening a federal grand jury arose immediately after the shootings, because the next day the FBI began its massive investigation for the Justice Department, which would use the FBI report to determine the need for a federal grand jury. According to a copyrighted story by David Hess which appeared in the *Akron Beacon Journal* on May 20, 1975, the initial reaction to the FBI report came from Robert A. Murphy, then deputy chief of the Civil Rights Division, Criminal Section, U.S. Department of Justice, with whom the report was filed. In an internal departmental memorandum of June 19, 1970, Murphy, the chief federal investigator in the case, is reported to have stated that he did "not believe any legal grounds existed to prosecute guards, officers, or state officials on *criminal* charges."[58] (Emphasis added) Hess quotes Murphy directly from the memo: " 'Although their conduct showed fool-hardiness and negligence, such is not the stuff of which specific intent is made.' "[59]

In a November 25, 1970 memo to Jerris Leonard, assistant attorney general in charge of the Civil Rights Division, Murphy did argue for the possibility of pursuing a *civil* case against the entire Ohio National Guard. The memo was "a rather long and complicated legal brief outlining the rationale for a civil suit."[60] Portions of the brief read:

Criminal sanctions imposed upon the individual guardsmen who fired their weapons at Kent State are not an adequate remedy. . . .

National Guardsmen act under the close supervision of their superior officers whom we feel share responsibility for the shooting at Kent State.

These officers, by their decisions and their actions, placed their men in a difficult situation and they promptly lost control of both the situation and the men.[61]

Hess reports that Murphy concluded: "Since the purpose of the federal law 'is clearly to protect against incidents such as Kent State and to forestall their occurrence,' . . . the case called for some civil court action designed to enjoin the guard from using tactics and procedures that might lead to another confrontation."[62]

Murphy's arguments were ultimately rejected by his immediate superior, K. William O'Connor, and by Leonard, although the memos involved "show an undisguised contempt for the quality of leadership exercised by high-ranking state and guard officials and university leaders."[63] In a memo to Leonard dated March 9, 1971, O'Connor agreed that individual guardsmen could not be criminally prosecuted. O'Connor's position was that there did not exist proof, beyond a reasonable doubt, concerning which guardsmen shot the students; FBI ballistics reports "were absolutely inconclusive in establishing which guardsman shot which weapon at which demonstrator. . . ."[64] Furthermore, O'Connor argued, it would be most difficult to prove that there was intent by the guardsmen to deprive the students of their rights, as the law requires. O'Connor did, however, find grave fault, although not legal responsibility under criminal law, with National Guard and university officials.

Youthful, poorly trained, ill-equipped, and poorly led National Guardsmen . . . were placed in a confrontation with student elements engaged in protest of a national policy.

The entire university leadership was incapable of making decisions which might have averted the deaths and injuries of May 4.

Command responsibility of the National Guard units was in the hands of an incompetent who was later discharged.[65]

Finally, O'Connor wrote: "The injury to the country cannot be undone by anyone. . . . The only fruit of prosecution now would be the revival of the divisive forces which rent the nation in May 1970. . . ."[66]

In addition to recommending against prosecution of enlisted guardsmen, O'Connor rejected Murphy's argument for pursuing a civil suit against the Ohio National Guard as a whole. O'Connor's argument was that the changes in Guard procedures which could be sought in a civil suit had already been made by the National Guard.[67]

The question must be raised here about the impact of Ehrlichman's "eyes only" memo to Mitchell, ordering that no grand jury should be impaneled. Unfortunately, we do not know how far down the orders went from Mitchell to torpedo the grand jury investigation. Murphy has rejected the charge of improper intrusions. In a 1975 interview in the *Akron Beacon Journal* with reporter John Dunphy, Murphy stated:

You know people have theorized because of Watergate and other reasons
that somehow or other there was corrupt influence on closing the case and I
don't agree with that.

I thought it should have gone to the grand jury, but I don't know of
any . . . there's nothing in our files and I don't know of any influence to get
the case closed . . . closed by the White House.[68]

An analysis of the legal reasoning behind his memos lends support to
Murphy's argument. As subsequent events were to reveal, the evidence was not present for successful criminal action against the
guardsmen. Quite clearly, however, Mitchell and Leonard were involved in grave improprieties. Leaders of the U.S. Justice Department were leading the obstruction of justice.

The first public announcement concerning the question of convening a federal grand jury came in a *Washington Post* story on March
21, 1971, in which it was reported that the Justice Department had
decided reluctantly to recommend to Attorney General John Mitchell
that a federal grand jury should not be convened because of the
reasons identified by O'Connor in his memorandum to Leonard.[69]
The reactions which arose to this story created strong pressures on
the Justice Department, and Mitchell's official announcement that
there would be no federal grand jury probe did not come until August 13, 1971. These pressures are described in detail elsewhere,[70]
so they can be summarized here. The most important leader in these
activities was Reverend John Adams of the Office of the Department
of Law, Justice, and Community Relations of the Board of Christian
Social Concerns of the United Methodist Church. Working through
the Civil Liberties Task Force of the Washington Inter-Religious Staff
Council, Adams led an extensive effort "to research the issue and to
bring every appropriate influence to bear upon those who were in
the strategic positions of authority in the federal and state gov-
ernments."[71] One of the most important results of these efforts was
the publication of a 226-page study by Peter Davies, a New York
insurance broker who had been deeply involved in researching the
May 4 shootings. In his study—"An Appeal for Justice"[72]—Davies
advanced the thesis that certain guardsmen had conspired a few
minutes before the shooting to fire upon the students.[73] This report
was distributed, under the auspices of the Department of Law, Jus-

tice and Community Relations of the Board of Christian Social Concerns of the United Methodist Church, to the U.S. Department of Justice on June 21, 1971. After a month when no acknowledgement or response was forthcoming,[74] the study was released to the news media on July 23, 1971.[75] In addition to the activities led by Adams, the parents of the four dead students and the wounded students made appeals for the convening of a federal grand jury;[76] the Ohio chapter of the American Civil Liberties Union provided some support for these efforts;[77] and nineteen Congressmen, led by William Moorhead, Democrat of Pennsylvania, also called for a federal grand jury probe.[78] All of these efforts met with failure, however, when Attorney General Mitchell announced on August 13 that the Justice Department had decided against convening a federal grand jury to investigate the shootings.

Reaction to Mitchell's announcement was, of course, intense and polarized, as all previous reactions to major developments had been. For the purposes of this study, attention needs to be focused upon the reactions of opponents of the decision, who continued to struggle for two more years before finally gaining a victory with the Justice Department's decision to reopen consideration of the case in August of 1973.

The parents of the dead students and the wounded students continued their quest, speaking out on the issue in various forums and filing suit on October 12, 1972, in an effort to compel a federal grand jury investigation;[79] this was dismissed in January of 1973 on the grounds that the court "could not interfere in a matter of discretion lying within the authority of the Federal prosecutor."[80] Kent State University students presented two petitions to the federal government; the first, containing more than 10,000 Kent State student signatures, was presented to the White House on October 21, 1971, and the second, with some 50,000 signatures, was presented on May 11, 1973, to the Justice Department. The official response to both petitions was negative. The results of the state criminal trials also led to revived calls for a federal grand jury.[81] Various religious groups also continued to press for a federal grand jury, and again John Adams was a leader in the efforts. Also during this period of time, Peter Davies published his book, *The Truth About Kent State: A Challenge to the American Conscience;*[82] and a movie entitled "Kent

State 1970" was produced, based upon the Davies book and narrated by E. G. Marshall. Finally, both the House and Senate Judiciary Committees exerted pressures on the Justice Department.[83]

All of these activities did not alter the decision of Mitchell nor did the government's position change when Mitchell was succeeded by Richard Kleindienst. But with Kleindienst's resignation, the linking of both Mitchell and Kleindienst to the Watergate scandal, and the new appointment of Elliot Richardson to the position of attorney general in April of 1973, new directions began to emerge in the Justice Department, leading to an announcement on August 3, 1973, that the case would be formally reopened. In making the announcement, J. Stanley Pottinger, assistant attorney general in charge of the Civil Rights Division, indicated that the decision did not reflect upon the integrity or probity of Mitchell; rather the decision was made in order to answer the gnawing doubts and questions in the public mind and "make sure that the department knows as much as can possibly be learned as to whether there were violations of Federal law."[84] Pottinger cautioned, however, that the decision to reopen the file "does not mean we have reason to believe the prior decision to discontinue active investigation was wrong or made for improper reasons, nor does it mean that we think that the additional inquiry is likely to lead to a different prosecutive judgment."[85]

Although the evidence is not strong as to why this important reversal was made by the Justice Department, bits and pieces of information can be put together to suggest the reasons. It appears that Pottinger played the key role, for he was responsible for initiating a fresh examination of the Kent State shootings after taking office in January, 1973.[86] The central role of Pottinger was emphasized by Robert Murphy in his 1975 interview by John Dunphy of the *Beacon Journal*:

Q. Can you give a running summary of what transpired within the Justice Department from the time former Atty. Gen. John Mitchell closed the case in August 1971 until the time former Atty. Gen. Elliot Richardson opened it in August 1973?

A. Not much happened between the time it was closed and reopened. The reason why it was reopened has been dealt with on one or two other occasions by Pottinger. But he said as the third anniversary of the shootings was coming up and he—having just become assistant attorney general and having received inquiries and knowing nothing about it since he was not in the Justice Department—he started to ask me and others, "What's this all about?" He became interested in it and finally went to Richardson.

Q. Did Peter Davies' appeal in June, 1971, charging conspiracy on the part of the Guardsmen, or the petition for a grand jury submitted by the Kent State students have any effect on reopening the case?

A. No, I don't think either one had anything to do with the case being reconsidered, frankly. (Davies is a New Yorker who wrote a book on Kent State.)

Q. Are you saying it was Pottinger's inquisitiveness that led to it?

A. Yes, I think the inquiries of whatever kind and nature that Mr. Pottinger got sparked his curiosity.[87]

Murphy's statements give rise to the question of what inquiries sparked Pottinger's curiosity. The evidence here is slender at best, but Pottinger's own statement to Bill Moyers in an interview is perhaps instructive:

MOYERS: Pottinger admits that part of the reason for re-opening Kent State was the persistence of private citizens.

What impressed you about the people who were coming in, saying; "Re-open the case?"

MR. POTTINGER: I think, most of all, it was a degree of intense concern—not to punish anyone. It didn't seem to be a vindictive kind of petition—it was: "Can we find the truth? Can we discover the truth? There are so many questions unanswered." I think that's got to impress anybody who works on an incident of this magnitude.[88]

Pottinger's word choice suggests that it was contact with people like Reverend John Adams, Arthur Krause, and others deeply and personally affected by the tragedy who may have had this impact upon Pottinger.

Unquestionably, many other factors need to be included in explaining the final decision to reopen the case. In a press interview, Pottinger cited a number of possible reasons: the rash of lawsuits stemming from the shootings, the books written on the subject, continuous congressional inquiries, student petitions, pressure from the press.[89] Pottinger also stated, "We have concluded there are some areas into which an additional inquiry is desirable,"[90] implying that new evidence would be examined.

During the fall of 1973, activities proceeded on two main fronts, one investigative and one political. On the investigative front, Robert Murphy, chief of the civil rights criminal section who had originally recommended guardsmen prosecution in 1970, was appointed by Pottinger as the head of the new investigation. According to an *Akron Beacon Journal* story on October 25, 1973,

> Murphy assembled a five-man team, two of whom are in Ohio now, to sift through old evidence, including state and local law enforcement reports, a State grand jury transcript, ballistics data, films, and a voluminous FBI reports (sic).
>
> Murphy and the team also are interviewing scores of witnesses and others close to the case in an apparent effort to expand on old evidence and develop new.
>
> Accounts of these interviews indicate that Murphy is determined to build a strong evidentiary case to uphold a recommendation that the case go to a grand jury.[91]

On the political front, considerable controversy arose over the appointment of Ohio Senator William Saxbe to replace Richardson as Attorney General when the latter resigned over a conflict with Richard Nixon stemming from the Watergate affair. Saxbe was at the time an inactive Ohio National Guard Colonel and a long-time friend of Ohio Governor Rhodes, and Saxbe indicated he might shut down the Kent State investigation if he were confirmed.[92]

Despite the controversy that arose over Saxbe's nomination and subsequent confirmation, the investigation proceeded unencumbered, and on December 12, 1973, Pottinger announced that a federal grand jury would investigate the Kent State shootings. On December 18, a twenty-three member jury was sworn in by U.S. District Court Chief Judge Frank Battisti, and a four-lawyer team headed by Murphy began presenting evidence to the grand jury. The lengthy and complicated probe—Murphy called it "one of the most complicated civil rights cases ever conducted"[93]—involved 39 sessions and lasted three-and-one-half months, during which time the jury heard from 173 witnesses including most of the 28 guardsmen who fired weapons.[94]

A process that had begun almost four years before came to an end on March 29, 1974, when the federal grand jury handed down indictments against eight guardsmen in three separate counts.[95] Five guardsmen were named in one felony civil rights count, being charged with aiding and abetting each other and with willfully assaulting and intimidating the dead and wounded students by firing M-1 rifles and

did thereby willfully deprive said persons of the right secured and protected by the Constitution and laws of the United States not to be deprived of liberty without due process of law; and death resulted to the said Allison Krause, Jeffrey Miller, Sandra Scheuer, and William Schroeder from such deprivation.[96]

Three guardsmen were named in two additional misdemeanor civil rights counts, one guardsman being charged with "willfully discharging a loaded .45 caliber automatic pistol" and two guardsmen being charged with "willfully discharging loaded 12 gauge shotguns" at the dead and wounded students and "did thereby willfully deprive said persons of the rights secured and protected by the Constitution and laws of the United States not to be deprived of liberty without due process of law."[97] The five indicted on the felony count faced a possible sentence of life imprisonment if they were convicted, and the three charged with misdemeanors faced maximum sentences of one year in jail and a $1,000 fine or both if convicted.

Public reaction to the decision of the grand jury was predictably strong and divided. Critics of the decision expressed both surprise and bitterness. Republican Senator Robert Taft told reporters that he was " 'mildly surprised' at the indictments. 'I said before that I didn't think there was the basis for any indictable offenses. . . .' "[98] Paul Brown, Ohio Attorney General in May 1970, commented, "On the evidence which we had available to us, our grand jury decided not to indict any guardsmen and I agree with their refusal to indict."[99] The bitterness felt by many was expressed by Major John I. Martin, a guard leader on the Kent State campus on May 4: "These young men have civil rights, too. . . . I'm wondering if anybody is looking after them."[100] Reaction by supporters of the decision was rather varied. For many of the parents and wounded students, the decision served to reaffirm their shaken confidence in the American judicial system. Sandy Scheuer's father stated: "Justice works very, very slowly. But this shows we still have a civilized country."[101] Dean

Kahler, one of the wounded students, expressed a similar view: "I think it reassures the faith I have in our system of justice. If you had asked me about it yesterday, I would have said no."[102] Another frequently mentioned viewpoint was that of basic support for the decision but disappointment that those in charge of the guardsmen were not indicted. Democratic Representative John Seiberling of the Kent-Akron area told reporters: "Morally, at least, people much higher than those Guardsmen have a responsibility for what happened...."[103] Former Senator Stephen Young was even more adamant: "At least some semblance of justice is being meted out, even if they didn't indict Rhodes and those generals." Young continued, "(Rhodes) came there (to Kent) screaming and pounding on the table and demanding law and order, running scared because he was trailing behind Congressman Taft in the primary election. He caused the deaths of the students."[104] This same general viewpoint was taken by two wounded students, Alan Canfora and Tom Grace: "In the final analysis, the few triggermen must bear the blame for these deaths.... At the same time, the blame must also be shared equally by their superior officers, former Governor Rhodes and Richard Nixon."[105]

Federal Criminal Trial

Ironically, the federal criminal trial that had taken four and one-half years to begin lasted only ten days when, on November 9, 1974, U.S. Federal District Judge Frank Battisti acquitted the eight former national guardsmen of charges, ruling that the federal government had failed to prove its case beyond a reasonable doubt.

A set of complex motions was initiated almost immediately after the grand jury handed down its indictments, thus delaying the start of the trial until late October of 1974. In the opening statement to the twelve-member jury, chief government prosecutor Robert Murphy admitted that there was no ballistic evidence to link any of the defendants to the weapons fired on May 4, but he told the jury that the government would prove its case on the basis of guardsmen statements to the FBI and the Ohio Highway Patrol. Murphy also told the jury:

The evidence will show there was no massive rush of students toward the Guard.

We will prove to you that the Guardsmen were not surrounded at the time of the shooting; that no student was within 60 feet of the Guard at the time of the shooting; that only about 15 students who were within as much as 50 yards of the Guard were moving toward the Guard, and that the Guard was in its best and safest position, that is, high ground.

And we will prove to you that the firing was indiscriminate and unjustified. . . .[106]

Ten days and thirty-three witnesses later, Judge Battisti's acquittal of the guardsmen meant that the government had not succeeded in producing evidence sufficient to establish its contentions. In concluding his opinion, Battisti emphasized the limited scope of his ruling. He stressed that the relevant statute—Section 242 of Title 18 of the U.S. Code—required that the government establish beyond a reasonable doubt that the guardsmen were possessed of *specific intent* to deprive students of their constitutional and federal rights. Specific intent is enormously difficult to establish, for it requires either explicit testimony about the defendants' motivation or the existence of extremely obvious circumstances. An example of such circumstances cited by Battisti was a case in which two police officers clamped a bicycle lock around a suspect's testicles to persuade him to confess to a crime. The government prosecutors had neither direct testimony from the guardsmen nor such obvious circumstances to show specific intent. While the lack of evidence required acquital of the guardsmen, Battisti emphasized that the decision did not hold that the guardsmen were justified in shooting.

. . . it must be clearly understood that the conduct both of the guardsmen who fired, and of the guard and state officials who placed these guardsmen in the situation . . . is neither approved nor vindicated by this opinion.

. . . .

The events at Kent State University were made up of a series of tragic blunders and mistakes of judgment. It is vital that state and national guard officials not regard this decision as authorizing or approving the use of force against unarmed demonstrators, whatever the occasion or the issues involved. Such use of force is, and was, deplorable.[107]

This dramatic, mid-trial decision brought to an end the lengthy criminal law activities associated with the May 4 shootings, for prosecution at both the state and federal levels had now failed. The judicial proceedings were far from over, however, for looming on the immediate horizon was a massive federal civil case.

CIVIL TRIALS

The decision in the federal criminal trial was a disappointment for the wounded students, the parents of the dead students, and their supporters, while the outcome was a source of deep satisfaction for the guardsmen and their supporters. Reaction to the verdict was muted, however, because of the widespread awareness that the issue of responsibility for the shootings would receive its final judgment through a pending federal civil case. This trial would for the first time place the enlisted guardsmen, guard officers, Governor Rhodes, and former Kent State President White as defendants against the wounded students and the parents, and few restrictions would be placed on the evidence brought into the trial. After five years of struggle, the plaintiffs were to have their day in court, their opportunity to establish who was really responsible for the shootings. The plaintiffs' day in court was to last for nearly four years.

The 1975 Federal Civil Trial

The pursuit of civil suits by the parents of the four dead students and the nine wounded students began shortly after the shootings occurred. These suits followed two general lines: suing the state of Ohio and its officers, and suing the various officials and guardsmen in their individual capacities. The former approach did not prove successful; for after a lengthy struggle through Ohio state courts, the U.S. Supreme Court in 1973 refused to hear the case of *Krause v. Ohio*,[108] thus in effect upholding the doctrine of sovereign immunity, which basically is the principle that a sovereign entity cannot be sued without its consent. The second approach was to prove more fruitful for the plaintiffs, despite a series of initial setbacks. The attempt to sue officials and guardsmen in their individual capacities was unsuccessful at the state level in a series of suits intiated at the lowest court levels and ultimately appealed to the Ohio Supreme Court, which ruled that the doctrine of sovereign immunity protected the state officials and guardsmen from being sued. A parallel effort to bring the suits before the federal courts under federal civil rights actions and federal wrongful death and personal injury actions was to prove successful, however. The suits were rejected in federal district court in mid-1971 when the late Judge James C. Connell upheld the doctrine of sovereign immunity, ruling that the state of Ohio could not be sued without its consent. By a 2–1 vote, the U.S. Sixth Circuit Court of Appeals in Cincinnati in late 1972 upheld the lower court's ruling.[109] However, a further appeal to the U.S. Supreme Court reversed the two previous decisions. Speaking for a unanimous Court in *Scheuer v. Rhodes,*[110] Chief Justice Warren Burger ruled on April 17, 1974 that the doctrine of sovereign immunity was not absolute and that the federal district court should hear the plaintiff's claim.

The Eleventh Amendment to the Constitution of the United States provides: "The judicial power of the United States shall not be construed to extend to any suit in law or equity, commenced or prosecuted against one of the United States by citizens of another State. . . ."

. . . .

However, since *Ex parte Young* . . . it has been settled that the Eleventh Amendment provides no shield for a state official confronted by a claim that he had deprived another of a federal right under color of state law.

. . . .

While it is clear that the doctrime of *Ex parte Young* is of no aid to a plaintiff seeking damages from the public treasury, . . . damages against individual defendants are a permissible remedy in some circumstances notwithstanding the fact that they hold public office.[111]

Following the Supreme Court's decision, the U.S. Sixth Circuit Court of Appeals remanded the suits back to the federal district court for hearing, and in July, 1974 Judge Donald Young of Toledo was assigned to hear the suits. The trial date was finally set for May, 1975, by Judge Young in order to allow the conclusion of the federal criminal trial stemming from the federal grand jury indictments and also to allow attorneys adequate time to prepare for the complex trial. During the pretrial period, Judge Young also determined that all of the suits would be heard in one trial,[112] thus placing the parents and the wounded students as plaintiffs against Governor Rhodes, former Kent State President White, former Ohio National Guard Adjutant General Sylvester Del Corso, National Guard officers, and enlisted guardsmen as defendants.[113] Finally, Judge Young decided that the trial would proceed in two parts; the first segment would focus on the liability of the defendants, and, if liability were to be established, the second part of the trial would focus on the determination of damages.

Perhaps the most interesting and important pretrial development involved a conflict among lawyers for the plaintiffs, which resulted in an eleventh hour change in the head of the lawyers' team. Originally, the plaintiffs' lawyers were to be headed by former U.S. Attorney General Ramsey Clark. Disagreements between Clark and Cleveland lawyer Steven Sindell led to Clark's withdrawal from the case in mid-May, just before jury selection began.[114] Clark was replaced by Joseph Kelner of New York, who had been involved for four years as the attorney for Mrs. Elaine Holstein, mother of Jeffrey Miller. Speculation arose following the trial as to the adverse effects on the plaintiffs' cases of this last minute change. Most observers believed that the plaintiffs' attorneys were poorly organized and were badly outshown by the defendants' lawyers.[115]

The 1975 federal civil trial of *Krause v. Rhodes* was of a magnitude and significance that defy easy description. An enormous amount of money was potentially at stake, $46 million. The sheer length of the trial, which lasted fifteen weeks, made it "one of the longest courtroom dramas in the history of American law," and the complexity of the issues led Judge Young to conclude that it may have been the most difficult civil case for a jury in the history of the American legal system.[116] The jury was faced with the testimony of 101 witnesses, resulting in a trial transcript of over 12,000 pages; it was presented with seventy-six pages of legal instructions from Judge Young; and it was faced with at least 500 individual verdicts.[117] As the trial progressed, one juror was assaulted and threatened,[118] while Kelner, chief counsel for the plaintiffs, received three separate threats to "lay off the defendants, or we'll get you...."[119] The significance of the trial was underscored by attorneys for both the defendants and the plaintiffs in closing statements. Kelner told the

jurors: "I dare say that the case, perhaps, has no rival in its importance in the history of American justice."[120] Charles Brown, defense
attorney, placed this perspective on the trial: "Ladies and gentle-
men, in this historic case, you are not only the conscience of the
community, you are the conscience of the United States of
America."[121]

The jury's basic decisions, as set forth by Judge Young in his 76
pages of instruction given on August 23, 1975, centered on the
following issues raised by the plaintiffs:

(1) Did the defendants "knowingly subject the plaintiffs to the deprivation
of the following rights and privileges secured and protected to them by the
Constitution and laws of the United States, namely the right to assemble
peaceably and petition for redress of grievances; their right not to be deprived of life or liberty without due process of law; the right not to suffer cruel
and unusual punishment; and the right to protection against excessive government force?"[122]

(2) Did the shootings by defendants constitute "assault and battery by the
defendants upon the persons of the plaintiffs or the plaintiffs descen-
dants?"[123]

(3) Were the injuries and deaths from the shootings "the result of the
willful or wanton misconduct or of the negligence of some or all of the
defendants?"[124]

After five days of deliberation, the jury of six men and six women
issued their verdict late in the afternoon of August 27: "We the jury,
on the issues joined, find in favor of all the defendants and against
the plaintiffs. . . ."[125] By a vote of 9-3 the jury decided that none of
the thirteen plaintiffs had been denied their civil rights nor had they
been victims of the violation of state laws relating to assault and
battery and negligence. Subsequent interviews with two of the jurors
suggested: the jury was convinced from the outset that Rhodes was
not liable, but more disagreement existed concerning the other defendants;[126] especially critical pieces of evidence were a blurry film of
the shootings and two sound tapes recorded a few seconds before
the shooting containing chants of "Charge! Charge!" and "Lay
down your guns. You're surrounded. Go home;"[127] and the jury
may have believed responsibility for the disturbance lay with the
students because of evidence that some students brought gas masks

and rocks to the noon rally.[128] One jury member, Ellen Gaskalla, stated furthermore that Judge Young's decision to group the defendants into five groups—Rhodes, White, Del Corso, nine guard officers, and seventeen enlisted men—"made a difference in people's minds."[129] According to a Cleveland *Plain Dealer* story:

> The jurors tended to feel that they had to find in favor of or against all of the men in each group, Mrs. Gasdalla said. She said she would have preferred considering the guardsmen "more on an individual basis."
> The guardsmen were discussed individually, she said, but the judge's instructions as to these two groups influenced the voting.[130]

Reactions to the decision by plaintiffs and defendants alike were more intense than after any previous judicial decision, reflecting the tensions and uncertainties of the prolonged trial. All the deeply personal emotions which had been building for over five years poured forth as the jury's decision was announced. Cries from student plaintiffs of "Murderers!" "This is an outrage! There's no justice!" nearly drowned the voice of the court clerk as he read the verdicts.[131] Mrs. Scheuer, tears streaming down her face, cried, "They're still murderers!"[132] For some of the defendants, the tears were those of joy rather than sorrow; one national guardsman, who heard the verdict over his car radio, said, "My emotions took over. I just pulled to the side of the road and cried like a baby I was so happy"[133] In general, however, a sense of deep relief rather than joy seems to have characterized the feelings of the guardsmen. Lawrence Shafer's reaction was typical: "I hope it's the end. It's hard to tell how long I've been hoping that."[134] Other defendants saw the verdict not only as a personal exoneration, but also as a victory for American justice; former guard officer Sylvester Del Corso called the verdicts "a great day for justice and law enforcement in this country."[135] Former Portage County Prosecutor Ron Kane echoed these sentiments, calling the trial and verdict "democracy in its purest form."[136] In stark contrast, Allison Krause's father, reflecting the views of the plaintiffs, despaired over the jury's verdict:

> They don't understand what the Constitution is about.
> They have just destroyed the most wonderful document ever made by man. Thanks to them, murder by the state is correct. The Constitution does not protect anyone against armed barbarians.[137]

Responses by the general public formed a much more ambiguous pattern. The local newspaper of Kent, the *Record-Courier*, reported that "public reaction from residents around Portage County, with few exceptions indicated approval of the verdict...."[138] The next day, however, the *Akron Beacon Journal* reported the results of phone calls received in response to their "Action Line" daily opinion poll, which had asked the question "Do you agree with the verdict of the Kent State jury?" The second largest response in the history of the poll—1,900 calls—resulted in a majority of 51 percent answering "no."[139]

1977 Appellate Case

Little question existed in the minds of the parents, students, and their lawyers that they would appeal the case. The only questions that had to be resolved were, what lawyers would be involved in the appeals case, and what issues would be focused upon in the appeal? Sanford Rosen, a San Francisco lawyer with longstanding ties with the American Civil Liberties Union, was selected to head the team of lawyers for the parents and students. Joining him were Nicholas Waranoff and Amitai Schwartz of San Francisco; three lawyers associated with the American Civil Liberties Union of Ohio Foundation, Nelson Karl, Michael Geltner, and Clyde Ellis; and David Engdahl of the University of Colorado. The team of lawyers was confronted with a massive task, for their basic working document—the 1975 civil trial transcript—was approximately 13,000 pages, and over 100 possible avenues of legal appeal should be researched and discussed before the written brief could be prepared and filed with the 6th U.S. Circuit Court of Appeals in Cincinnati.

After almost one and one-half years of work, the brief for the parents and wounded students was filed on May 3, 1976. In the brief, six major issues were presented for review:

I. Does the absence of substantial evidence to support the verdict require reversal of judgments?

II. Where a juror has been threatened and assaulted before deliberations, did the court err by telling the jury that the court took the threat seriously, and by refusing to voir dire the threatened juror or any other juror?

III. Were the jury instructions needlessly intricate, confusing, and obfusca-
tory?

IV. Whether prejudicial errors in the (charge) require reversal?

V. Whether numerous rulings concerning the conduct of the trial and the
admissibility of evidence deprived plaintiffs of a fair trial?

VI. Whether the trial court erroneously refused to allow plaintiffs to use at
trial federal grand jury testimony of the defendants?[140]

Oral arguments occurred in Cincinnati on June 21, 1977, with
Rosen representing the students and parents. The issue in which the
three-judge panel showed the most interest was Judge Young's handling of the threat to the juror. Rosen emphasized the arguments on
this issue raised in the written brief:

On Wednesday, August 20, 1975 (two days before the jury went out), the
trial court informed counsel that one of the jurors had been threatened, physically assaulted and told that he had better not vote the wrong way. The
person making the threats was unidentified and neither his bias nor the
identity of the threatened juror was revealed to counsel. The court decided to
sequester the jury for its deliberations, and to inform the jury of the reason
for sequestration.[141]

. . . .

The judge cleared the courtroom and, over plaintiffs' strenuous objections,
delivered a terrifying speech:

"I am very much troubled and disturbed by information that has come
to my ears that threats have been made to at least one of your number
in an attempt to influence your decision in this case.

I was brought up in an old school that threats of the type that were made
are not to be ignored and not to be taken lightly.

There have been times when I have ignored such threats and I have
blood on my hands and it is not easy to carry blood on your hands for
ignoring things, and I don't propose to have it happen again if I can
avoid it."[142]

. . . .

On August 22, the judge said that he was not going to excuse the juror. He
gave as his reason his assumption (he never interrogated the juror) that the

juror would not consider the threats, and said that it was not the juror's fault and he or she had tried to do the right thing. This failure to question the juror was error.[143]

. . . .

. . . the prejudice resulting from the trial court's action is patent. His "blood on my hands" speech and his refusal to question either the threatened juror or other jurors about the impact upon them of the threat result in a presumption of prejudice that was not overcome. Hence the judgments must be reversed.[144]

The appeals court on September 12, 1977 concluded that a new trial must be held. The court offered the following rationale for its decision:

The Supreme Court laid down the following rule in *Mattox* v. *United States,* 1892: Private communications, possibly prejudicial, between jurors and third persons or witnesses or the officers in charge are absolutely forbidden and invalidate the verdict, at least unless their harmlessness is made to appear.

. . . .

The intrusion in this case represents an attempt to pervert our system of justice at its very heart. No litigant should be required to accept the verdict of a jury which has been subjected to such an intrusion in the absence of a hearing and determination that no probability exists that the jury's deliberations or verdict would be affected. Although we are reluctant to do so, particularly in face of the obvious good faith efforts of the trial judge to deal with a most difficult problem which arose near the end of an exhausting trial, we conclude that reversal for a new trial is required.[145]

The court made some important additional rulings in the case as well. The opinion stated that all claims against former Kent State president Robert White should be dropped because he had no control over the National Guard. The court also dismissed the claim of the plaintiffs that their right of peaceable assembly had been denied on May 4, 1970:

It is settled that violent demonstrations do not enjoy First Amendment protection.

The plaintiff's argument is . . . "prior restraint" is never justified and the authorities must always indulge the presumption that the next assembly will be peaceful no matter how violent the preceding ones have been. That is not the law, particularly in a school or college setting.[146]

Finally, the court also ruled that it was permissible to use federal grand jury testimony which had not been allowed in the earlier trial.

The decision of the federal appellate court thus opened the door for a second federal civil trial over the May 4 shootings. No jury decision was ever to be announced in this second civil trial, however, for an out-of-court settlement was reached in mid-trial.

The 1979 Federal Civil Trial

Negotiating an out-of-court settlement is rarely an easy task, and the complexities of the May 4 civil trial seemed to present insurmountable barriers to such a solution. Common agreement had to be reached among thirteen plaintiffs and twenty-eight defendants. Not only did a monetary settlement have to be set, but also the wording of a statement by the defendants had to be made acceptable to all involved. Further, the source of the monetary settlement was to be the state of Ohio, and this required the involvement of the state legislature. And all of this had to be accomplished in a case of great emotional intensity and symbolic significance. This Gordian knot was to be untied by Judge William K. Thomas. Our concern in this section is to describe the process by which the settlement was reached, analyze the reasons why the plaintiffs and defendants agreed to the terms of the settlement, and survey reactions to the outcome of the case.

Initial attempts to reach an out-of-court settlement were unsuccessful by Judge Donald Young, the trial judge in the 1975 civil case who had been assigned the retrial of the case. The plaintiffs had criticized Young sharply for his handling of the 1975 case,[147] and he was not able to gain the confidence of the plaintiffs or their lawyers as he tried to achieve a settlement. In September of 1978 Young announced that he was stepping down from the case because of his inability to achieve a settlement. In a statement concerning his withdrawal from the case, Young was critical of the plaintiffs. He suggested that they should settle for about $380,000, the amount the state had allocated for the retrial, and further noted:

I realize that settlement for so small a sum would not be very palatable to the plaintiffs, but something is better than nothing.

I do not believe that the plaintiffs can ever win these cases, no matter how often they are tried or retried.[148]

With the assignment of Judge Thomas to the case in late September of 1978, new possibilities for a settlement emerged. Thomas did not bear the stigmatism from the 1975 civil trial, and the plaintiffs remembered with favor his ruling in 1971 to expunge the report of the Special State Grand Jury. Both sides were impressed by the abilities and dedication of Thomas, and an agreement slowly began to emerge on the financial terms and the wording of the statement. By the time the trial was ready to begin in December, terms of the settlement had been reached. The wording of the statement had been the most difficult part of the settlement, but getting the financial issue resolved took the longest period of time. The $675,000 was to be paid by the state of Ohio, and this unprecedented action required approval by the State Controlling Board, which was controlled by state Democratic legislators who were initially uncertain about the financial arrangements.[149] Questions were raised about the legality of the Board paying such a settlement, the potential liability of individual Board members if suits were brought against them, the type of precedent that might be set, and the reactions that voters might have to the settlement.[150] When the Controlling Board met on December 19 to consider the proposal, a motion was passed 5-2 to postpone action indefinitely, with the four Democrats all voting for postponement. This action was taken not only because of doubts about the legality, precedent, and political acceptability of the settlement, but also because of poor communication. Democratic legislators had not had time to discuss the settlement in the hectic closing days prior to the holiday break, leaving the Democrats on the Board with little party guidance. Further, the Board began its meeting at 12:30 P.M., unaware until then that they had to approve the funds by 1:30 when the trial was scheduled to begin. The failure of the Board to approve the funds meant the trial had to commence. The trial lasted only a few days in December, however, for after opening statements were given and two witnesses were called, Judge Thomas recessed the trial on December 21. The reason given was to provide time for the judge to deal with matters relating to a strike by independent steel truckers, but the recess also allowed time for the Board to reconsider its decision.

While the chances for reaching an out-of-court settlement did not look good, several developments during the holiday period altered the situation. Ohio Attorney General William J. Brown provided assurances to the legislators that they had the authority to approve such a payment. The concern of Democrats about adverse public reaction appears to have been calmed by a series of editorials in major Ohio newspapers which expressed their support for the settlement.[151] Thus, when Democratic legislators caucused on January 3, 1979 to discuss the political acceptability of the settlement, agreement was reached to support the allocation of funds. On January 4 the Board approved the payment by a vote of 6-1.

With the monetary settlement approved, Judge Thomas was able to announce on January 4 the full terms of the settlement. The plaintiffs would receive $675,000, divided as follows:

Dean Kahler, $350,000
Joseph Lewis, $42,500
Thomas Grace, $37,500
Donald MacKenzie, $27,500
John Cleary, $22,500
Alan Canfora, $15,000
Douglas Wrentmore, $15,000
Robert Stamps, $15,000
James Russell, $15,000
Parents of the four slain students, $15,000 each
Attorneys' fees and expenses, $75,000

The statement signed by the twenty-eight defendants read:

In retrospect, the tragedy of May 4, 1970 should not have occurred. The students may have believed that they were right in continuing their mass protest in response to the Cambodian invasion, even though this protest followed the posting and reading by the university of an order to ban rallies and an order to disperse. These orders have since been determined by the Sixth Circuit Court of Appeals to have been lawful.

Some of the Guardsmen on Blanket Hill, fearful and anxious from prior events, may have believed in their own minds that their lives were in danger. Hindsight suggests that another method would have resolved the confrontation. Better ways must be found to deal with such confrontation.

We devoutly wish that a means had been found to avoid the May 4 events culminating in the Guard shootings and the irreversible deaths and injuries. We deeply regret those events and are profoundly saddended by the deaths of four students and the wounding of nine others which resulted. We hope that the agreement to end this litigation will help to assuage the tragic memories regarding that sad day.[152]

Finally, the plaintiffs agreed to end all litigation against the defendants stemming from the May 4 shootings.

Why did the plaintiffs and the defendants agree to these terms? Looking first at the plaintiffs, a public statement issued after the settlement by the parents of the slain students reasoned that the basic objectives they sought over the long legal struggle had been "accomplished to the greatest extent possible under present law. . . ."[153] The five objectives identified were:

1. Insofar as possible, to hold the State of Ohio accountable for the actions of its officials and agents in the event of May 4, 1970.

2. To demonstrate that the excessive use of force by the agents of government would be met by a formidable citizen challenge.

3. To exhaustively utilize the judicial system in the United States and demonstrate to an understandably skeptical generation that the system can work when extraordinary pressure is applied to it, as in this case.

4. To assert that the human rights of American citizens, particularly those citizens in dissent of governmental policies, must be effected and protected.

5. To obtain sufficient financial support for Mr. Dean Kahler, one of the victims of the shooting, that he may have a modicum of security as he spends the rest of his life in a wheelchair.[154]

Each of these objectives was important for the plaintiffs, but they are not sufficient for understanding the decision to accept the settlement. A fundamental stimulus was the fear of losing the case. The plaintiffs' chief attorney, Sanford Rosen, described the trial outcome as a "crapshoot."[155] This was probably too optimistic. It was unlikely that any jury selected would have been initially sympathetic to the parents and students. For example, the Kent State Jury Project,[156] involving random telephoning of registered voters in Northeast Ohio, found that a majority of the respondents rejected the plaintiffs' basic argument, that the guardsmen fired upon the students without provocation.[157] Jury selection in the 1979 trial reinforced strongly the situation facing the plaintiffs. Thirty-three persons were excused from jury duty because of fixed opinions in the case. Thirty of the thirty-three were prejudiced against the plaintiffs.[158] Even assuming that twelve truly impartial jurors were selected, a most unlikely probability, the plaintiffs still faced enormous obstacles. The 1975 jury had voted 9-3 against the plaintiffs, and Rosen and his colleagues had no major new evidence to introduce. Most critically, the plaintiffs' attorneys still lacked the major piece of evidence they needed, an explanation as to why the guardsmen fired. Rosen in his opening statement to the jury admitted "we do not know. . . ."[159] But lawyers for the defendants had an answer. The guard fired because they were in serious danger of injury or death from the riotous students.

Even assuming the plaintiffs could win the case, a careful examination of the implications of winning pushed the plaintiffs toward accepting the out-of-court settlement. How much money would a jury return in damages in a case like this? Rosen believed that $40,000 would probably be the best that the plaintiffs could receive, with the exception of Dean Kahler.[160] By the time the costs were deducted, plaintiffs could well have received less than they received through the out-of-court settlement. In an interview after the trial, Judge Thomas did not challenge Rosen's assessment, and he stressed the difficulty in predicting a jury's decisions about damages in a civil rights case.[161] A further consideration was whether the plaintiffs would ever get their money if a jury awarded damages against the defendants. While Rhodes probably had the wealth to pay any damages, could the enlisted guardsmen meet their financial obligations if damages were assessed against them? Garnishment of their wages would certainly be a slow process for the plaintiffs to receive their damages. Yet a final consideration had to be taken into account: winning the case posed many problems for the plaintiffs. A victory would have undoubtedly resulted in an appeal by the defendants. This would have meant additional years of litigation with its attendant costs and personal anguish. Also, there was always the possibility of having the victory turned into defeat on appeal.

The decision by the plaintiffs to accept the terms of the settlement was thus an eminently reasonable one. The advantages accruing from an acceptance of the settlement were substantial, especially in light of the likelihood of losing the case and the questionable advantages even of winning the case. Yet it was not an easy decision, for acceptance of the decision meant that neither Rhodes nor guard officers and enlisted men would ever be held legally responsible for their actions.

But why did the defendants agree to the terms of the settlement? While the defendants probably felt they would win, there was always a possibility that they could lose. Even if they did win, the defendants knew that this meant more appeals and thus the continued prolonging of the litigation which had already covered nearly a decade. The enticement of ending the litigation forever was a powerful force. Furthermore, the terms of the settlement meant that all of the defendants would be freed of any personal financial liability. Finally, the wording of the statement did not require the admission of guilt or liability for the shootings. Thus, the defendants also found that the benefits of the settlement far outweighed its disadvantages.

Reactions to the settlement varied widely. Plaintiffs, defendants, and their lawyers expressed basic satisfaction with the settlement, but their respective interpretations of the meaning of the settlement were in sharp conflict. Rosen argued that the students and parents achieved "a great victory. It is an unprecedented settlement. Never before has a government apologized and paid money for injuries and deaths it caused."[162] Defendants' lawyers viewed the settlement in quite different terms. When asked if the settlement was an apology, Burton Fulton replied, "I don't read it as an apology, but as an expression of grievance. It is an acknowledgement that a tragedy occurred."[163] Plaintiff Arthur Krause and defendant Sylvester Del Corso expressed similarly opposing interpretations. Krause stated: "Everyone in the world knows that a monetary settlement is not made unless there is guilt and liability involved."[164] Del Corso argued "there is no apology"[165] and further "this is no admission of liability."[166]

Several plaintiffs and defendants spoke primarily in terms of the great emotional stress associated with the long ordeal. Defendant Lawrence Shafer expressed a widely held feeling: "I'm glad it's over with."[167] Plaintiff Dean Kahler stated: "I hope some day I'll be able to go to sleep and spend eternity in peace. Now, I don't feel that."[168] The somber mood of the plaintiffs was reflected in the remarks of Jeffrey Miller's mother: "My initial thought (about a settlement) was, I'm not satisfied; I'm upset, I'm horrified. But I realized that nothing would satisfy me. I wanted the impossible. I wanted Jeffrey back."[169]

Reaction from the general public was quite mixed. Some supporters of the plaintiffs expressed satisfaction with the settlement; one student observed, "It seemed as much as we could have hoped for."[170] Others sympathetic to the students and parents were critical of the outcome. Greg Rambo, who had led the petition drive for a federal grand jury, told reporters: "I'm disappointed that after eight years of struggle, it should end like this."[171] Joseph Kelner, chief counsel for the plaintiffs in 1975, stated, "I'm stunned at the utterly inadequate amount of money that has been paid. I feel that justice has not been served."[172] A view that was expressed by several individuals was disappointment that the out-of-court settlement meant there would be no opportunity to resolve the many unanswered questions about the shootings. The most prevalent reaction, however, seems to have been one of relief. Rob Tomsho, campus reporter for the Record-Courier paper of Kent, observed: "Many people, both on the campus and in the community, are hesitant to discuss the shootings. Most of those who will, express relief that another episode in the tragedy is behind us."[173]

Unanimous support for the settlement came from the three major newspapers of Northeast Ohio, the Akron Beacon Journal,[174] the Cleveland Plain Dealer,[175] and The Cleveland Press.[176] The editorial in the Beacon Journal stated some common themes:

... debate as to who was guilty of what will doubtless continue as long as memory of that tragic day persists.

But Thursday's out-of-court settlement ... should at least put an end to painful judicial probing of the old wounds and help the long, slow process of healing.

And the terms of the settlement perhaps come as close to "justice" as any neutral observer could hope for.[177]

CONCLUSIONS

While the May 4 trials spanned the decade of the 1970s, no clear judgments emerged from these extensive legal activities about who was responsible for the shootings. A state grand jury investigation and state criminal trial resulted in three protesters being found guilty of charges relating to the burning of the ROTC building on May 2, but twenty-two of the indictees were not convicted. Members of the Ohio National Guard were acquitted in a federal criminal trial. Guard officers, Guard enlisted men, Governor Rhodes, and Kent State president White were found not liable for damages in a 1975 federal civil suit, and no legal liability was established for any defendants in the 1979 out-of-court settlement of the retrial of the 1975 civil suit. The court proceedings have thus failed to establish who was responsible for the May 4 shootings, although several decisions have exonerated people from responsibility.

The question of responsibility will probably always be a subject of debate and disagreement. While that question remains unresolved, we can examine the impact of these various judicial activities upon people's perceptions of responsibility for the shootings.

NOTES

1. The legal actions not considered in this paper include a false arrest action brought by former Kent State University student body president Craig Morgan and others against KSU and Kent city police officers; the judicial decisions to close Kent State after the shootings and then to reopen the university; a suit filed by the American Civil Liberties Union involving the search of KSU dorms after the shootings; a suit on the constitutionality of Ohio's "Campus Riot Act;" contempt cases involving state grand jury prosecutor Seabury Ford and KSU professor Glenn Frank for violating a "gag" rule relating to the state grand jury probe; a suit by Ohio National Guard Sergeant Myron Pryor against Peter Davies and others regarding his book which suggested Pryor was a central figure in an Ohio National Guard conspiracy to punish the students; a suit filed by three former KSU students involving the training and weapons given Ohio National Guardsmen; a CBS suit against Donald Young's "gag" rule in the 1975 federal civil trial; and finally, the numerous cases stemming from the 1977 controversy over building a gymnasium annex on part of the area where students and guardsmen confronted each other in 1970. For an analysis of the gymnasium controversy, see Thomas R. Hensley, "Kent State 1977: The Struggle to Move the Gym," in Hensley and Jerry M. Lewis, eds., *Kent State and May 4th: A Social Science Perspective* (Dubuque, Ia: Kendall/Hunt, 1978), pp. 121–48, and Hensley and Glen W. Griffin, "The Kent State University Board of Trustees and the 1977

Gymnasium Controversy: Victims of Groupthink?" paper presented at the 1978 meeting of the Midwest Political Science Association.

2. The most important scholarly research on the Kent State trials has been done by David Engdahl: "Immunity and Accountability for Positive Governmental Wrongs," *University of Colorado Law Review* 44, 1 (1972); "The Legal Background and Aftermath of the Kent State Tragedy," *Cleveland State Law Review* 22, 1 (Winter 1973): 3–25; "The Legislative History of the Law Revision Center, a Comprehensive Study of the Use of Military Troops in Civil Disorders, with Proposals for Legislative Reform," *University of Colorado Law Review* 42 (1972); and "Soldiers, Riots, and Revolution: The Law and History of Military Troops in Civil Disorders," *Iowa Law Review* 57, 1 (October 1971). Other useful articles include John P. Adams, "Kent State: Justice and Morality," *Cleveland State Law Review* 22, 1 (Winter 1973): 26–47; Robert Howarth, "Sovereign Immunity—An Argument Pro," *Cleveland State Law Review* 22, 1 (Winter 1973): 48–55; Gordon Keller, "Middle America Against the University: The Kent State Grand Jury," *The Humanist* 31 (March/April 1973): 28–29; Jerry M. Lewis, "The Quest for a Federal Grand Jury," in Hensley and Lewis, eds., *Kent State and May 4th: A Social Science Perspective*, pp. 59–65; Steve Sindell, "Sovereign Immunity—An Argument Con," *Cleveland State Law Review* 22, 1 (Winter 1973): 55–71; and Judge William K. Thomas, "Jury Selection in the Highly Publicized Case," *Columbus Bar Association Journal* 35, 5 (May 1979): 3–4 ff. A recent book on the 1975 civil trial is Joseph Kelner and James Munues, *The Kent State Coverup*, New York: Harper and Row, 1980.

3. *Akron Beacon Journal*, 22 July 1970, p. A1.

4. Ibid.

5. *Akron Beacon Journal*, 23 July 1970, p. A1.

6. *New York Times*, 31 October 1970, p. 15. The Justice Department Summary of the FBI Report can also be found in chapter 4 of I. F. Stone, *The Killings at Kent State: How Murder Went Unpunished* (New York: New York Review Book, 1971) and in Ottavio Casale and Louis Paskoff, eds., *The Kent Affair: Documents and Interpretations* (Boston: Houghton Mifflin Co., 1971), pp. 119–26.

7. The full summary appears in *Congressional Record* 119, 1 (January 3, 1973 to January 16, 1973): 1113–19.

8. For example, I. F. Stone, *The Killings at Kent State: How Murder Went Unpunished* (New York: New York Review Book, 1971), chapter 4; Peter Davies, *The Truth About Kent State: A Challenge to the American Conscience* (New York: Farrar, Straus, and Giroux, 1973), Appendix III; and Engdahl, "The Legal Background and Aftermath of the Kent State Tragedy," 19–21.

9. For example, the summary states:
As with the Guardsmen the students tell a conflicting story of what happened just prior to the shootings. A few students claim that a mass of students who had been following the Guard on its retreat to Taylor Hall from the practice football field suddenly "charged" the Guardsmen hurling rocks. These students allege in general that the Guard was justified in firing because otherwise they might have been overrun by the onrushing mob.

10. *Congressional Record*, 119, 113–19.

11. *Akron Beacon Journal,* 25 August 1970, p. A1.

12. See Kent *Record Courier,* 22 December 1978, pp. 1,5.

13. See Charles Thomas, "The Kent State Massacre: Blood on Whose Hands?" *Gallery* 7,5 (April 1977): 98.

14. Ibid., p. 104.

15. The President's Commission on Campus Unrest, *The Kent State Tragedy* (Washington, D. C.: U. S. Government Printing Office, 1970), p. 87.

16. Ibid., p. 90.

17. Ibid., p. 89.

18. Ibid., p. 90.

19. Ibid., p. 91.

20. Ibid., pp. 91–92.

21. Henry J. Abraham, *The Judicial Process,* 3rd ed., (New York: Oxford University Press, 1975), p. 22.

22. Ibid.

23. *Akron Beacon Journal,* 21 May 1970, p. A10.

24. *Akron Beacon Journal,* 29 June 1970, p. B1.

25. *Akron Beacon Journal,* 3 August 1970, p. A1.

26. Ibid.

27. Ibid.

28. Ibid.

29. Ibid.

30. Adams, "Kent State—Justice and Morality," p. 29.

31. "Report of the Special Grand Jury," Supplemental Order, Portage County Court of Common Pleas, October 15, 1970, p. 6.

32. Ibid.

33. Ibid., p. 8.

34. Ibid., pp. 8–9.

35. Ibid., p. 10.

36. Ibid., pp. 10–11.

37. Ibid., pp. 11–12.

38. Ibid., p. 14.

39. Ibid.

40. Ibid., p. 12. The twenty-three faculty issued a statement on May 3 which was sharply critical of Governor Rhodes and President Nixon.

41. Ibid., p. 13.

42. *Hammond v. Brown,* 323 F. Supp. 326, at 357.

43. *Hammond v. Brown,* 323 F. Supp. 326 *aff'd,* 450 F. 2d 480.

44. *Akron Beacon Journal,* 8 December 1971, p. A1.

45. Ibid.

46. Ibid.

47. *Akron Beacon Journal,* 8 December 1971, p. A18.

48. Ibid.

49. *Akron Beacon Journal,* 8 December 1971, p. A1. *Beacon Journal* reporters have attempted to strike a balanced, neutral ground in all of their reporting.

50. *Akron Beacon Journal*, 8 December 1971, p. A18.
51. Ibid.
52. Ibid.
53. Two useful studies are by Adams, "Kent State—Justice and Morality" and Lewis, "The Quest for a Federal Grand Jury." Two very important interviews were conducted by *Akron Beacon Journal* reporters John Dunphy and David Hess with Justice Department official Robert Murphy and published on 4 May 1975 and 20 May 1975.
54. *Akron Beacon Journal*, 5 May 1978, p. A14.
55. Unfortunately, the Nixon memo itself has never been made public.
56. Thomas, "The Kent State Massacre," p. 104. Thomas did not know about the existence of the memo when he wrote his article, but its appearance provided confirming proof to Thomas of Nixon's activities and motivations.
57. See *Akron Beacon Journal*, 3 August 1970, p. A1.
58. *Akron Beacon Journal*, 20 May 1975, p. A1.
59. *Akron Beacon Journal*, 20 May 1975, p. A5. Specific intent would have to be established beyond a reasonable doubt in such a federal criminal trial.
60. Ibid.
61. Ibid.
62. Ibid. See also *Akron Beacon Journal*, 20 March 1977, p. A16.
63. *Akron Beacon Journal*, 20 May 1975, p. A1.
64. *Akron Beacon Journal*, 20 May 1975, p. A5.
65. Ibid.
66. Ibid.
67. Ibid.
68. *Akron Beacon Journal*, 4 May 1975, p. A8.
69. Adams, "Kent State—Justice and Morality," pp. 32–33.
70. Adams, "Kent State—Justice and Morality" and Lewis, "The Quest for a Federal Grand Jury."
71. Adams, "Kent State—Justice and Morality," p. 36.
72. Davies, "An Appeal for Justice," *Congressional Record*, (22 July 1971), E8143-58.
73. Adams states that Davies's involvement stemmed from a meeting on 17 May 1971, involving himself, Cleveland attorney Steven Sindell, and Deputy Attorney General Richard Kleindeinst in which the question of possible conspiracy was discussed. In that meeting, "Surprisingly, the Deputy Attorney General did not dismiss the suggestion and conceded that the Civil Rights Division had not explored this possibility at all. When I urged that any decision about a federal grand jury be delayed long enough for us to submit material concerning Michener's veiled hints of the more serious wrong-doing than deprivation of civil rights without due process of law, Kleindeinst readily agreed." This encouragement from the Justice Department led Adams to call upon Davies, for Davies had been involved in researching the question for almost a year. Adams, "Kent State—Justice and Morality," p. 40.
74. Ibid., p. 41.

75. Ibid.
76. Lewis, "The Quest for a Federal Grand Jury," p. 12.
77. Ibid., p. 8.
78. *Akron Beacon Journal,* 16 October 1971, p. A3.
79. *Schroeder et al. v. Kleindeinst,* Civ. Action No. 2048-72 (D.D.C.).
80. *Akron Beacon Journal,* 17 January 1973, p. C14.
81. Calls for a federal grand jury came from such diverse sources as former Senator Steven Young, a long-time critic of the state grand jury, and the *Akron Beacon Journal,* which has tried to steer a middle ground in its reporting. Cf. *Akron Beacon Journal,* 8 December 1971, pp. A6 and A18.
82. Davies, *The Truth About Kent State.*
83. *Akron Beacon Journal,* 1 August 1973, p. A11.
84. *Akron Beacon Journal,* 8 August 1973, p. A1.
85. Ibid., p. A2.
86. *Akron Beacon Journal,* 13 June 1973, p. A1.
87. *Akron Beacon Journal,* 4 May 1975, p. A8.
88. Lewis, "The Quest for a Federal Grand Jury," pp. 1-2, citing Bill Moyers, "Kent State: Struggle for Justice," (Transcript) (New York: Educational Broadcasting Corporation, 1974).
89. *Akron Beacon Journal,* 4 August 1973, p. A2.
90. Ibid., p. A1.
91. *Akron Beacon Journal,* 25 November 1973, p. D3.
92. *Akron Beacon Journal,* 4 November 1973.
93. *Akron Beacon Journal,* 30 March 1974, p. A6.
94. Ibid., pp. A1, A6.
95. Murphy stated that it was only these eight guardsmen who fired in the direction or at human beings on May 4. *Akron Beacon Journal,* 30 October 1974, p. C1.
96. *United States v. Shafer,* Indictment, p. 1. They were charged with violating Section 242 of Title 18, U. S. Code, which provides:

Whoever, under color of any law, statute, ordinance, regulation or custom, willfully subjects any inhabitant of any State, Territory or District to the deprivation of any rights, privileges, or immunities secured or protected by the Constitution or laws of the United States, . . . shall be fined not more than $1,000 or imprisoned not more than one year, or both; and if death results, they shall be subject to imprisonment for any term of years or life.

97. Ibid., pp. 2,3. These three guardsmen were also charged with violating Section 242 of Title 18, U. S. Code.
98. *Akron Beacon Journal,* 30 March 1974, p. A6.
99. Ibid.
100. Ibid.
101. Ibid.
102. Ibid.
103. *Akron Beacon Journal,* 30 March 1974, p. A1.

104. *Akron Beacon Journal,* 30 March 1974, pp. A1 and A6. Rhodes had earlier declared that the grand jury probe was an attempt to smear his reputation. Cf. *Akron Beacon Journal,* 10 February 1974, p. C4.

105. *Akron Beacon Journal,* 30 March 1974, p. A6.

106. *Akron Beacon Journal,* 30 October 1974, p. C1.

107. *United States v. Shafer,* 384 F. Supp. 496 (1974), at 503.

108. *Krause v. Ohio,* Civil No. 884,042 (Cuyahoga County, Ohio, C.P., Nov. 17, 1970); 28 Ohio App. 2d 1, 274 N.E. 2d 231 (1971), *rev'd,* 31 Ohio St. 2d 132, 285 N.E. 2d 736 (1972), *appeal dismissed,* 41 U.S.L.W. 3329 (U.S. Dec. 12, 1972) (No. 22), *petition for rehearing dismissed,* . . . U. S. . . . , 22 Jan. 1973.

109. *Krause v. Rhodes,* 471 F. 2d 430 (6th Cir. 1972).

110. *Scheuer v. Rhodes,* 416 U. S. 232 (1974).

111. *Scheuer v. Rhodes,* 416 U. S. 232 (1974), at 237, 238.

112. Thirteen separate suits were actually involved, filed by each of the parents of the dead students and the nine wounded students. Each suit was further directed at each of the officials, officers, and enlisted men individually.

113. Although there were originally fifty-three defendants, charges were dropped against many of the enlisted men, reducing the final number of defendants to twenty-nine.

114. *Akron Beacon Journal,* 10 June 1975, p. B2.

115. See, for example, *Akron Beacon Journal,* 31 August 1975, p. A2. In Kelner's book, heavy responsibility for the plaintiff's defeat is placed on Judge Donald Young's handling of the trial.

116. *The Cleveland Press,* 28 August 1975, p. B6.

117. See note 112 above. Judge Young, however, placed the defendants into five groups to simplify the process. The significance of this decision is mentioned below.

118. *Akron Beacon Journal,* 22 August 1975, p. A1.

119. *Akron Beacon Journal,* 20 August 1975, p. D6.

120. Trial Transcript, *Krause v. Rhodes,* 390 F. Supp. 1072 (N.D. Ohio 1975), p. 12,189.

121. Ibid., p. 12,361.

122. Ibid., p. 12,445.

123. Ibid., p. 12,469.

124. Ibid., p. 12,473.

125. *Akron Beacon Journal,* 28 August 1975, p. A1.

126. *The Cleveland Press,* 29 August 1975, p. A1.

127. *The Cleveland Press,* 29 August 1975, p. A16.

128. *Cleveland Plain Dealer,* 30 August 1975.

129. *Plain Dealer,* 30 August 1975, p. 13A.

130. Ibid.

131. *Akron Beacon Journal,* 28 August 1975, p. A1.

132. Ibid.

133. *Akron Beacon Journal,* 28 August 1975, p. A1.

134. Ibid.

135. *Akron Beacon Journal,* 28 August 1975, p. A11.

136. *Record Courier,* 28 August 1975, p. A11.

137. *Plain Dealer,* 28 August 1975, p. 17-A.

138. *Record Courier,* 28 August 1975, p. 1.

139. *Akron Beacon Journal,* 29 August 1975, p. A1.

140. Brief for Appellants at 1, 2, *Krause v. Rhodes,* 390 F. Supp. 1072 (N.D. Ohio, 1975), on appeal.

141. Ibid., p. 88.

142. Ibid., p. 89.

143. Ibid., p. 91.

144. Ibid., pp. 96, 97.

145. *Krause v. Rhodes,* 570 F. 2d 563 (6th Cir. 1977), at 567, 570.

146. Ibid., at 570−71.

147. The plaintiffs believed that many of Young's decisions as well as his general demeanor, showed favoritism to the defendants. The incident cited most frequently was Young's addressing Governor James Rhodes as "Your Excellency" when Rhodes took the witness stand. See Trial Transcript, *Krause v. Rhodes,* 390 F. Supp. 1072 (N. D. Ohio, 1975), p. 8786.

148. *Akron Beacon Journal,* 22 September 1978, p. A1.

149. The State Controlling Board of Ohio is a seven-person group which is empowered to release funds which the state legislature has appropriated and to make certain transfers of funds. The Board was composed of six legislators, four Democrats and two Republicans, and a representative of the Ohio Office of Budget and Management. The latter is appointed by the governor. Interestingly, Governor Rhodes had appointed Robert F. Howarth, Jr. to the Board, and Howarth had been an attorney for Rhodes in the earlier state court cases over the May 4 shootings.

150. A specific concern of the Democratic legislators was the potential reaction against a payment which would free Republican Governor Rhodes from any personal financial liability.

151. Editorials favoring the settlement appeared in several of Ohio's major newspapers, and after the settlement Judge Thomas expressed his appreciation to the papers for their editorial positions. See *The Cleveland Press,* 6 January 1979, p. B2; *Record-Courier,* 8 January 1979, p. 4; and *The Plain Dealer,* 7 January 1979, p. A27.

152. Statement issued in Cleveland, Ohio, January 4, 1979, by the defendants in the federal civil trial. This statement was printed in many of the major newspapers in the northeast Ohio area.

153. Statement issued in Cleveland, Ohio, January 4, 1979, by the parents of the students killed at Kent State University on 4 May 1970.

154. Ibid.

155. Interview with Sanford Rosen on 4 May 1979, by Thomas R. Hensley.

156. This was a project, led by Columbia University sociologists, seeking to provide valuable data on potential jurors for attorneys for the plaintiffs.

157. *Akron Beacon Journal,* 12 December 1978, p. B2.

158. Thomas, "Jury Selection in the Highly Publicized Case," p. 8.

159. *Akron Beacon Journal,* 20 December 1978, p. B1.

160. Interview with Sanford Rosen on 4 May 1979 by Thomas R. Hensley.

161. Interview with Judge William K. Thomas on 19 July 1979 by Thomas R. Hensley.
162. *Plain Dealer,* 5 January 1979, p. A1.
163. Ibid.
164. *Record-Courier,* 5 January 1979, p. 11.
165. *Plain Dealer,* 5 January 1979, p. A8.
166. *Daily Kent Stater,* 5 January 1979, p. 1.
167. *Akron Beacon Journal,* 5 January 1979, p. A1.
168. *Record-Courier,* 5 January 1979, p. 11.
169. Ibid.
170. *Daily Kent Stater,* 5 January 1979, p. 1.
171. *Record-Courier,* 5 January 1979, p. 11.
172. *Akron Beacon Journal,* 5 January 1979, p. A12.
173. *Record-Courier,* 12 January 1979, p. 4.
174. *Akron Beacon Journal,* 5 January 1979, p. A6.
175. *Plain Dealer,* 5 January 1979, p. A18.
176. *The Cleveland Press,* 5 January 1979, p. A8.
177. *Akron Beacon Journal,* 5 January 1979, p. A6.

4

Attitude Change and the Judicial Process*

What impacts do the decisions of judicial bodies have upon people's attitudes? When a jury makes a decision in a controversial case, do people, when they disagree with the decision, change their attitude on the case to conform with the jury's decision? Or do they maintain their attitude toward the issue and change their opinion of the judicial structure? If individuals lower their evaluations of a specific judicial structure, does this also carry over into a more negative attitude about the general judicial system, or is this more general attitude relatively stable? Having analyzed in detail the events of May 1–4, 1970 at Kent State University as well as the various judicial proceedings stemming from the shootings, we are now able to focus our attention upon these important questions.

THEORETICAL FOUNDATIONS

In chapter one we discussed the basic theoretical concerns of the study, which are rooted in cognitive consistency theory. We need to summarize that discussion in order to review the basic propositions guiding our analysis. We will also examine the existing literature on judicial support, which will provide the contextual framework for setting forth hypotheses based upon cognitive consistency theory.

*Portions of this chapter were published in an article entitled "The Impact of Judicial Decisions on Attitudes of an Attentive Public: The Kent State Trials," *Sociological Focus* 13, 3 (August 1980): 273–92.

Cognitive Consistency Theory

Cognitive consistency theory postulates that attitude change can occur when an individual's attitudes are in conflict; dissonance is created, which can be reduced by changing one of the dissonance producing attitudes, thereby achievieng attitude consistency or balance. For example, person A may believe strongly in civil rights and may also like person B. When A discovers that B is a member of the Ku Klux Klan, which A dislikes, A would likely experience attitudinal conflict and dissonance. In this case A might reevaluate his attitude toward B, or possibly toward the Ku Klux Klan, thereby achieving attitudinal consistency.

These ideas can be used to study the attitudinal impact of the Kent State trials. Using four diagrams in Figure 4.1, we see that students in (1) and (4) find themselves in a state of attitude consistency or balance following a judicial decision that the National Guard was responsible for the shootings. In (1) before the trial the student believed that the Guard was responsible for the shootings and had positive support for the specific judicial structure. The court then ruled that the Guard was responsible for the shootings, conforming with the student's viewpoint. Hence, the student's attitudes would be consistent with each other. In situation (4) a student believes before the trial that the Guard was not responsible for the shootings and had a negative attitude toward the judicial structure. The court rules that the Guard was responsible; presumably no dissonance would be created for the student who would not expect the court to make the "right" decision. While students in situations (1) and (4) should not experience dissonance, students in situations (2) and (3) should feel dissonance. In (2) the student believes before the trial that the Guard was responsible for the shootings and has a negative attitude toward the judicial structure. However, the court makes a decision consistent with the student's attitude about Guard responsibility, potentially creating attitude inconsistency or dissonance for the student. A situation is thus created in which dissonance could be eliminated by changing either his attitude toward the issue of Guard responsibility or toward the judicial structure. Finally, a student represented in (3) should also experience dissonance; he believes the Guard was not responsible for the shootings and has an attitude of positive support for the legal structure. The court, however, finds that the Guard was

FIGURE 4.1: THE FOUR POSSIBLE SITUATIONS OF ATTITUDE CONSISTENCY/DISSONANCE IMMEDIATELY FOLLOW-
ING AN AUTHORITATIVE DECISION BY A LEGAL STRUCTURE

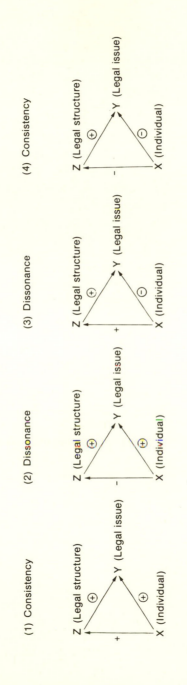

(1) Consistency   (2) Dissonance   (3) Dissonance   (4) Consistency

⊖ Position that the Guard was not responsible for the shootings

⊕ Position that the Guard was responsible for the shootings

− Negative attitude toward the legal structure

+ Positive attitude toward the legal structure

137

responsible for the shootings, a finding that conflicts with the student's view of responsibility. Again dissonance is created, and the student may seek to achieve attitude consistency or balance by changing either his attitude about responsibility or his attitude toward the legal structure.

The analysis to this point has dealt with specific support, that is, support for a specific judicial structure involved in a controversial decision. This logic can be extended in a straightforward manner to diffuse the general support for the entire system. One merely substitutes "judicial system" for "legal structure" in Figure 4.1.

In the two dissonance-producing situations, the individual can change one of two attitudes to reduce or eliminate dissonance. Which attitude will change? Cognitive consistency theory posits that the attitude held least strongly will be the one most likely to change. This provides relatively little guidance to us, however, because we have no reliable or valid direct measure of which attitude people hold most strongly.[1] For assistance we must look to the scholarly research on judicial support.

Judicial Support

David Easton, whose original writing on support for governmental institutions in the American political system still remains the seminal work,[2] states that support can be classified as diffuse or specific. Diffuse support consists of those "strong ties of loyalty and affection" held by members of a political system "independent of any specific rewards which the member may feel he obtains from belonging to the system."[3] In contrast, specific support involves satisfactions which members of the political system experience in regard to particular demands to which the system has responded. Thus, specific support involves perceptions of benefits and advantages stemming from particular decisions and policies of the political system.[4] Both diffuse and specific support can be directed toward persons, groups, goals, ideas, or institutions of the political system.

Easton suggests that diffuse support is generally stable and constant, while specific support is more susceptible to change. When demands are not met, "discontent and disaffection may be stimulated," and specific support may decline; but "whatever the grievances a member expresses, he may still remain fundamentally true to the system."[5] Specific support is thus more likely to vary over time because it is responsive to the daily actions of political actors and institutions, while diffuse support is unlikely to be affected by any one action or short-term series of actions. Thus, Easton suggests, we should expect that "diffuse support is independent of the effects of daily outputs."[6] Nonetheless, the consistent failure of a system to maintain or gain specific support from its members can have serious long range consequences for the continued validity of the system.[7]

Easton's analysis of support provides important insights for us. It suggests that we may expect students' support for specific judicial structures to diminish if those structures make decisions which are inconsistent with the students' attitudes. We should not anticipate significant changes in student support for the broader judicial system, however, for such attitudes are stable, at least in the short run.

Easton's work has provided the stimulus for a substantial amount of research on support for the judicial system. We now turn to an examination of that research, looking first at the studies on people's perceptions of a court's decision and their attitudes toward that court, and then looking at research dealing with people's general attitudes toward the judicial system.

SPECIFIC SUPPORT

Walter Murphy and Joseph Tanenhaus have been the leading scholars in the study of judicial support,[8] and the results of their research buttress Easton's argument that disagreement with specific policies of an institution may result in a lowered evaluation of that institution rather than a change in one's policy views. In an analysis of data gathered in a 1966 Survey Research Center national sample of 1,200 Americans of voting age, they report a number of findings relevant to our concerns. Of greatest interest were the responses to a hypothetical Supreme Court decision. Respondents were first asked if they thought newsstands should be able to sell adult magazines which some people might think were obscene; then respondents were asked to imagine that the Supreme Court had ruled in the opposite direction; and finally the respondents were asked if the adverse decision would lower their opinion of the Court. Although the situation is hypothetical, it is a direct test of dissonance theory. The authors found that 47 percent of the respondents said their opinion of the Court would be lowered, suggesting that a substantial amount of attitude change toward a judicial structure may occur as a direct result of a decision with which people disagree. Other analyses undertaken by Murphy and Tanenhaus reinforce this finding, for they conclude that there is solid grounding for the basic hypothesis that "respondents who approved the particular decisions of the Court should have been more supportive than those who were neutral and much more supportive than those who were opposed to the rulings."[9]

Other empirical studies of public opinion and the courts have also found support for the Murphy and Tanenhaus hypothesis. Studies by A. S. Miller and A. W. Scheflin,[10] Gregory Casey,[11] and Richard Lehne and John Reynolds[12] have concluded that the public's agreement or disagreement with a court's decision affects the public's evaluation of the court.

Applying these research findings to our research, it would seem that we are now on solid ground in offering the hypotheses that students' attitudes toward responsibility for the shootings are not likely to change significantly in response to the decision of a judicial structure, while students' attitudes toward the judicial structure may well change if the decision creates cognitive dissonance for the student.

Unfortunately, our hypotheses are not as firmly grounded as we would like. None of the research cited above has had exactly the same focus as our research, and, more importantly, none has involved study before and after, making the accurate assessment of attitude change difficult. One study—William Muir's analysis of the impact of the school prayer decisions[13]—has raised questions similar to ours and has utilized a before-and-after research design. His findings point in somewhat different directions than the studies noted above.

Muir studied twenty-eight educators in "Midland, U.S.A." before and after the Schempp decision on school prayer. Muir's intensive analysis revealed interesting patterns regarding attitude change toward the issue of schoolhouse religion as well as toward the Supreme Court. A majority of the educators—fifteen—changed their views on schoolhouse religion after the Court's decision, and eleven of the fifteen moved toward the position of the Court. His statistical analysis and in-depth personal interviews led Muir to conclude:

Can law change deep-rooted attitudes? Of course it can. . . . Indeed, it is hard to think of any widely held attitude upon which law has not had a significant influence: our attitudes about loyalty, sex, privacy, honesty, responsibility, innovation, democracy, freedom, tolerance, progress, patriotism, economics, and of course religion have all been affected by the legal context within which we live. Judiciously used, law can and does manipulate our deep-rooted attitudes, our personalities.[14]

Muir also found attitude change regarding the Supreme Court.[15] Thirteen of the twenty-eight changed their attitudes toward the Court, with nine becoming more positive and four becoming more negative. The attitudes of fifteen did not change.

Muir's results raise doubts about the hypotheses we suggested earlier. However, Muir's respondents did have alternative methods of dissonance reduction available to them so that attitude change may not have been the best test of how his respondents coped with dissonance.[16]

What, then, are we to conclude? With a certain degree of caution, we offer the following hypotheses:

H_1: Students will not significantly alter their attitudes about responsibility for the shootings in response to the decision of an authoritative judicial structure.

H_2: Students who are placed in a situation of cognitive dissonance following a decision of an authoritative judicial structure will significantly change their attitude toward the judicial structure. More precisely,

H_{2a}: If dissonant students disagree with the decision, they will significantly lower their support.

H_{2b}: If dissonant students agree with the decision, they will significantly increase their support.

These hypotheses follow from the preponderance of the prior research, Muir's findings notwithstanding, and they also conform to our own intuitive understanding of the situation which confronted Kent State students during the 1970s with regard to the shootings. Many pressures existed on Kent State students to come to their own judgments regarding the issues of May 4 early in their academic careers. The campus newspaper frequently printed stories, letters, and editorials about the shootings. Activist student organizations scheduled programs throughout the year on the shootings. Dormitory, sorority, fraternity, and off-campus "bull" sessions frequently focused on the events of May 4. And most students, returning home for vacations, were asked to explain what "really happened at Kent State." Thus, Kent State students, because they attended the university where the shootings took place, were forced to come to grips with the question of responsibility; and having made up their minds, they were not likely to change them easily.

DIFFUSE SUPPORT

What about diffuse support? Easton's original formulation posits that diffuse support is stable and not susceptible to change in the short run. Most research has focused upon the Supreme Court, and the general pattern revealed by the research is consistent with Easton's formulation.[17] While individuals may disagree with specific decisions of the Court, their general belief in the legitimacy and authority of the Court does not change quickly. This leads us to conclude that we would not expect to see significant changes in diffuse support, even among those students who find a judicial structure making a decision conflicting with their evaluation of responsibility for the shootings. Thus, a change in diffuse support should not be a way of reducing cognitive dissonance when students disagree with a court's decision in a specific case.

A study by Harrell Rodgers and Roger Hansen[18] raises some doubts about the validity of this line of argument, however. Rodgers and Hansen were interested in what happens when a general principle of the law in which one believes, which they define as diffuse support, comes into conflict with a specific action which happens to be a violation of that principle. In studying the issue of Amish parents in Iowa violating the law by not sending their children to public schools, Rogers and Hansen found that a sample of Iowa citizens did not change their attitude about the specific issue of the right of Amish parents to educate their children as they saw fit but rather altered their diffuse support attitude concerning behavior in compliance with the law.

As with specific support, then, our literature search leaves us in a somewhat uncertain position. The weight of the literature leads us, however, to the following hypothesis:

H_3: Students will not significantly alter their diffuse support for the judicial system in response to the decision of a judicial structure, regardless of the outcome of the decision.

When we take this hypothesis in conjunction with the previous two, we are suggesting the following pattern. Students at Kent State University tend to have rather strong attitudes about responsibility for the May 4 shootings, and these attitudes are not likely to change. If a judicial structure makes a decision which creates cognitive dissonance for a student, we believe that this dissonance will probably be reduced by altering one's support for the specific judicial structure which issued the decision. But the attitude of diffuse support for the judicial system is relatively stable and is not likely to change significantly. Thus, students will still have faith in the judicial system even if an important judicial decision goes contrary to their views on the particular issue.

METHODOLOGY

Having set forth the hypotheses which will guide our analysis, we now move to a consideration of methodology. We believe that an experimental design/analysis of variance orientation best serves the purposes of our research, and in this section we shall first discuss the quasi-experimental design which we are using and then explain our use of analysis of variance for testing our hypotheses.

Experimental Design

The use of experimental and quasi-experimental designs in political science research is comparatively new, and while such studies are not widespread, their frequency is increasing.[19] Political scientists who use experimental designs appear to be attracted to the rigorous logic, the control over—or at least awareness of—contaminating variables, and the statistical elegance of experimental research. We too are impressed by these qualities and hence have chosen to approach our analysis from an experimental design perspective. Our study is quasi-experimental in nature, however, and, as such, it lacks some of the rigor of a true experimental design.

Our design is a "one-group, pretest-posttest study." For each of the three judicial decisions under analysis, we selected before the decisions were announced a random sample of Kent State University students to whom we mailed questionnaires designed to measure the attitudes in which we were interested. After the judicial structures in each of the three cases had made their decisions, we sent follow-up questionnaires to those students who had responded to the first round, measuring the same attitudes measured in the first round. This design is far superior to those used in almost all previous studies of judicial impact on public opinion, for these studies have been ex post facto in nature.[20] Because these studies have had no "before" measures, there is no accurate way to access the nature and degree of attitude change in response to court actions.

It must be recognized, however, that a one-group, before-after study is not the strongest possible type of experimental design. For that reason we must discuss the weaknesses associated with this type of research design. For this analysis we will draw heavily from the work of several authors: Donald Campbell and Julian Stanley, who have produced a succinct but seminal study of experimental and quasi-experimental designs;[21] Fred Kerlinger, who has authored a classic work on behavioral research;[22] Roger Kirk, the author of a sophisticated study on experimental designs;[23] and Richard Lempert, who has adapted some of Campbell and Stanley's ideas to the research of legal impact.[24]

Our one-group, pretest-posttest design, presented in Figure 4.2, lacks important qualities contained in more ideal designs.[25] In Figure 4.3, representing a pretest-posttest, control group design, two impor-

FIGURE 4.2: THE ONE-GROUP, PRETEST-POSTTEST DESIGN

$$O_1 \quad X \quad O_2$$

FIGURE 4.3: THE PRETEST-POSTTEST CONTROL GROUP DESIGN

$$R \quad O_1 \quad X \quad O_2$$

$$R \quad O_3 \quad \quad O_4$$

tant improvements have been made upon the one-group, pretest-posttest design. First, a control group has been added. The control group is not exposed to the experimental treatment (X); if change occurs between O_1 and O_2 but not between O_3 and O_4, the researcher is much more confident that the change was a result of the experimental treatment rather than other events occurring between the two measurements, sensitization to the testing instrument, or individual maturation.[26] The second improvement is that randomization increases confidence that all extraneous variables are randomly distributed and effectively controlled. Hence, any differences between the experimental and control groups should be due to the treatment effect of the experimental variable (X) rather than prior differences between the two groups.

Unfortunately, the nature of our research did not lend itself to utilization of this more sophisticated design. Working with random samples of Kent State University students, there was no way that we could select a control group of Kent State students that would not have been exposed to the experimental treatment variable (X)—announcement of the decision—unless we had isolated the control group from hearing the decision of the judicial body. And if we have no way of randomly assigning students to control and test groups, then the randomly assigned, pretest-posttest, control group design is impossible.

Lacking random assignment, we might have used a quasi-experimental design alternative, the nonequivalent control group design, represented in Figure 4.4. This design is much weaker than the pretest-posttest, control group design, because it lacks random assignment of subjects, although it does have the strength of a control group with which to compare the attitude changes of the experimen-

FIGURE 4.4: THE NONEQUIVALENT CONTROL GROUP DESIGN

$$O_1 \quad X \quad O_2$$

$$O_3 \qquad O_4$$

tal group. While the researcher cannot be certain whether the differences found are due to the experimental effects or to prior differences between the two groups, this design does control for the contaminating effects of history, maturation, and testing. Once again, however, the characteristics of our research project did not lend themselves to the adaptation of this design because we had no viable control group. We could not use Kent State students because they would be exposed to the experimental "treatment," and we could not use students at other campuses because they would be quite different from Kent State students on many important characteristics.

Social science research is never ideal, and Campbell and Stanley recognize that research in natural settings will rarely lend itself neatly to experimental designs. The best that we can do is to recognize and discuss the inherent limitations of our design and then use the necessary caution in interpreting the results of our data analysis. We turn, then, to a list of weaknesses developed by Campbell and Stanley in their analysis of the various experimental and quasi-experimental designs.[27]

One problem identified by Campbell and Stanley is the potential effects of reactions to the survey instrument, whereby the process of measurement could affect the respondents and their responses. One way this could occur in our studies would be if students, having responded to the first-round questionnaires before the judicial decision, had felt the need to be consistent in their answers to the second round questionnaires, regardless of how they were affected by the decision. This should not be a serious problem for our research, however. Students were not told they would be getting a second questionnaire, and several weeks passed between the two surveys, making it difficult for students to remember what they had answered in the first round. Another possible problem is that the very action of answering the questions in the first-round survey may have sensitized some students to the judicial activity, and they may have paid more attention to it than they would have done otherwise. This sensitization may have occurred, but its effects were probably not widespread. One reason for selecting Kent State students for study is that their already high level of interest in and awareness of the judicial activities insures sensitivity, regardless of the research. In addition, the campus newspaper, the *Daily Kent Stater,* provided continuous coverage of the various court activities and may have been much more influential in sensitizing students to the relevant judicial activity than our research efforts.

A second problem identified by Campbell and Stanley is the effect of history, or the impact of events other than the experimental variable. Thus, any changes in attitude might be the result of events other than the outcome of the judicial proceedings we are studying. We tried to protect against this problem by sending out the second-round questionnaire within two weeks of the decision, when media attention had diminished sharply but hopefully before other events occurred which might have contaminated students' responses. In this way we tried to minimize the impact of external events.

Another possible problem with our design is that single measurements before and after an event may not coincide with the time frame in which attitudes change. Lempert notes:

Two arbitrarily chosen points in time may not be typical periods at which to measure the incidence of behavior which is supposed to be affected . . . and the investigator may well find a seeming change which is actually the result of regression artifacts, i.e., a stochastic probability that extreme phenomena will appear less extreme on remeasurement.[28]

Alternatively, attitude change might be slow in developing and a measurement later in time might show greater change. These are difficult arguments to address. As we noted earlier, we sent the second-round questionnaires about two weeks after the decisions to control for the "history contamination" of external events. Should we have then sent out another questionnaire several months later? Ideally, perhaps, yes, but good reasons existed not to do so. A third questionnaire would have heightened the sensitization problem discussed above, and our return rate would probably have been very low for two reasons: one, given the extreme mobility of students, we would have had great difficulty in getting the questionnaires to them; and second, we would have been severely trying the patience of our respondents with yet a third questionnaire.

A fourth problem discussed by Campbell and Stanley is sample representativeness. The issue here, of course, is whether the students who returned the questionnaires are truly representative of the population of Kent State students. This is not a problem directly associated with the research design itself, but rather is a sampling problem. We will therefore discuss the problem later in the chapter when we compare characteristics of our respective samples with the same characteristics of the respective Kent State student populations.

Perhaps the most difficult issue is the control of extraneous variables associated with students in our respective samples. If our analysis is undertaken at a level where we simply compare students' scores before and after a judicial decision, then this is not a problem because all variables are controlled by using each subject as his or her own control in a repeated measures study. Dissonance theory involves the analysis of more complex relationships, however. For example, we will be concerned with knowing whether judicial support changed more for students who disagreed with a decision than for students who agreed with a decision. This will require us to divide our sample into two groups—those who agreed with the decision and those who did not—and then to compare changes in judicial support scores. But when we divide the sample into two groups on the basis of their agreement or disagreement with the decision, we are creating two groups which could differ on many other characteristics as well. Thus, if we do find differences between the two groups on judicial support, how can we know that it is due to their agreement or disagreement with the judicial decision rather than to one or more extraneous variables also associated with the respective groups? We cannot, because we have not been able to assign students randomly to groups. Some extraneous variables can be introduced into the analysis as treatment variables, providing a type of statistical control, but it is not possible to know if other important variables have been excluded. This is a problem without a good solution.

This discussion of the potential weaknesses of our quasi-experimental design can be concluded on a positive note, despite the difficulties we have identified. Perhaps most importantly, it needs to be recognized that our design is a noticeable improvement over almost all previous empirical studies of judicial impact because of our before-and-after measurements of the same subjects. Furthermore, we believe that the presentation and rigorous analysis of the strengths and weaknesses of one's research design are a necessary step toward greater methodological sophistication in judicial impact research. Far too few studies engage in such analysis, and we hope that our discussion can help create a greater awareness of this need.

Analysis of Variance

Having discussed in detail the strengths and weaknesses of our research design, we now turn to a discussion of our data analysis strategy. A rather substantial literature has developed regarding alternative statistical procedures for analyzing attitude change.[29] One option favored by some is the use of multiple regression analysis, and we have utilized this technique in an earlier study of the 1974 federal grand jury investigation,[30] as well as in another study of attitude change.[31] For the purposes of our research, however, an analysis of variance strategy seems most useful and appropriate. Analysis of variance allows us to test our hypotheses more directly than multiple regression, for the structuring of the variables in analysis of variance corresponds precisely to the logical structure of dissonance theory as presented in this chapter and in chapter 1. In addition, analysis of variance is intuitively easier to understand than multiple regression analysis, because with analysis of variance we can discuss most of the data analysis results in terms of simple means, allowing the reader without substantial statistical background to follow our data analysis discussion.

Our analysis is based upon the work of Roger Kirk, whose book *Experimental Design: Procedures for the Behavioral Sciences*[32] is a sophisticated exposition of the use of analysis of variance in association with a wide variety of experimental research designs. Using Kirk's terminology, we will be employing analysis of variance for a split-plot design, which is also called a repeated measures design, or, more technically, a factorial design with block-treatment confounding.[33] To better understand this, we need to refer to our just completed discussion of alternative research designs. If we take our basic design—$O_1 \times O_2$—and assume that we are measuring specific judicial support scores before and after a judicial decision, then we can perform a simple analysis of variance for the repeated measures of our dependent variable, specific judicial support. As we have already seen, however, cognitive consistency theory requires that we take into account at least one other independent variable,[34] students' agreement or disagreement with the decision. This means that we now have a factorial design, which Kerlinger defines as "the structure of research in which two or more independent variables are juxtaposed in order to study their independent and interactive effects on a dependent variable."[35] In other words, a split-plot or factorial design with block-treatment confounding is simply a logical extension of our basic one-group, pretest-posttest design, an extension involving the introduction of one or more additional independent variables.

The use of some example data can make all of this more clear and can also save us from making methodological explanations when we analyze the data later in this chapter. Table 4.1 represents the basic form our data will take when we analyze our hypotheses about changes in students' attitudes about specific judicial support:

> H_2: Students who are placed in a situation of cognitive dissonance following a decision of an authoritative judicial structure will significantly change their attitude toward the judicial structure. More precisely,
> H_{2a}: If dissonant students disagree with the decision, they will significantly lower their support.
> H_{2b}: If dissonant students agree with the decision, they will significantly increase their support.

In this mock table, let us assume that we have measured the specific support scores of ten students before and after a trial in which none of the members of the Ohio National Guard were found responsible for the shootings. Our dependent variable of specific support can have scores which range from a low of 2 to a high of 6. In addition to dividing these scores into before and after categories, our hypothesis also requires that we know students' attitudes about responsibility for

**Table 4.1: EXAMPLE OF SPECIFIC JUDICIAL SUPPORT SCORES
PRESENTED IN A SPLIT-PLOT DESIGN**

Attitude Toward Guard Responsibility	Subjects	Specific Judicial Support Scores		Totals	Means
		Time			
		Before the Decision	After the Decision		
Guard responsible	1	5	3		
	2	4	3		
	3	6	2	40	4.0
	4	4	4		
	5	6	3		
Guard not responsible	6	4	6		
	7	3	4		
	8	5	6	46	4.6
	9	5	5		
	10	3	5		
Totals		45	41	86	
Means		4.5	4.1		4.3

*Support scores can range from a low of 2 to a high of 6.

the shootings.[36] Thus, we have measured and classified our students as viewing the Guard as either responsible or not responsible. From this table we can test two main treatment effects and an interaction effect of both treatments. The two main treatment effects are "time" (before/after) and "responsibility" (Guard responsible/Guard not responsible). Looking at "time," we see that support scores declined from a mean of 4.5 before the trial to a mean of 4.1 after the trial. In regard to "responsibility," it can be observed that those students who viewed the Guard as responsible had a mean of 4.0 while students who believed the Guard was not responsible had a higher mean score of 4.6.

These main treatment effects are *not* of primary interest to us, however, for our main hypothesis on change in specific judicial support posits as *interactive* relationship between time and responsibility.[37] More specifically, dissonance theory suggests that students who believed the Guard was responsible for the shootings could find dissonance created by the court's decision finding the Guard not responsible, and hence their support for the court could decline between the before and after measurements. Also, those students who find themselves in agreement with the court's decision could raise their support for the court. An examination of Table 4.2, which contains mean support scores for both "responsibility" groups before and after the decision, reveals that the scores have shifted as we hypothesized. For those students who believed the Guard was responsible, and hence found themselves in conflict with the decision, the mean support score dropped from 5.0 before the trial to 3.0 after the trial. But for those students in agreement with the decision—the Guard was not responsible—we see an increase in mean support scores from 4.0 to 5.2. How nice to have such control over one's data!

These results can be seen graphically in Figure 4.5. In this figure we can easily observe the rather dramatic changes that have occurred in the before-and-after scores of the students in our example. Such graphs are frequently utilized in conjunction with analysis of variance because of their utility in visually summarizing data. A key point for us to recognize is that when interaction is present, the lines in the graph will not be parallel; conversely, if the lines are parallel, then no interaction is present. This is important because nonparallel lines indicating interaction may mean that attitude change has occurred as hypothesized.

Our final concern with this example is whether the differences

Table 4.2: EXAMPLE OF STUDENTS' MEAN SPECIFIC SUPPORT SCORES BEFORE AND AFTER A TRIAL

Attitude Toward Guard Responsibility	Specific Judicial Support Scores	
	Time	
	Before the Decision	After the Decision
Guard responsible	$\bar{X} = 5.0$	$\bar{X} = 3.0$
Guard not responsible	$\bar{X} = 4.0$	$\bar{X} = 5.2$

FIGURE 4.5: EXAMPLE GRAPH OF STUDENTS' SPECIFIC SUPPORT SCORES
BEFORE AND AFTER A TRIAL

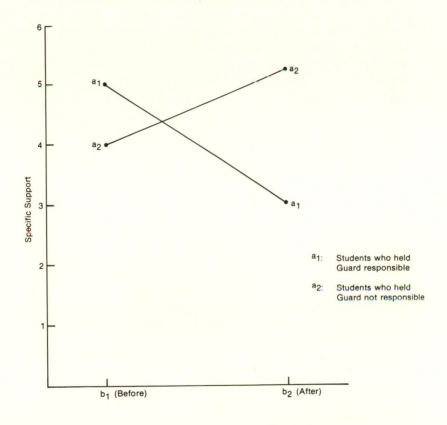

153

which we have seen are large enough for us to accept our hypothesis. Here we turn to formal analysis of variance. Table 4.3 contains the results of an analysis of variance for the data in Table 4.1. We are primarily concerned in the interaction effect (A × B).[38] If the probability of the interaction is less than 5 percent (.05), then we can accept our general interaction hypothesis. Because the probability is less than .05 (it is actually less than .01), we are in a position to accept our hypothesis.

An important technical point needs to be added here, however, for further testing of the interaction effect is possible and necessary. The interaction effect which we have just examined in Table 4.3 is the *overall* interaction, but we need to be even more precise by examining our specific hypotheses:

H_{2a}: If dissonant students disagree with the decision, they will significantly lower their support.

H_{2b}: If dissonant students agree with the decision, they will significantly increase their support.

We can test these hypotheses by undertaking "tests of simple main effects,"[39] which in our example involves testing for the significance of the difference between the scores of the "Guard responsible" group (a_1) before and after the trial and also testing the before and after scores of the "Guard not responsible" group (a_2). Looking at

Table 4.3: **EXAMPLE OF ANALYSIS OF VARIANCE SOURCE TABLE FOR STUDENTS' SPECIFIC JUDICIAL SUPPORT SCORES BEFORE AND AFTER A TRIAL**

Source	df	MS	F	p
Between subjects	9			
A (Responsibility)	1	1.8	2.22	>.10
Error	8	.8		
Within subjects	10			
B (Time)	1	.8	1.00	>.25
A × B (Interaction)	1	12.8	16.00	<.01
Error	8	.8		

the graph in Figure 4.5, we are testing the differences of the a_1 scores at b_1 and b_2 as well as the differences between a_2 at b_1 and b_2. This analysis, employing Fisher's least significant difference test,[40] reveals that both differences are statistically significant.[41] We can thus accept our hypotheses completely. In this example with fictional data, students who were placed in a dissonance situation by a decision did significantly change their attitudes toward the judicial structure, with students who disagreed with the decision significantly lowering their support, and students who agreed with the decision significantly increasing their support.

One final methodological matter which must be raised in our discussion of analysis of variance involves the basic assumptions which underlie the split-plot design. We need to determine which assumptions can be met and which cannot, and we need to discuss the implications of the failure to meet certain assumptions. Kirk lists four general assumptions for all analysis of variance designs and four specific assumptions for a split-plot design. The four general assumptions are:

1. Observations are drawn from normally distributed populations. 2. Observations represent random samples from populations. 3. Variances of populations are equal. 4. Numerator and denominator of F ratio are independent.[42]

The four additional assumptions which underlie the split-plot design are:

5. Two or more treatments, with each treatment having two or more levels, that is, p levels of A, which is designated as a between-block or nonrepeated measurements treatment, and q levels of B, which is designated as a within-block or repeated measures treatment, where p and q $\geq$ 2. 6. The number of combinations of treatment levels is greater than the desired number of observations within each block. 7. If repeated measurements on the subject are obtained each block contains only one subject. 8. For the repeated measurements case, p samples of n subjects each from a population of subjects are randomly assigned to levels of the nonrepeated treatment (A).[43]

Looking first at the assumptions associated with the split-plot design, we can see from an examination of Table 4.1 that assumptions 5, 6, and 7 are each met. Assumption 8, random assignment of subjects to the nonrepeated treatment, cannot be met in our study, as we noted earlier. This means we do not have control over extraneous variables, and hence we can never be certain that differences we may find are due to the independent variables we are studying. We must therefore exercise caution in the interpretation of our results.

Turning to the more general assumptions of analysis of variance, it is important to recognize that "the F distribution is very robust with respect to violation of many of the assumptions associated with its mathematical derivation."[44] This is fortunate, because we cannot be absolutely certain that we have met all of the general assumptions. Three of the four general assumptions are closely related. If observations are randomly sampled from normally distributed populations (assumptions 1 and 2), then the numerator and denominator of the F ratio are independent (assumption 4).[45] While we have used random sampling in gathering data for the three decisions, we cannot be certain that the completed questionnaires truly represent the student populations being sampled because of our use of mailed questionnaires. This is a problem inherent in the use of mailed questionnaires, and we did not have the resources to employ any other technique for gathering the data. All that we can do is to test our samples against known characteristics of the respective student populations in regard to such items as sex and class standing to see if the samples appear to be representative. Fortunately, as will be seen in the later discussions, our samples are closely representative on these characteristics. Further, visual inspection of the data reveals that the scores of our samples on important variables do not depart severely from normal distributions. Kirk states that "it is impossible to be certain that all required assumptions are exactly specified by a set of data,"[46] and hence we have cautious optimism in regard to our assumptions 1, 2, and 4.

Assumption 3 requires separate consideration, but it can be discussed quickly. While elaborate procedures exist for testing this assumption, such tests are rarely reported in the literature, because, as Kirk notes, "the F distribution is so robust with respect to violation of the assumption of homogeneity of error variance, it is not customary to test this assumption routinely."[47] We can therefore make assumption 3 with some degree of confidence.

Before moving into an analysis of the 1974 federal grand jury data, a concluding comment needs to be made about the use of analysis of variance in examining our data and testing our hypotheses. While analysis of variance will play a central part in our statistical analysis, we will also be placing substantial emphasis upon the tables and graphs containing simple means. At certain points, these tables and graphs can provide important insights that may be hidden in the analysis of variance tables. Kirk places an appropriate perspective on the use of analysis of variance with experimental designs:

> Hypothesis-testing procedures should be viewed as tools that aid an experimenter in interpreting the outcome of research. Such procedures should not be permitted to replace the judicial use of logic by an alert analytic experimenter. In particular, the technique of analysis of variance . . . should be considered an aid in summarizing data. It should be used to help an experimenter understand what went on in an experiment; it is not an end in itself.[48]

THE 1974 FEDERAL GRAND JURY INVESTIGATION

"Justice works very, very slowly. But this shows we still have a civilized country."[49] This reaction by Sandra Scheuer's father to the indictment by the federal grand jury of eight Ohio National Guard enlisted men was shared by many of those closely associated with the nearly four-year struggle by the parents and wounded students to have a federal grand jury investigate the May 4 shootings. Dean Kahler's comments mirrored those of Mr. Scheuer: "I think it reassures the faith I have in our system of justice. If you had asked me about it yesterday, I would have said no."[50]

Reactions to the grand jury's decision were by no means uniformly supportive, however. Two wounded students expressed mixed feelings about the indictments: "In the final analysis, the few triggermen must bear the blame for these deaths. . . . At the same time, the blame must also be shared equally by their superior officers, former Governor Rhodes, and Richard Nixon."[51] Many people expressed sympathy for the indicted guardsmen. For example, an Ohio National Guard officer who was at Kent State on May 4, 1970 stated: "These young men have rights, too. . . . I'm wondering if anybody is looking after them."[52]

Kent State University students participating in our survey had mixed reactions to the outcome of the grand jury investigation. It was found that 48 percent of the students expressed agreement with the decision, while 32 percent were in disagreement, and 20 percent were undecided. While nearly 50 percent of the students agreed with the decision, the majority of the students did not believe the grand jury had answered fully the unresolved questions about the shootings nor did the students believe that the grand jury had finally determined who was responsible for the shootings. Not one student in our sample believed the grand jury had answered all the important questions about May 4, and only 9 percent felt that most of the questions had been answered; 53 percent believed some questions had been resolved, while 38 percent felt that few or none had been answered. In response to a question asking if the federal grand jury had determined, once and for all, who was responsible for the shootings, an overwhelming 86 percent responded that the grand jury had not made such a determination. Thus, Kent State students, while not strongly disagreeing with the grand jury's actions, believed that many important questions had not been answered, including who was responsible for the shootings.

What impacts did the federal grand jury decision have upon the attitudes of Kent State University students? We hypothesized earlier in this chapter that in the aftermath of an authoritative judicial decision about the shootings, students' attitudes regarding responsibility for the shootings will not change, students' attitudes toward the specific judicial structure will change if the decision creates dissonance for the students, and students' general support for the judicial system will not change. In analyzing the 1974 federal grand jury decision, we will focus on attitude change regarding responsibility for the shootings and specific judicial support, but we will not be able to study diffuse support because we did not build in the necessary questions in the 1974 questionnaires we sent to students. We will be able to analyze diffuse support for both the civil trials, however.

As we test these hypotheses, we need to be aware of the unique features of a grand jury which distinguish it from a trial jury. A grand jury has the responsibility for making an initial investigation of facts to determine whether there is sufficient evidence in a criminal matter to bring a case to a trial, where guilt or innocence is determined. As such, the grand jury investigation is an early stage in the judicial process, not the last. Because of its unique role, the activities of a grand jury are controlled by the prosecuting attorneys; they call all the witnesses, and witnesses are not cross-examined by attorneys for the potential defendants. Also, the proceedings of a grand jury are conducted in closed session to protect both witnesses and potential defendants who might not be indicted. Thus, the end product of the Kent State grand jury investigation was clear, but the process was quite the opposite, making it difficult for the public to judge how and why the grand jury indicted the eight guardsmen.

The Questionnaires

While the federal grand jury was being conducted, we developed a questionnaire which was sent to a random sample of 500 students drawn from the university's student directory. Of the 500 questionnaires mailed, we received 188, or 37.5 percent of the sample. A sizeable portion of the nonresponses can be attributed to our use of the student directory to draw our sample. Given the nature and mobility of the Kent State student body, the student directory is outdated before it is published in the fall of each year. The Kent State Registrar's Office estimates that accurate addresses may be missing for as many as one-third of the students who drop out of school, move to new locations, or provide inaccurate addresses. Nonetheless, the directory was readily available, convenient, and quick, important factors when we had to get into the field with the study before the grand jury completed its deliberations. And, unfortunately, no alternative listing of students existed.

The response rate might have been higher had extensive follow-ups of nonrespondents been possible. But the timing of the grand jury investigation and uncertainty regarding when it would complete its work made extensive follow-ups virtually impossible. As it was we barely finished the first round of the study, arbitrarily halting data collection on March 15, 1974 when the federal grand jury issued its indictments on March 29. Two weeks after this announcement, a second questionnaire, similar in content to the first, was mailed to the 188 students who had participated in the first round of the study. We received completed questionnaires from 141 of those students, a 70 percent return rate. The 141 students who participated in both the before and after rounds are the subjects of our analysis.[53]

The questionnaire used in both rounds was largely closed-ended. Respondents were asked in both rounds for their assessment of the degree of responsibility for eleven major actors frequently mentioned in analyses of the shootings: Governor Rhodes, National Guard officers, National Guard enlisted men, Richard Nixon, Spiro Agnew, radical students, nonstudent radicals, nonradical students, Kent State faculty members, Kent State administrators, and KSU president Robert White.[54] In addition, students were asked their evaluation of the 1970 state grand jury, whether they thought the federal grand jury investigation was necessary, and whether the investigation would be fair and unbiased. In Round 2, after the grand jury's indictments, students were asked whether they agreed with the grand jury's actions and whether they felt the grand jury had been necessary, fair, and unbiased. A set of demographic questions was used to determine such things as family income, party affiliation, ideological stance, class in college, and academic major. The before questionnaire can be found in Appendix A and the after questionnaire in Appendix B.

Although our sample is relatively small, Table 4.4 shows that it is fairly representative of the total university population from which it is drawn. On a class-by-class basis, the sample somewhat overrepresents freshmen, seniors, and graduate students and underrepresents sophomores and juniors, but the differences are not substantial. The enrollment pattern for the university, which is reflected in our sample, represents the realities of enrollment at the university in the aftermath of the 1970 shootings. Beginning in 1971 the enrollment fell sharply, recovering briefly in 1974 and 1975 before beginning to decline again. As a result, at the time we were conducting our research, the freshman and senior classes were proportionately larger than the sophomore and junior classes. Our sample tends to overemphasize those differences between the classes. In comparing our sample and the population on the characteristic of sex, we find that men are somewhat underrepresented in the sample. Thus, while the sample and population do not match exactly on the characteristics of class standing and sex, the differences are not extreme.

Table 4.4: COMPARISON OF STUDENT SAMPLE AND STUDENT BODY OF KENT STATE UNIVERSITY IN WINTER 1974 ON SELECTED CHARACTERISTICS

Characteristic	Sample ($N = 141$)	Student Body ($N = 16,675$)
Sex		
Male	42%	53%
Female	58%	47%
Total	100%	100%
Class		
Freshman	23%	21%
Sophomore	12%	19%
Junior	16%	19%
Senior	29%	26%
Graduate Student	20%	16%
Total	100%	101%*

*The total does not come to 100% because of rounding error.

Attitudes Toward Responsibility for the Shootings

We can now turn our attention to an examination of students' attitudes of responsibility for the shootings and the impact of the grand jury decision on those attitudes. One might expect Kent State students to defend youthful protestors' actions in May of 1970 and to point the finger of responsibility at political leaders and members of the Ohio National Guard. This is not the case. Instead, Kent State students in 1974 believed that political officials, National Guard members, and radicals—students and nonstudents—all shared responsibility for the events of May 4, 1970. In Table 4.5 we see that before the 1974 federal grand jury decision, Kent State students placed primary responsibility for the shootings upon National Guard officers, but they also attributed a high level of responsibility to Governor Rhodes, radical students, nonstudent radicals, and National Guard enlisted men. These data parallel rather closely the findings of Stuart Taylor and his colleagues, who received questionnaires from

**Table 4.5: MEAN SCORES OF KENT STATE STUDENTS' PERCEPTIONS
IN 1970 AND 1974 OF VARIOUS ACTORS' RESPONSIBILITY
FOR THE MAY 4 SHOOTINGS**

Individuals and Groups	Mean Responsibility Scores[a]	
	1974	1970[b]
Guard officers	1.58	1.79
Rhodes	1.90	1.79
Radical students	1.96	1.61
Nonstudent radicals	1.98	1.99
Guard enlisted men	2.01	2.11
Nixon	2.67	2.15
White	2.72	
KSU administrators	2.95	2.58
Agnew	3.23	2.36
KSU faculty	3.44	3.05
Nonradical students	3.57	

[a]Responsibility scores can range from 1 (Very Responsible) to 4 (Not Responsible)
[b]Source: Stuart Taylor et al., *Violence at Kent State: The Students' Perspective* (New York: College Notes and Texts, 1971). Taylor's survey did not ask students to assess the responsibility of KSU president Robert White or nonradical students.

nearly 7,000 Kent State students in the immediate aftermath of the shootings in 1970.[55] As can be seen in Table 4.5, the same actors were ranked high in responsibility. The 1970 students, however, considered radical students to have the highest responsibility for the shootings, and the 1970 students also placed much greater responsibility on Richard Nixon and Spiro Agnew than did the 1974 students.

Our primary concern is not, however, with a description of students' perceptions of responsibility for the shootings per se, but rather with assessing whether the decision of the federal grand jury to indict eight Ohio National Guard enlisted men had an impact on students' attitudes about responsibility for the shootings. The specific hypothesis we have set forth is:

H_1: Students will not significantly alter their attitudes about responsibility for the shootings in response to the decision of an authoritative judicial structure.

The decision of the federal grand jury was directed at one specific group, Guard enlisted men, and we are therefore most interested in analyzing whether students' attitudes about the enlisted men's responsibility underwent significant change. It is also interesting, however, to examine if changes in perceptions of responsibility occurred in regard to other major actors, for there was uncertainty about whom the federal grand jury would indict, if anyone. It was possible that radical students, nonstudent radicals, and possibly even Kent State professors might be indicted. Speculation also existed concerning whether National Guard officers might be indicted. The decision of the grand jury not to indict any of these people could therefore be interpreted to mean that they were not responsible for the shootings.

Looking first at the data on the enlisted men of the Ohio National Guard contained in Tables 4.6 and 4.7, we find a surprising result: students' attitudes toward enlisted men responsibility did change, but the change occurred in the direction *opposite of the grand jury's decision*. A significant number of students viewed the guardsmen as *less responsible* for the shootings after the grand jury indicted the eight enlisted men. In Table 4.6 we see that while a substantial number of students did not change their views on responsibility of the enlisted men for the shootings, many students lowered their ranking on responsibility after the indictments. Of those who held the guardsmen very responsible before the decision, 33 percent saw them as only moderately responsible and 10 percent saw them as minimally responsible after the decision; 43 percent of those who saw the enlisted men as moderately responsible before the decision viewed them as minimally responsible afterward; and 15 percent of those who ranked the guardsmen as minimally responsible before the indictments saw them as not responsible afterward. Table 4.7 provides us with an analysis of variance summary which clearly leads us to reject the hypothesis of no attitude change in regard to students' views of the responsibility of the Guard enlisted men.

An analysis of variance for students' before and after scores on the

Table 4.6: STUDENTS' PERCEPTIONS BEFORE AND AFTER THE 1974 FEDERAL GRAND JURY INVESTIGATION OF OHIO NATIONAL GUARD ENLISTED MEN'S RESPONSIBILITY FOR THE MAY 4 SHOOTINGS

Perceptions of Guard Enlisted Men's Responsibility After the Decision	Perceptions of Guard Enlisted Men's Responsibility Before the Decision				
	Very	Moderately	Minimally	None	Totals
Very	55%	6%	4%	7%	(32) 25%
Moderately	33%	46%	23%	13%	(41) 32%
Minimally	10%	43%	58%	13%	(37) 29%
None	2%	6%	15%	67%	(17) 13%
Totals	100%	101%	100%	100%	(127) 99%
	(51)	(35)	(26)	(15)	

Some columns do not add to 100% because of rounding error.

**Table 4.7: ANALYSIS OF VARIANCE TABLE FOR STUDENTS'
PERCEPTIONS BEFORE AND AFTER THE 1974 FEDERAL
GRAND JURY INVESTIGATION OF NATIONAL GUARD
ENLISTED MEN'S RESPONSIBILITY FOR THE MAY 4
SHOOTINGS**

Source	df	MS	F	p
Between subjects	122			
Within subjects	123			
Time	1	4.699	13.553	.0006
Error	122	.347		

responsibility of each of the other major actors—Governor Rhodes, National Guard officers, nonstudent radicals, and student radicals—reveals that no significant changes occurred. It thus appears that students did not view the grand jury's decision as an exoneration of responsibility for these groups. The students still found them responsible, even if the grand jury did not issue indictments against them.

We must return to our surprising finding that the students lowered their perceptions of the degree of responsibility of the Guard enlisted men despite the fact that the grand jury issued indictments against eight enlisted men. How do we account for these findings? Unfortunately, the data do not provide us with insights as to why some students found the guardsmen less responsible after the decision. Ideology was not a factor; liberals, moderates, and conservatives showed similar patterns of attitude change. One strong possibility which occurred to us was that some students may have believed that the enlisted men were being used as scapegoats to protect elected officials and Guard officers. We therefore looked at students' agreement and disagreement scores with the following statements taken from newspapers after the 1974 decision: "The Guardsmen were sold down the river in order to protect Rhodes and some of the other officials," and "Morally, at least, people much higher than these guardsmen have a responsibility for what happened." In correlating students' responses to these statements with attitude changes on guardsmen responsibility, however, no statistically significant results emerged. We also tested the possibility that the students who lowered their perceptions of responsibility of the guardsmen did so because they saw them as being placed in a difficult situation which they did not create. Again, however, no significant results emerged from our analysis.

Attitudes Toward Specific Judicial Support

We next turn to the question of attitude change among Kent State students in regard to specific judicial support. At the beginning of this chapter we set forth the following hypotheses:

> H_2: Students who are placed in a situation of cognitive dissonance following a decision of an authoritative judicial structure will significantly change their attitude toward the judicial structure. More precisely,
>
> H_{2a}: If dissonant students disagree with the decision, they will significantly lower their support.
>
> H_{2b}: If dissonant students agree with the decision, they will significantly increase their support.

These hypotheses were based upon cognitive consistency theory and assumed that students' attitudes about responsibility for the shootings would not change. Because we believed attitudes about responsibility would not change, we posited that if students found themselves in a condition of dissonance because of the decision, then students' attitudes toward the judicial structure would change to create cognitive balance.

We reconsidered these hypotheses on judicial support when we found significant change in students' attitudes toward the responsibility of the Guard enlisted men whom the grand jury indicted. Cognitive consistency theory could still guide our analysis, but we had to make some special efforts to determine which students found themselves in a state of dissonance following the decision of the grand jury. Once this was done, we could test whether those students who found themselves in a dissonant state changed their attitude about the federal grand jury.

We made this determination by dividing the student sample into four groups: those who viewed the Guard enlisted men as responsible before the grand jury decision and also viewed them as responsible after the decision;[56] students who perceived the guardsmen as responsible before the grand jury announcement but not responsible afterwards; students who viewed the guardsmen as not responsible before and responsible after; and students who believed the guardsmen were not responsible before and not responsible after.

These four groups are represented in Table 4.8, which contains the mean specific support scores for each group before and after the decision.[57] It can be seen from comparing the before and after scores of each respective group that relatively slight change occurred for each group except those students who viewed the guardsmen as not

Table 4.8: STUDENTS' MEAN SPECIFIC SUPPORT SCORES FOR THE
FEDERAL GRAND JURY BEFORE AND AFTER THE 1974
INVESTIGATION

Attitude Toward Guardsmen Responsibility Before the Decision	Attitude Toward Guardsmen Responsibility After the Decision	Specific Judicial Support Scores*	
		Time	
		Before the Decision	After the Decision
Guardsmen Responsible (N = 67)	Guardsmen Responsible (N = 48)	4.90	5.17
	Guardsmen Not Responsible (N = 19)	4.73	4.62
Guardsmen Not Responsible (N = 27)	Guardsmen Responsible (N = 7)	5.43	5.48
	Guardsmen Not Responsible (N = 20)	4.40	3.55

*Scores can range from a low of 2 to a high of 6.

responsible both before and after the decision; this group's mean support scores declined sharply from 4.40 to 3.55. The graphs presented in Figure 4.6 contain the mean scores for each group before and after the decision and can help us to examine the specific propositions within hypothesis 2.

Graph 1 contains the mean support scores of those students who viewed the guardsmen as responsible for the shootings after the grand jury's decision. Within this group, the students who had viewed the guardsmen as responsible before the decision (a_1) found themselves in agreement with the decision, and hence our hypothesis leads us to expect this group of students to increase their support for the grand jury. We do see an increase, from a mean of 4.90 to 5.17. While this is not a large increase, the mean support score before the decision was very high, and hence we could not expect a dramatic increase. The second group represented in Graph 1, students who viewed the guardsmen as not responsible before the decision (a_2), changed their attitude about responsibility for the shootings in conformity with the grand jury's decision. We thus would not expect them to change their judicial support scores, and we do see little change for this group, although there is a slight increase in the mean support scores from 5.43 to 5.48.

In Graph 2 we see the mean support scores for those students who viewed the guardsmen as not responsible after the decision. Of these students, one group had viewed the guardsmen as responsible before the decision (a_1), and thus they changed their attitude about responsibility in opposition to the grand jury decision. Because this group of students changed their attitude about responsibility, we might not expect them to change their attitude on judicial support; however, their disagreement with the grand jury decision could lead them to lower their judicial support scores. We do observe a slight decrease in support for this group, whose mean scores were 4.73 before the decision and 4.62 after the decision. The other group of students in Graph 2 viewed the guardsmen as not responsible before the decision as well as after the decision (a_2). They thus found themselves in a dissonant situation because the federal grand jury had found the guardsmen responsible, and as we hypothesized their support scores declined substantially, from a mean of 4.40 to a mean of 3.55.

FIGURE 4.6: GRAPHS OF STUDENTS' MEAN SPECIFIC JUDICIAL SUPPORT SCORES BEFORE AND AFTER THE 1974 FEDERAL GRAND JURY INVESTIGATION

Graph 1: Students Who Viewed
Guardsmen as responsible
After the Decision

Graph 2: Students Who Viewed
Guardsmen as Not Responsible
After the Decision

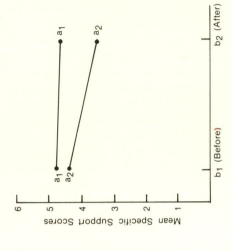

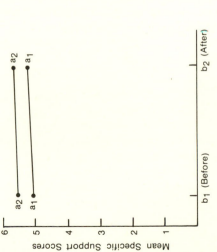

a_1: Students who viewed guardsmen as responsible before decision

a_2: Students who viewed guardsmen as not responsible before decision

169

We turn now to the analysis of variance presented in Table 4.9 to reach final judgments about the significance of these changes. Our concern is with the overall interaction (A × B × C), and we see that the probability is quite high (.312) that such an interaction could occur by chance. This indicates that there was no statistically significant overall interaction. This overall result could hide important patterns within the data, however, and we know that one group—those who believed the guardsmen not responsible both before and after the decision—showed a substantial decline in support. We can therefore test to see whether the change for this group was statistically significant, and Fisher's least significant difference test reveals that this change is statistically significant.[58]

Summarizing these findings, we are not in a position to accept the overall interaction hypothesis (H₂) that students who were placed in a situation of cognitive dissonance by the grand jury decision significantly changed their attitudes toward the federal grand jury. The testing of changes for particular groups of students provides us with

Table 4.9: ANALYSIS OF VARIANCE TABLE FOR STUDENTS' SPECIFIC JUDICIAL SUPPORT SCORES BEFORE AND AFTER THE 1974 FEDERAL GRAND JURY INVESTIGATION

Source	df	MS	F	p
Between subjects				
A (Attitude on Responsibility Before)	1	.369	0.199	.661
B (Attitude on Responsibility After)	1	2.652	14.316	.001
A × B (Interaction)	1	1.000	5.399	.021
Error	89	1.853		
Within subjects				
C (Time)	1	.556	.835	.634
A × C (Interaction)	1	1.395	2.093	.148
B × C (Interaction)	1	3.510	5.265	.023
A × B × C (Interaction)	1	.693	1.040	.312
Error	89	.667		

important additional insights, however. Hypothesis 2b stated that students who were in agreement with the decision would significantly increase their support, but we did not find this occurred. The support scores for these students were quite high before the decision, and hence it would have been difficult for their scores to have gone significantly higher. Hypothesis 2a stated that students who disagreed with the decision would significantly decrease their support, and this hypothesis was confirmed for those students who considered the guardsmen not responsible for the shootings both before and after the decision. The hypothesis was not confirmed for students who viewed the guardsmen as responsible before the decision but not responsible afterward.

THE 1975 FEDERAL CIVIL TRIAL

"Murderers! This is an outrage! There's no justice!"[59] These cries came from several of the wounded students following the announcement on August 27, 1975 that the jury had found all of the defendants—Rhodes, White, Guard officers, and Guard enlisted men—not liable for damages in the federal civil trial that had spanned the entire summer of 1975. The trial was one of the longest, most costly, and most complex civil actions in American history, and it was the culmination of five years of struggle by the parents and wounded students to have their complaints fully presented in a court of law.

Given the financial and emotional commitments involved, the reactions following the trial were intense. With tears streaming down her face, Sandra Scheuer's mother cried as the decision was read: "They're still murderers!"[60] Allison Krause's father lamented the jury's decision:

They don't understand what the Constitution is about.

They have just destroyed the most wonderful document ever made by man. Thanks to them, murder by the state is correct. The Constitution does not protect anyone against armed barbarians.[61]

In sharp contrast, the defendants and their supporters perceived the decision in much different terms. Sylvester Del Corso, Ohio National

Guard Adjutant General in 1970, called the verdicts "a great day for justice and law enforcement in this country."[62] Ronald Kane, Portage County prosecutor in 1970, expressed a similar sentiment, labeling the trial and outcome "democracy in its purest form."[63]

Kent State students responding to our survey generally echoed the sentiments expressed by the parents of the slain students and the wounded students. Sixty-four percent of our sample disagreed with the decision, while only 20 percent were in agreement with it; 16 percent were undecided. Furthermore, most students felt the trial had not resolved the unanswered questions about the shootings. Two-thirds of the sample believed that the trial had resolved few or none of the important questions, and only 10 percent felt the trial had resolved most or all of the salient questions about the shootings. And most students—70 percent—agreed with the statement that "in regard to the shootings of May 4, 1970, justice has not yet been realized in the American courts."

The central questions concerning us are whether the trial had any impacts upon the attitudes of Kent State students. Did the students maintain their attitudes about responsibility for the shootings, or did they alter their attitudes to conform to—or perhaps to oppose—the results of the federal civil trial? Did students' attitudes toward the federal district court change because of the decision? Did the outcome of the case have an impact upon students' attitudes toward the American judicial system?

The results we found in analyzing the 1974 federal grand jury investigation give us some confidence in the hypotheses we originally set forth in this chapter, even though they were not completely confirmed. As we analyze the 1975 federal civil trial, we must recognize that it differed in important ways from the 1974 federal grand jury investigation. One important difference was that the federal grand jury was veiled in secrecy, whereas the civil trial was open to the public and was reported upon daily by the papers. A second important difference involved the more definitive judgment on responsibility in the 1975 trial, where the jury stated clearly that the defendants were not responsible on any of the grounds claimed by the parents and students. In contrast, the decision of the grand jury was that eight guardsmen *might* be guilty, but this would have to be decided by a trial jury. Thus, the 1975 decision was less ambiguous than the earlier trial decision, hence we might expect clearer patterns of responses to the decision. We therefore will test the same set of hypotheses, based upon cognitive consistency theory, which we set forth earlier: students' attitudes toward responsibility for the shootings will not alter significantly; students' attitudes toward the federal district court will change significantly for those students who were placed in a dissonance producing situation by the decision of the jury; and students' attitudes toward the American judicial system will not change significantly.

The Questionnaires

Before we can test the specific hypotheses, we need to discuss the data-gathering procedures we used, which were essentially the same that we employed in the 1974 grand jury study. We again used two mailed questionnaires, one sent out before the jury's decision was announced and a second sent after the decision to all those who responded to the first round questionnaire. The questionnaires sought basically the same type of information we sought in 1974, and many of the questions were the same. We were primarily concerned with determining students' attitudes toward responsibility for the shootings, their attitudes toward the federal district court, and, in this study, their attitude toward the American judicial system. We also asked a variety of questions concerning their personal characteristics, their awareness of and interest in the trial, and their agreement with a variety of statements taken from area newspapers after the trial. The before and after questionnaires appear in Appendices C and D, respectively.

The first-round questionnaires were initially sent in May of 1975 to a random sample of 500 Kent State students whose names were drawn from the 1974–1975 student directory. Follow-up letters and questionnaires were sent to those who did not respond to the initial mailing, and we ended with 222 completed responses to the first-round mailing. About two weeks after the announcement of the decision in August, we sent the second-round questionnaire to the 222 students who had completed the first round. After follow-ups were sent, we eventually received 135 of these questionnaires, which constitutes the number of subjects we shall be analyzing.[64]

The question of the representativeness of our sample must be raised before we move to the data analysis. Our total number of respondents is not overly impressive—135 of 500, or 27 percent. As with the 1974 study, this return rate does not mean necessarily that we had a large number of refusals. The high number of nonrespondents is more likely the result of our questionnaires never reaching the students. We sent out the first-round questionnaire in the spring of 1975, but our sampling source, the student directory, is published each fall. In the 1974–1975 school year, Kent State went through its normal decline in students, dropping from an enrollment of 18,458 in the fall of 1974 to 17,122 in the spring quarter of 1975. In addition to students who left the university, we faced the problem of students moving from one residence to another during the school year with no forwarding address. Our second-round questionnaire mailing faced even more severe problems, for these were sent out in late summer after most students had left Kent State for summer vacation. We felt fortunate to get back 135 of the 222 questionnaires.

The critical question for us is not the number of students who never received the questionnaire, however, for we have no way of answering this. What is possible is to compare our sample against the known characteristics of the Kent State student body in the spring of 1975 to see if the sample seems to be representative. Table 4.10 indicates that the sample matches the student population rather closely. The breakdown by sex is exactly the same for the sample and the population, 53 percent males and 47 percent females. Some differences emerge when we compare the class make-up of our sample with the population. The largest difference involves senior students, for our sample has 35 percent seniors, whereas the student body was composed of only 23 percent seniors. The other class differences are not large, however, and overall the sample seems to be rather representative.

Attitudes Toward Responsibility for the Shootings

Our first analytic task is to test hypothesis 1 regarding responsibility for the shootings:

H_1: Students will not significantly alter their attitudes about responsibility for the shootings in response to the decision of an authoritative judicial structure.

**Table 4.10: COMPARISON OF STUDENT SAMPLE AND
STUDENT BODY OF KENT STATE UNIVERSITY
IN SPRING 1975 ON SELECTED
CHARACTERISTICS**

Characteristics	Sample (N = 135)	Student Body (N = 17,122)
Sex		
Male	53%	53%
Female	47%	47%
Total	100%	100%
Class		
Freshman	13%	22%
Sophomore	16%	19%
Junior	12%	20%
Senior	35%	23%
Graduate Student	24%	17%
Total	100%	101%*

*The total does not come out to 100% because of rounding error.

We are interested in only two groups of defendants, Ohio National Guard enlisted men and Ohio National Guard officers. Ohio Governor James Rhodes and former Kent State president Robert White were also defendants, but we are excluding both of them from our analysis. Rhodes was an active and controversial political figure in Ohio throughout the 1970s, and by 1975 he was again serving as Governor after winning reelection in 1974. Because students' attitudes toward Rhodes could have changed due to many factors other than the trial, we exclude him from our analysis. White is excluded because he was a unique figure in the trial, a defendant used primarily as a legal tactic by the plaintiffs' lawyers to enhance their ability to question witnesses. On several occasions, the students and parents stated that they did not hold White responsible for the shootings. Furthermore, White hired his own lawyer, who sought to defend him independently of the other defendants.

As a preliminary step to testing this hypothesis, we can first look briefly at Kent State students' perceptions of all actors' responsibility for the shootings, just as we did with the 1974 data. Table 4.11 reveals that Ohio National Guard officers were considered to be most

Table 4.11: MEAN SCORES OF KENT STATE
STUDENTS' PERCEPTIONS IN
1974 AND 1975 OF VARIOUS
ACTORS' RESPONSIBILITY FOR
THE MAY 4 SHOOTINGS

Individuals and Groups	Mean Responsibility Scores*	
	1975	1974
Guard officers	1.57	1.58
Rhodes	1.64	1.90
Nonstudent radicals	1.90	1.98
Radical students	1.96	1.96
Guard enlisted men	2.21	2.01
White	2.37	2.72
Nixon	2.57	2.67
KSU administrators	2.76	2.95
Agnew	3.14	3.23
KSU faculty	3.40	3.44
Nonradical students	3.55	3.57

*Responsibility scores can range from 1 (Very Responsible) to 4 (Not Responsible).

responsible for the shootings by the students in our sample before the trial, followed by Rhodes. Radicals, students and nonstudents, were also assessed as bearing a high degree of responsibility, and the Guard enlisted men were also held responsible by many students. In comparing Kent State students' perceptions of responsibility before the 1975 trial with students' views before the 1974 grand jury investigation, we see from Table 4.11 that the scores were remarkably similar. The only noticeable shifts occurred for Rhodes, who was held more responsible by the students in 1975; White, who was also held more responsible in 1975; and Guard enlisted men, who were viewed as less responsible in 1975. The increase in Rhodes' responsibility may have been attributable to his reemergence in public life with his upset victory for reelection as governor in the fall of 1974.

Similarly, White may have been considered more responsible because the question of his responsibility became a publicized issue as a result of his defendant role in the 1975 civil case. Finally, the drop in students' perceptions of responsibility of the guardsmen may have been related not only to the reaction we saw against the grand jury indictments but also to the results of the fall 1974 federal criminal trial in which all charges were dropped against the eight indicted guardsmen.

Turning our attention to testing hypothesis 1, an examination of Tables 4.12 and 4.13 suggests that we can accept this hypothesis, for relatively little change is seen in regard to both Guard officers and enlisted men. From Table 4.12 we see that for the Guard officers, 77 percent of the students who saw them as very responsible before the trial saw them as very responsible afterwards; 42 percent of the students who viewed them as moderately responsible before the trial also saw them as moderately responsible after the trial; 62 percent of the sample that ranked them as minimally responsible before the trial ranked them the same after the trial; and of those who did not believe the officers were responsible at all before the trial, 67 percent kept this view after the trial. Overall, 66 percent of the sample had exactly the same perception of responsibility before and after the

Table 4.12: STUDENTS' PERCEPTIONS BEFORE AND AFTER THE 1975 FEDERAL CIVIL TRIAL OF OHIO NATIONAL GUARD OFFICERS' RESPONSIBILITY FOR THE MAY 4 SHOOTINGS

Perceptions of Guard Officers' Responsibility After the Trial	Perceptions of Guard Officers' Responsibility Before the Trial				Totals	
	Very	Moderately	Minimally	None		
Very	77%	39%	12%	0%	(75)	58%
Moderately	19%	42%	25%	0%	(33)	25%
Minimally	4%	18%	62%	33%	(20)	15%
None	0%	0%	0%	67%	(2)	2%
Totals	100%	99%	99%	100%		
	(78)	(33)	(16)	(3)	(130)	100%

Not all column percentages add to 100 because of rounding error.

Table 4.13: STUDENTS' PERCEPTIONS BEFORE AND AFTER THE 1975 FEDERAL CIVIL TRIAL OF OHIO NATIONAL GUARD ENLISTED MEN'S RESPONSIBILITY FOR THE MAY 4 SHOOTINGS

Perceptions of Guard Enlisted Men's Responsibility After the Trial	Perceptions of Guard Enlisted Men's Responsibility Before the Trial					
	Very	Moderately	Minimally	None	Totals	
Very	42%	18%	11%	0%	(27)	21%
Moderately	42%	61%	39%	0%	(56)	44%
Minimally	14%	20%	46%	33%	(33)	26%
None	3%	0%	4%	67%	(12)	9%
Totals	101%	99%	100%	100%		
	(36)	(49)	(28)	(15)	(128)	100%

Not all column totals add to 100 because of rounding error.

trial. It is also interesting to note that the vast majority of shifts were slight, from one category to the next adjacent one, among those who did give different rankings in their before and after scores. The pattern for Guard enlisted men is similar, although somewhat more change can be detected in Table 4.13. Overall, a majority of the sample maintained exactly the same ranking of responsibility of the Guard enlisted men. As with the Guard officers, those students who ranked the enlisted men in a different category after the trial overwhelmingly shifted the responsibility only slightly, to an adjacent category.

Analysis of variance will allow us to accept or reject hypothesis 1 for both Guard officers and Guard enlisted men based upon probability theory. The results presented in Tables 4.14 and 4.15 give strong confirmation to this hypothesis. The differences in the respective before-and-after scores could have occurred easily by chance. We thus conclude that student attitudes regarding responsibility for the shootings by Guard officers and Guard enlisted men did not change as a result of the 1975 civil trial.

**Table 4.14: ANALYSIS OF VARIANCE TABLE FOR STUDENTS'
PERCEPTIONS BEFORE AND AFTER THE 1975 FEDERAL
CIVIL TRIAL OF NATIONAL GUARD OFFICERS'
RESPONSIBILITY FOR THE MAY 4 SHOOTINGS**

Source	df	MS	F	p
Between subjects	133			
Within subjects	134			
Time	1	.239	.694	.589
Error	133	.344		

Attitudes Toward Specific Judicial Support

Because our hypothesis regarding the lack of change in perceptions of responsibility held up, we can move directly to the testing of the hypotheses regarding attitudes toward the specific judicial structure, the federal district court. These hypotheses are:

H_2: Students who are placed in a situation of cognitive dissonance following a decision of an authoritative judicial structure will significantly change their attitude toward the judicial structure. More precisely,

H_{2a}: If dissonant students disagree with the decision, they will significantly lower their support.

H_{2b}: If dissonant students agree with the decision, they will significantly increase their support.

**Table 4.15: ANALYSIS OF VARIANCE TABLE FOR STUDENTS'
PERCEPTIONS BEFORE AND AFTER THE 1975 FEDERAL
CIVIL TRIAL OF NATIONAL GUARD ENLISTED MEN'S
RESPONSIBILITY FOR THE MAY 4 SHOOTINGS**

Source	df	MS	F	p
Between subjects	133			
Within subjects	134			
Time	1	.451	.822	.631
Error	133	.549		

An examination of Tables 4.16 and 4.17 leads us to accept these hypotheses. Significant change occurred in students' support for the federal district court; and students who agreed with the decision of the court increased their support for the court, while those students who disagreed with the court's verdict decreased their support for the court. Looking first at Table 4.16, we see the mean support scores[65] for two groups of students, those who viewed the National Guard as responsible for the shootings and those who did not hold the Guard responsible.[66] Those who viewed the Guard as responsible for the shootings showed a decrease in support from a mean of 3.87 before the decision to a mean of 3.42 after the decision, while those students who did not believe the Guard was responsible increased their support scores from a mean of 4.06 to 4.54. Table 4.17 provides a more formalized testing of these differences through analysis of variance. As explained in the major methodological section of this chapter, we are interested in testing the interaction effects, for we are hypothesizing that attitudes of specific support will change significantly based upon students' agreement or disagreement with the outcome of the trial. We see in Table 4.17 that our general hypothesis is confirmed, for the overall interaction effect is statistically significant. Furthermore, when we apply the Fisher's least significant difference test to both groups of students, we find both hypotheses

Table 4.16: STUDENTS' MEAN SPECIFIC SUPPORT SCORES FOR THE FEDERAL DISTRICT COURT BEFORE AND AFTER THE 1975 TRIAL

Attitude Toward Guard Responsibility	Specific Judicial Support Scores*	
	Time	
	Before the Decision	After the Decision
Guard Responsible (N = 92)	$\bar{X} = 3.87$	$\bar{X} = 3.42$
Guard Not Responsible (N = 35)	$\bar{X} = 4.06$	$\bar{X} = 4.54$

*Specific support scores can range from a low of 2 to a high of 6.

Table 4.17: ANALYSIS OF VARIANCE TABLE FOR STUDENTS' SPECIFIC JUDICIAL SUPPORT SCORES BEFORE AND AFTER THE 1975 FEDERAL CIVIL TRIAL

Source	df	MS	F	p
Between subjects				
A (Responsibility)	1	31.76	13.91	.001
Error	124	2.28		
Within subjects				
B (Time)	1	2.29	2.91	.089
A × B (Interaction)	1	10.20	12.96	.001
Error	124	.79		

2a and 2b confirmed. The graph in Figure 4.7 helps us to see this clearly. Those students who found themselves in agreement with the court's decision increased their support substantially, while those in disagreement with the court's decision substantially decreased their support. Thus, while the support scores for the two groups were rather close before the decision, after the decision they were substantially different.

Attitudes Toward Diffuse Support

What about attitudes toward the broader judicial system? We have established that students did not significantly alter their attitudes about responsibility for the shootings following the trial, and for many students this would possibly create dissonance with their attitude toward the American judicial system. For students who disagreed with the decision, did this lessen their faith in the judicial system? If students agreed with the decision, did their support for the system increase?

In examining the judicial process literature earlier in this chapter, we offered the following hypothesis:

H$_3$ Students will not significantly alter their diffuse support for the judicial system in response to the decision of a judicial structure, regardless of the outcome of the decision.

FIGURE 4.7: A GRAPH OF STUDENTS' MEAN SPECIFIC SUPPORT SCORES
BEFORE AND AFTER THE 1975 FEDERAL CIVIL TRIAL

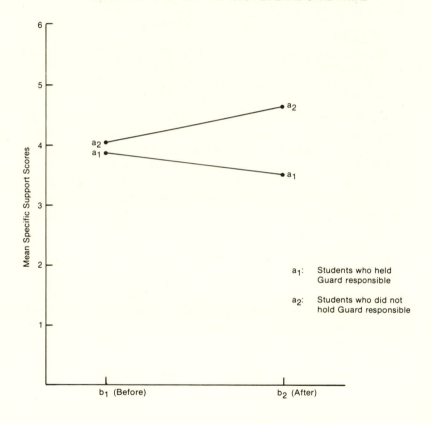

General support for the judicial system seems to be deeply ingrained and hence not susceptible to easy change. Further, our analysis of specific judicial support has revealed that students did appear to reduce dissonance by altering their attitudes toward the specific court. This form of dissonance reduction may make it easier to maintain one's view about the general judicial process.

The data to test this hypothesis appear in Tables 4.18 and 4.19. They lead us to accept the hypothesis: students' attitudes concerning diffuse support for the American judicial system did not change significantly as a result of the decision of the jury in the 1975 May 4 civil trial. Looking first at Table 4.18, we see that diffuse support scores[67] for students who believed the Guard was responsible shifted only slightly, dropping from a mean score of 8.67 before the trial to a mean of 8.53 after the trial. A somewhat larger change can be observed for the students who did not believe the National Guard was responsible. The mean diffuse support score for these students increased from 9.66 to 10.14. Thus, we do see some shifts in mean support scores, and they do move in the directions we would expect; diffuse support scores decreased slightly for those students whose attitudes of responsibility were in disagreement with the court's decision, and diffuse support scores increased for students who found the court's decision compatible with their views of responsibility for the shootings. Table 4.19 reveals, however, that these differences are

Table 4.18: STUDENTS' MEAN DIFFUSE SUPPORT SCORES FOR THE AMERICAN JUDICIAL SYSTEM BEFORE AND AFTER THE 1975 FEDERAL CIVIL TRIAL

Attitude Toward Guard Responsibility	Diffuse Judicial Support Scores*	
	Time	
	Before the Decision	After the Decision
Guard Responsible (N = 95)	$\bar{X} = 8.67$	$\bar{X} = 8.53$
Guard Not Responsible (N = 35)	$\bar{X} = 9.66$	$\bar{X} = 10.14$

*Diffuse support scores can range from a low of 3 to a high of 15.

Table 4.19: ANALYSIS OF VARIANCE TABLE FOR STUDENTS' DIFFUSE JUDICIAL SUPPORT SCORES BEFORE AND AFTER THE 1975 FEDERAL CIVIL TRIAL

Source	df	MS	F	p
Between subjects				
A (Responsibility)	1	86.45	13.37	.001
Error	124	6.46		
Within subjects				
B (Time)	1	.03	.02	.891
A × B (Interaction)	1	5.13	2.53	.109
Error	124	2.01		

not large enough for us to accept them as being statistically significant, and hence we accept hypothesis 3 that students' diffuse support scores did not change significantly.[68]

We have thus found that each of our hypotheses has been confirmed for the 1975 federal civil trial. Student attitudes toward responsibility of the Ohio National Guard enlisted men and officers did not change significantly. We did see significant attitude change in regard to specific judicial support, and the changes occurred as predicted through cognitive consistency theory. Students in disagreement with the decision significantly lowered their support for the federal district court, and students in agreement with the decision significantly increased their support for the court. Finally, we did not find significant change in students' diffuse support for the American judicial system.

THE 1979 FEDERAL CIVIL TRIAL

There is no stirring among the spectators, no display of emotion. Of the nine students wounded that day at Kent State, only Robert Stamps is present. The final legal act of a historic drama has played to a sparse audience and a strangely muted reception. Besides the jury, the lawyers and officers of the court, there are 34 people in the room, many of them representatives of news organizations. Folding chairs have been set up but they haven't been needed.

Lawyers shuffle papers, shake hands, offer mutual respects for the excellence of their performances. The spectators talk quietly and then depart. Before long the courtroom is cleared and a young woman goes about collecting the folding chairs.[69]

The contrast between the end of the first May 4 civil trial in 1975 and the culmination of the second civil trial in 1979 could hardly have been more stark. The 1975 trial outcome was a clear victory for Governor Rhodes and members of the Ohio National Guard, and it was a bitter defeat for the parents and students. Reactions were also clear and unrestrained; on the one side there was deep bitterness and on the other side great relief and joy. The 1979 federal civil trial lacked any such clarity of outcome. All thirteen plaintiffs received financial awards, and they received a statement of regret from the defendants. But none of the defendants personally had to pay any money, and the statement of regret did not explicitly contain any admission of guilt or liability.

The ambiguity of the out-of-court settlement was reflected in the reactions of our sample of Kent State students. When asked about their general reaction to the overall settlement, no clear consensus emerged; 37 percent of the respondents expressed dissatisfaction with the settlement, 25 percent were satisfied, and 38 percent were either undecided or had no response. Kent State students did not see either side as a clear winner in the settlement. Twenty-five percent of the students believed the defendants had won, 13 percent saw the parents and wounded students as the winners, and 8 percent felt both sides won; but the majority—54 percent—responded that neither side had won. The students were extremely negative about the extent to which the trial and settlement resolved important questions about the shootings. Eighty percent of the respondents indicated that few or none of the questions were resolved, and only 3 percent believed all or most of the questions had been resolved. Finally, Kent State students did not believe that justice had yet been achieved in regard to the May 4 shootings. Only 17 percent of the student respondents felt that justice had been realized in regard to the shootings, one-third were undecided, and one-half believed justice had not yet been realized.

This unexpected, ambiguous, and controversial out-of-court settlement that ended the 1979 civil trial provided us with yet a third opportunity to analyze the impact of an authoritative judicial decision on attitudes of an attentive public toward a specific issue, a specific court, and the American judicial system. The hypotheses set forth at the start of this chapter were only partially confirmed in analyzing the impact of the 1974 federal grand jury decision, but each hypothesis was confirmed in testing the data on the 1975 federal civil trial. We therefore will test these same hypotheses again: students' attitudes toward responsibility for the shootings will not change in response to the outcome of the judicial settlement; students' attitudes toward the federal district court will change if students are placed in a dissonance condition because of the outcome of the case; and students' attitudes regarding the American judicial system will not change significantly.

The Questionnaires

Our questionnaires and sampling procedures were similar to those used in our 1974 and 1975 studies. We did this to assure comparability; but we were also reasonably satisfied with our procedures from the earlier studies, and we lacked the resources to approach the study differently if we had so desired.

The questionnaires again focused primarily upon students' attitudes toward responsibility for the shootings, toward the federal district court, and toward the American judicial system. The before and after questionnaires appear in Appendices E and F, respectively.

We sent first-round questionnaires in November of 1978 to a random sample of 600 students drawn from the 1978–1979 student directory. We increased the sample size from the 500 we had selected in our earlier studies for the purpose of increasing the total number of respondents to both the before-and-after questionnaires. The approach was successful. By mid-December we had received 312 questionnaires. About two weeks after the announcement of the out-of-court settlement on January 4, 1979, we sent the second-round questionnaire to each student who had responded to the first-round. We eventually received 184 second-round questionnaires.

Looking at the question of the representativeness of the sample, we did receive a larger number of responses than in the previous studies, but our percentage of respondents is still rather low at 31 percent. The reason our response rate is somewhat better than the 1975 study (27 percent) is probably because the settlement of the 1979 case came rather early in the school year, whereas in 1975 most of the students had left campus for the summer by the time the decision was announced. Again with the 1979 study, however, we faced the problem of the mobility of the students, which probably meant that as many as one-third of the students did not receive their questionnaires. Table 4.20 presents comparative data for our sample and the Kent State student body in the fall quarter of 1978. The sample is almost identical to the population in regard to gender, but the differences for the variable of class standing are somewhat larger. Freshmen and sophomore students are somewhat underrepresented in our sample, and juniors, seniors, and graduate students are over-represented. These differences are not large enough to cause us serious concern, however.

Table 4.20: COMPARISON OF STUDENT SAMPLE AND STUDENT BODY OF KENT STATE UNIVERSITY IN FALL 1978 ON SELECTED CHARACTERISTICS

Characteristic	Sample (N = 184)	Student Body (N = 18,331)
Sex		
Male	48%	49%
Female	52%	51%
Total	100%	100%
Class		
Freshman	14%	25%
Sophomore	13%	17%
Junior	19%	17%
Senior	23%	17%
Graduate Student	30%	24%
Total	99%*	100%

*The total does not add to 100% because of rounding error.

Attitudes Toward Responsibility for the Shootings

Once again we begin our analysis by examining the hypothesis that there will be no change in students' perceptions of responsibility for the shootings:

> H₁: Students will not significantly alter their attitudes about responsi-
> bility for the shootings in response to the decision of an authorita-
> tive judicial structure.

We saw in analyzing the impact of the 1975 federal civil trial that the hypothesis was supported; students' attitudes concerning the responsibility of the Ohio National Guard officers and enlisted men did not change significantly. It would seem that this hypothesis should again hold true, for the ambiguous nature of the 1979 out-of-court settlement did not seem to provide any clear-cut statements about who was responsible for the shootings.

Before we test this hypothesis for the Guard officers and enlisted men, we will once again examine Kent State students' attitudes toward responsibility of all the individuals and groups associated with the shootings, comparing the 1978 student sample with the 1974 and 1975 samples. We see in Table 4.21 that our sample of Kent State students in the fall of 1978 had somewhat different perceptions of primary responsibility for the shootings than did the students in our 1974 and 1975 studies, for the 1978 students ranked radicals—student and nonstudent—as most responsible for the shootings. Also, while Rhodes and Guard officers and enlisted men were all given considerable responsibility for the shootings, the 1978 students ranked them somewhat less responsible than did the 1975 students. While we do not have data to explore why these shifts occurred, they may have resulted from the protest activities in 1977 surrounding the decision to build a gymnasium annex on part of the site where protestors and guardsmen confronted each other on May 4, 1970. This protest in its early stages involved primarily Kent State students using peaceful, legal means. As the protest continued into the late summer and fall, however, the movement came increasingly under the control of more radical students and radical elements from outside the university. The activities of these radicals resulted in serious confrontations between protestors and law enforcement personnel in the fall

Table 4.21: MEAN SCORES OF KENT STATE STUDENTS' PERCEPTIONS IN 1974, 1975, AND 1978 OF VARIOUS ACTORS' RESPONSIBILITY FOR THE MAY 4 SHOOTINGS

Individuals and Groups	Mean Responsibility Scores*		
	1978	1975	1974
Nonstudent radicals	1.55	1.90	1.98
Radical students	1.69	1.96	1.96
Guard officers	1.75	1.57	1.58
Rhodes	1.87	1.64	1.90
Guard enlisted men	2.33	2.21	2.01
White	2.55	2.37	2.72
Nixon	2.77	2.56	2.67
KSU administrators	2.84	2.76	2.95
Agnew	3.22	3.14	3.23
KSU faculty	3.49	3.40	3.44
Nonradical students	3.62	3.55	3.57

*Responsibility scores can range from 1 (very responsible) to 4 (not responsible).

of 1977, and the university received extremely bad publicity with an accompanying sharp drop in enrollment in 1977 and 1978.[70] These developments may have led students responding to our questionnaire to heighten their perceptions of radical responsibility for the events of 1970.

Turning our attention back to hypothesis 1, we find in examining the relevant data that the hypothesis is confirmed. Students' attitudes regarding the responsibility of both Guard officers and Guard enlisted men did not change significantly between the first and second rounds.[71] Looking first at the Guard officers, we see from Table 4.22 that most of the respondents maintained exactly the same perception of Guard officer responsibility after the trial as before; 72 percent of those who held the officers very responsible before the trial saw them as very responsible after the trial, and 55 percent of the students who believed before the trial that the officers were moderately responsible held the same view afterward. The analysis of variance presented in Table 4.23 provides clear confirmation that the change which did occur was not statistically significant. We see a similar pattern in

Table 4.22: STUDENTS' PERCEPTIONS BEFORE AND AFTER THE 1979 FEDERAL CIVIL TRIAL OF NATIONAL GUARD OFFICERS' RESPONSIBILITY FOR THE MAY 4 SHOOTINGS

Perceptions of Guard Officers' Responsibility After the Trial	Perceptions of Guard Officers' Responsibility Before the Trial				
	Very	Moderately	Minimally	None	Totals
Very	72%	22%	15%	29%	46% (76)
Moderately	26%	55%	30%	14%	37% (61)
Minimally	1%	20%	35%	14%	13% (21)
None	0%	3%	20%	43%	5% (9)
Totals	99%	100%	100%	100%	101% (167)
	(80)	(60)	(20)	(7)	

Not all column percentages add to 100 because of rounding error.

Tables 4.24 and 4.25 in regard to students' perceptions of the responsibility of Guard enlisted men. As shown in Table 4.24, one-half of the students maintained exactly the same view of responsibility, and the shifts that did occur were primarily to an adjacent category rather than dramatic shifts. The analysis of variance presented in Table 4.25 provides strong confirmation that students' views of the responsibility of Guard enlisted men did not change significantly in response to the out-of-court settlement in the 1979 civil trial.

Table 4.23: ANALYSIS OF VARIANCE TABLE FOR STUDENTS' PERCEPTIONS BEFORE AND AFTER THE 1979 CIVIL TRIAL OF NATIONAL GUARD OFFICERS' RESPONSIBILITY FOR THE MAY 4 SHOOTINGS

Source	df	MS	F	p
Between subjects	180			
Within subjects	181			
Time	1	.224	.427	.521
Error	180	.524		

Table 4.24: STUDENTS' PERCEPTIONS BEFORE AND AFTER THE 1979 FEDERAL CIVIL TRIAL OF NATIONAL GUARD ENLISTED MEN'S RESPONSIBILITY FOR THE MAY 4 SHOOTINGS

Perceptions of Guard Enlisted Men's Responsibility After the Trial	Perceptions of Guard Enlisted Men's Responsibility Before the Trial				
	Very	Moderately	Minimally	None	Totals
Very	38%	19%	3%	10%	19% (31)
Moderately	42%	54%	26%	5%	39% (64)
Minimally	18%	24%	49%	33%	29% (47)
None	2%	3%	23%	52%	13% (22)
Totals	100%	100%	101%	100%	100% (164)
	(40)	(68)	(35)	(21)	

Not all columns add to 100 because of rounding error.

Attitudes Toward Specific Support

Having established that students' attitudes toward the National Guard's responsibility for the shootings did not change significantly, we can now turn our attention to the question of whether the attitudes of students toward the federal district court underwent significant changes. Cognitive consistency theory leads us to believe that such changes may have occurred for those students who were placed

Table 4.25: ANALYSIS OF VARIANCE TABLE FOR STUDENTS' PERCEPTIONS BEFORE AND AFTER THE 1979 CIVIL TRIAL OF OHIO NATIONAL GUARD ENLISTED MEN'S RESPONSIBILITY FOR THE MAY 4 SHOOTINGS

Source	df	MS	F	p
Between subjects	180			
Within subjects	181			
Time	1	.398	.599	.554
Error	180	.664		

in a dissonant condition by the outcome of the case. Our specific hypotheses are:

H_2: Students who are placed in a situation of cognitive dissonance following a decision of an authoritative judicial structure will significantly change their attitude toward the judicial structure. More precisely,

H_{2a}: If dissonant students disagree with the decision, they will significantly lower their support.

H_{2b}: If dissonant students agree with the decision, they will significantly increase their support.

Unique methodological problems arise when we try to test these hypotheses. In studying the two previous decisions, the outcomes of the decisions were clear in regard to responsibility for the shootings. It was therefore an easy matter to determine if students' attitudes regarding responsibility for the shootings were in agreement with the decisions. The 1979 out-of-court settlement, however, was highly ambiguous in regard to the question of the defendants' responsibility. Hence, before we can look at changes in specific support, we first need to determine how students perceived the outcome of the settlement, for only then can we determine if a student's views on responsibility were in agreement or disagreement with the outcome of the case. Specifically, we need to assess which students perceived the settlement as finding the defendants responsible for the shootings and which students viewed the decision as not placing responsibility on the defendants. We did this by factor analyzing a number of newspaper statements about the settlement which we included in our second questionnaire. We labeled one of the factors which emerged the "responsibility factor." Two questions composed this factor:

The defendants' statement is an admission of moral responsibility and the compensation is an acknowledgement of legal liability.

Although there was no admission of guilt from the defendants, the settlement itself implies that those who acted for the state bore some responsibility for the tragedy.

Students responded to each statement by indicating on a 1 to 7 scale whether they agreed or disagreed with the statements. A score of 1 was given for strongly agree and a 7 was given for strongly disagree. To determine if students believed the settlement found the defendants responsible for the shootings, we summed the two scores for each student, giving us a scale ranging from 2 (strongly agreed that the settlement established defendants' responsibility) to 14 (strongly disagreed that the settlement established defendants' responsibility). We then divided the scale into three categories. Students with scores of two through six were classified as viewing the settlement as finding the Guard responsible; students with scores of seven through nine were considered to be uncertain as to whether the settlement found the Guard responsible; and those students with scores of ten through fourteen were classified as considering the settlement to find the Guard not responsible for the shootings.

The results of these classification procedures can be seen in Table 4.26, which contains the before-and-after scores on specific support for each group of students. Before testing the hypotheses on changes in specific judicial support, it is interesting to observe the patterns of perceived outcomes of the settlement. We had assumed that a process of cognitive transposition would occur for most students, by which they would interpret the outcome of the settlement consistently with their attitude about responsibility for the shootings.[72] This did not occur for a majority of the students. Forty-one percent of the students did interpret the outcome of the settlement consistently with their perceptions of responsibility; but 18 percent of the students perceived the outcome of the settlement inconsistently with their views of responsibility; and 41 percent of the students were uncertain about the meaning of the settlement in terms of Guard responsibility.

We are now in a position to test our hypotheses. The results of the data analysis reveal that a significant change occurred for only one group of students, those students who had perceived the Guard as responsible before the trial and viewed the settlement as finding the Guard not responsible. These students should thus have experienced dissonance, and we hypothesized that their support scores would decline significantly. Other groups should also have experienced dissonance, however, but they did not show significant changes.

We need to examine the data in closer detail to comprehend more fully these results. Table 4.26 contains the mean before and after specific judicial support scores[73] for each of the six groups of stu-

Table 4.26: STUDENTS' MEAN SPECIFIC SUPPORT SCORES FOR THE
FEDERAL DISTRICT COURT BEFORE AND AFTER THE 1979
CIVIL TRIAL

Attitude Toward Guard Responsibility	Perceptions of Outcome of the Settlement	Specific Judicial Support Scores*	
		Time	
		Before the Settlement	After the Settlement
Guard Responsible (N = 99)	Guard Responsible (N = 45)	$\bar{X} = 4.20$	$\bar{X} = 3.98$
	Uncertain (N = 44)	$\bar{X} = 3.93$	$\bar{X} = 3.82$
	Guard Not Responsible (N = 10)	$\bar{X} = 4.50$	$\bar{X} = 3.40$
Guard Not Responsible (N = 53)	Guard Responsible (N = 17)	$\bar{X} = 3.88$	$\bar{X} = 4.41$
	Uncertain (N = 18)	$\bar{X} = 4.18$	$\bar{X} = 3.71$
	Guard Not Responsible (N = 18)	$\bar{X} = 4.22$	$\bar{X} = 4.00$

*Specific support scores can range from a low of 2 to a high of 6.

dents. We see that five of the six groups showed a decline in support.
Only one group—those who viewed the Guard as responsible but
saw the settlement as finding the Guard not responsible—underwent
a large change, however, declining from a mean support score of
4.50 to 3.40.

We can better analyze the meaning of these scores in terms of cognitive consistency theory by placing them onto graphs, which are presented in Figure 4.8. We will analyze these graphs in conjunction with the analysis of variance results presented in Table 4.27. From this table we can see that the overall interaction effect (A×B×C) is not quite significant at the .05 level, but it is possible that specific main interaction effects will prove to be significant. The graphs in Figure 4.8 will help us to determine this.

Within Figure 4.8 we see three graphs based upon the three types of perceptions which students held about the outcome of the settlement in regard to determining Guard responsibility for the shootings. In Graph 1 we find those students who believed that the settlement found the Guard responsible. Within this group, we would expect those students who also viewed the Guard as responsible before the trial (a₁) to be more supportive of the court after the trial. This has not occurred, however, for these students decreased in mean support from 4.20 to 3.98. Those students included in Graph 1 who viewed the Guard as not responsible before the settlement (a₂) should have found themselves in a dissonant situation because their perception of the outcome of the trial—the Guard was found responsible—

Table 4.27: ANALYSIS OF VARIANCE TABLE FOR STUDENTS' SPECIFIC SUPPORT FOR THE FEDERAL DISTRICT COURT BEFORE AND AFTER THE 1979 CIVIL TRIAL

Source	df	MS	F	p
Between subjects				
A ((Responsibility)	1	.512	.317	.581
B (Perceptions of Outcome)	2	.838	.519	.602
A × B (Interaction)	2	.062	.038	.963
Error	145	1.610		
Within subjects				
C (Time)	1	4.019	5.429	.020
A × C (Interaction)	1	2.545	3.437	.062
B × C (Interaction)	2	3.139	4.240	.016
A × B × C (Interaction)	2	2.176	2.939	.054
Error	145	.740		

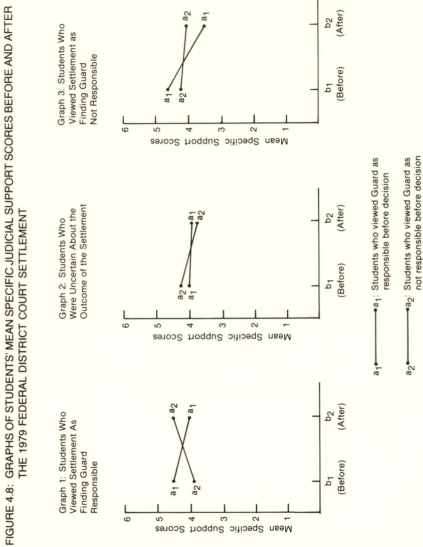

FIGURE 4.8: GRAPHS OF STUDENTS' MEAN SPECIFIC JUDICIAL SUPPORT SCORES BEFORE AND AFTER THE 1979 FEDERAL DISTRICT COURT SETTLEMENT

Graph 1: Students Who Viewed Settlement As Finding Guard Responsible

Graph 2: Students Who Were Uncertain About the Outcome of the Settlement

Graph 3: Students Who Viewed Settlement as Finding Guard Not Responsible

a₁: Students who viewed Guard as responsible before decision

a₂: Students who viewed Guard as not responsible before decision clashed with their perception of responsibility, and hence we would predict a decline in specific support. Instead, we see an increase from a mean of 3.88 to a mean of 4.41. Thus, the support scores for both these groups went in the opposite direction predicted by our cognitive consistency model. When we apply the Fisher's least significant difference test to each of these sets of scores, however, we find that neither difference is statistically significant.

Turning to Graph 2 in Figure 4.8, we have those students who were uncertain about whom the settlement found responsible for the shootings. These students should not have found themselves in a dissonance condition, given their ambiguity about the settlement, and hence we should not expect significant change. We find that little change has occurred for students who viewed the Guard as responsible before the trial (a_1), a shift from a mean support score of 3.93 before the trial to 3.82 afterwards. The other group of students, those who held the Guard not responsible before the trial (a_2), had a sharper decline in support, from a mean of 4.18 to 3.71. Neither of these changes is statistically significant, however, when the Fisher's least significant difference test is applied.

The final set of students we need to examine are those represented in Graph 3, students who viewed the settlement as finding the Guard not responsible for the shootings. Of these students, the group that perceived the Guard as responsible before the settlement (a_1) should have found themselves in a dissonant condition because of their view of the meaning of the settlement, and we have hypothesized that they would lower their support significantly. We see in Graph 3 that this has occurred. This group underwent the largest change of any of the six groups, dropping in mean support from 4.50 to 3.40, a statistically significant difference. The other group of students in Graph 3, those who viewed the Guard as not responsible before the trial (a_2), should have experienced an increase in specific support, but we find instead a slight decrease for this group of students from a mean of 4.22 before the trial to a mean of 4.00 after the trial. This difference was not statistically significant.

It is now possible to draw all of these findings together. At a general level, hypothesis 2 stated that we would find significant attitude change in specific judicial support for students who experienced dissonance because of the results of the 1979 out-of-court settlement.

More specifically, we hypothesized that students in agreement with the outcome would increase their support (H_{2b}), and students in disagreement would decrease their support (H_{2a}). Because of the complexity of the out-of-court settlement, we had to examine six groups of students. Two groups of students were uncertain about the meaning of the settlement in terms of responsibility, and they should not have experienced dissonance; as hypothesized they did not show significant change. Two groups of students perceived the outcome of the settlement to be consistent with their views of Guard responsibility, but neither group showed significant increases in support for the court. Thus, we reject hypothesis 2b which states that students in agreement with the decision will significantly increase their specific support. For the two groups that viewed the settlement as being opposed to their view of Guard responsibility, only one of the groups underwent a significant change, decreasing their support for the federal district court. Thus, for only one of the two groups can we accept hypothesis 2a that students who disagreed with the decision will lower their support for the judicial structure.

Attitudes Toward Diffuse Judicial Support

We now shift our attention to an analysis of changes in students' diffuse support for the American judicial system. Our analysis of the 1975 trial data led us to accept our hypothesis that no significant change would occur in students' diffuse support, and hence we expect this hypothesis to be confirmed again in regard to the 1979 trial:

H_3: Students will not significantly alter their diffuse support for the American judicial system in response to the decision of an authoritative judicial structure, regardless of the outcome of the case.

An examination of mean scores in Tables 4.28 and the analysis of variance in Table 4.29 leads to a clear conclusion: students' diffuse support for the American judicial system did not undergo significant change. Examining the mean diffuse support scores[74] in Table 4.28, we see rather small changes in the before and after scores for each of the six groups of students. Only two groups show changes of any

Table 4.28: STUDENTS' MEAN DIFFUSE JUDICIAL SUPPORT SCORES
FOR THE AMERICAN JUDICIAL SYSTEM BEFORE AND
AFTER THE 1979 CIVIL TRIAL

Attitude Toward Guard Responsibility	Perceptions of Outcome of the Settlement	Diffuse Judicial Support Scores*	
		Time	
		Before the Settlement	After the Settlement
Guard Responsible (N = 102)	Guard Responsible (N = 44)	$\bar{X}$ = 8.95	$\bar{X}$ = 9.07
	Uncertain (N = 48)	$\bar{X}$ = 9.25	$\bar{X}$ = 9.42
	Guard Not Responsible (N = 10)	$\bar{X}$ = 9.10	$\bar{X}$ = 8.70
Guard Not Responsible (N = 49)	Guard Responsible (N = 17)	$\bar{X}$ = 9.29	$\bar{X}$ = 9.29
	Uncertain (N = 18)	$\bar{X}$ = 9.89	$\bar{X}$ = 9.33
	Guard Not Responsible (N = 14)	$\bar{X}$ = 10.50	$\bar{X}$ = 10.64

*Diffuse support scores can range from a low of 3 to a high of 15.

noticeable size. Students who saw the Guard as responsible before
the trial and perceived the settlement as holding the Guard not responsible showed a decrease in diffuse support from 9.10 to 8.70,
and students who viewed the Guard as not responsible and were
uncertain about the outcome of the settlement also declined, from
9.89 to 9.33. Table 4.29 reveals that the overall interaction effect is
not significant (p = .365), and none of the simple main effects
proved to be statistically significant.[75] Thus, we can accept hypothesis
3 that students did not significantly alter their support for the Ameri-

Table 4.29: ANALYSIS OF VARIANCE TABLE FOR STUDENTS' DIFFUSE JUDICIAL SUPPORT SCORES BEFORE AND AFTER THE 1979 CIVIL TRIAL

Source	df	MS	F	p
Between subjects				
A (Responsibility)	1	30.250	4.972	.026
B (Perceptions of Outcome)	2	6.210	1.021	.364
A × B (Interaction)	2	11.752	1.932	.146
Error	145	6.083		
Within subjects				
C (Time)	1	.430	.240	.631
A × C (Interaction)	1	.130	.073	.784
B × C (Interaction)	2	.309	.173	.843
A × B × C (Interaction)	2	1.823	1.017	.365
Error	145	1.792		

can judicial system in the aftermath of the 1979 out-of-court settlement of the Kent State civil trial.

CONCLUSIONS

It is now possible to summarize the findings of the analyses of each of the three decisions. Table 4.30 contains the results of the hypothesis tests for each decision.

Hypothesis 1 stated: "Students will not significantly alter their attitudes about responsibility for the shootings in response to the decision of an authoritative judicial structure." We found confirmation of this hypothesis in studying both the 1975 and 1979 federal civil trials. We had to reject the hypothesis in regard to the 1974 federal grand jury decision. But this was not because Kent State students changed their attitudes to conform to the grand jury's decision. Rather, the significant change in attitude went against the grand jury's decision; students significantly lowered their assessment of enlisted guardsmen responsibility for the shootings even though the grand jury indicted eight guardsmen. It is therefore clear that Kent State students did not

Table 4.30: A SUMMARY OF THE RESULTS OF THE HYPOTHESIS TESTING

Hypotheses	Decisions		
	1974 Federal Grand Jury	1975 Federal Civil Trial	1979 Federal Civil Trial
H_1: Students will not significantly alter their attitudes about responsibility for the shootings.	Reject for Enlisted Men	Accept for Officers and Enlisted Men	Accept for Officers and Enlisted Men
H_2: Students who are placed in a situation of cognitive dissonance following a decision of an authoritative judicial structure will significantly change their attitude toward the judicial structure. Specifically,			
H_{2a}: If dissonant students disagree with the decision, they will significantly lower their support.	Accept for one group, reject for one group	Accept	Accept for one group, reject for one group
H_{2b}: If dissonant students agree with the decision, they will significantly increase their support.	Reject for two groups	Accept	Reject for two groups
H_3: Students will not significantly alter their diffuse support for the judicial system.	Did not test	Accept	Accept

201

change their attitudes about responsibility to conform to the decisions of authoritative judicial structures.

Hypothesis 2, involving students' attitudes of specific support for the judicial structures making the respective decisions, was derived from the basic postulates of cognitive consistency theory. The central idea here is that if two attitudes of an individual come into conflict, then an unpleasant condition of dissonance arises; this dissonant condition can be reduced or eliminated by changing one of the attitudes. Thus, if a judicial structure makes a decision which creates dissonance for an individual, then the individual may change his attitude about either the issue or the judicial structure. We hypothesized that Kent State students would not change their attitudes about responsibility for the shootings but rather about the judicial structure:

> H_2: Students who are placed in a situation of cognitive dissonance following a decision of an authoritative judicial structure will significantly change their attitude toward the judicial structure. More precisely,
> H_{2a}: If dissonant students disagree with the decision, they will significantly lower their support.
> H_{2b}: If dissonant students agree with the decision, they will significantly increase their support.

We found that students did not change their attitudes about responsibility for the shootings to conform to the decisions of the judicial structures. Did they change their attitudes about the structures? We do not have an unequivocal answer to this question. Hypothesis 2a was generally accepted, whereas hypothesis 2b was generally rejected. Thus, students in a dissonant situation who disagreed with a decision did appear to significantly lower their support for the judicial structure, thus presumably achieving cognitive consistency as hypothesized in H2a; this hypothesis did not hold for two groups, however. We found little support for hypothesis 2b, which stated that students in a dissonant condition who agreed with the decision would significantly increase their support for the judicial structure. This hypothesis was confirmed only for students in regard to the 1975 civil trial. The reason why this hypothesis was not generally confirmed may have been because students' support scores for the judicial structures before the decisions tended to be rather high, making it unlikely that the scores would increase to a significant degree. The final hypothesis involved diffuse support:

H_3: Students will not significantly alter their diffuse support for the judicial system in response to the decision of a judicial structure, regardless of the outcome of the decision.

This hypothesis was based upon the theoretical literature which conceptualizes diffuse support as a deeply ingrained, relatively stable attitude of general good will toward the American judicial system. Thus, even if students did find themselves in a dissonant situation, they would not change their attitudes on diffuse support; rather, dissonance would be resolved by altering specific support attitudes. This hypothesis was confirmed for all groups of students tested.

NOTES

1. For a recent discussion of some of the problems associated with measuring attitude intensity, see Dennis R. Goldenson, "The Measurement of Attitude Intensity," paper presented at the 1979 meeting of the Midwest Association for Public Opinion Research.

2. Easton's three major statements of systems analysis are: "An Approach to the Analysis of Political Systems," *World Politics* 9 (1957):383–400; *A Framework for Political Analysis* (Englewood Cliffs, N.J.: Prentice-Hall, 1965); and *A Systems Analysis of Political Life* (New York: John Wiley and Sons, 1965). Among the more important of Easton's recent writings are "A Re-Assessment of the Concept of Political Support," *British Journal of Political Science* 5, 4 (October 1975):435–58 and "Theoretical Approaches to Political Support," *Canadian Journal of Political Science* 9, 3 (September 1976):431–48.

3. Easton, *A Framework for Political Analysis*, p. 125.

4. Easton, *A Systems Analysis of Political Life*, p. 268.

5. Easton, *A Framework for Political Analysis*, p. 126.

6. Easton, *A Systems Analysis of Political Life*, p. 273.

7. Easton, *A Framework for Political Analysis*, p. 126.

8. An especially important study and the one we draw upon here is Walter Murphy, Joseph Tanenhaus, and Daniel Kastner, *Public Evaluations of Constitutional Courts: Alternative Explanations* (Beverly Hills: Sage Publications, 1973).

9. Ibid., p. 44.

10. A. S. Miller and A. W. Scheflin, "The Power of the Supreme Court in the Age of the Positive State: A Preliminary Excursus," *Duke Law Journal* (April 1967):273—320.

11. Gregory Casey, "Popular Perceptions of Supreme Court Rulings," *American Politics Quarterly* 4, 1 (January 1976):3—45.

12. Richard Lehne and John Reynolds, "The Impact of Judicial Activism on Public Opinion," *American Journal of Political Science* 22, 4 (November 1978):896—904.

13. William Muir, *Prayer in the Public Schools* (Chicago: University of Chicago Press, 1967).

14. Ibid., p. 138.

15. Muir's questionnaire was primarily concerned with the Supreme Court, but a few questions dealt with courts and lawyers more generally.

16. Alternative means of dissonance reduction are discussed in chapter one.

17. Among the studies that have examined diffuse support are: Murphy, Tanenhaus, and Kastner, *Public Evaluations of Constitutional Courts;* Casey, "Popular Perceptions of Supreme Court Rulings;" Austin Sarat, "Support for the Legal System: An Analysis of Knowledge, Attitudes, and Behavior," *American Politics Quarterly* 3, 1 (January 1975):3—24; Harrell Rodgers and Edward Lewis, "Political Support and Compliance Attitudes," *American Politics Quarterly* 2, 1 (January 1974):61—77; and R. Engstrom and M. Giles, "Expectations and Images: A Note on Diffuse Support for Legal Institutions," *Law and Society Review* 6, 4 (May 1972):631—36.

18. Harrell Rodgers and Roger Hansen, "The Rule of Law and Legal Efficacy: Private Values vs. General Standards," *Western Political Quarterly* XXVII, 3 (September 1974):387—94.

19. Recent examples of experimental research include Kenneth D. Wald and Michael B. Lupfer, "The Presidential Debate as a Civics Lesson," *Public Opinion Quarterly* 42, 3 (Fall 1978):342—53; James M. Carlson, "Politics and Interpersonal Attraction," *American Politics Quarterly* 7, 1 (January 1979):12—26; and Meredith M. Watts and David Sumi, "Studies in the Physiological Component of Aggression-Related Social Attitudes," *American Journal of Political Science* 23, 3 (August 1979):528—58. The journal *Experimental Study of Politics* has been founded to promote and disseminate experimental research, and panels on experimental political research have become a regular feature at major political science conferences.

20. An important exception is Muir, *Prayer in the Public Schools.*

21. Donald T. Campbell and Julian C. Stanley, *Experimental and Quasi-Experimental Designs for Research* (Chicago: Rand McNally and Co., 1963).

22. Fred N. Kerlinger, *Foundations of Behavioral Research,* 2nd ed. (New York: Holt, Rinehart & Winston, Inc., 1973).

23. Roger E. Kirk , *Experimental Design: Procedures for The Behavioral Sciences* (Belmont, Calif.: Brooks/Cole Publishing Co., 1968).

24. Richard Lempert, "Strategies of Research Design in the Legal Impact Study: The Control of Rival Hypotheses," *Law and Society Review* 1 (November 1966):111—32.

25. Our notation is based upon that used by Campbell and Stanley. 0_1 refers to the

observations of a group of subjects at one point in time, and O_2 refers to the observation of the same group of subjects at a later point in time. X is a treatment effect which may bring about a change in the subjects between O_1 and O_2. In Figure 4.3, the letter R refers to randomization, which means the subjects are assigned to experimental and control groups on a random basis.

26. These are among the most important factors which can jeopardize the validity of a research design. See Campbell and Stanley, *Experimental and Quasi-Experimental Designs for Research,* pp. 5–6.

27. For a full discussion of these weaknesses, see ibid., pp. 5–12.

28. Lempert, "Strategies of Research Design in the Legal Impact Study," p. 125.

29. For example, W. H. Manning and P. H. DuBois, "Correlational Methods in Research on Human Learning," *Perceptual and Motor Skills* 15 (1962):287–321; L. J. Cronbach and L. Furby, "How We Should Measure 'Change'—or Should We?" *Psychological Bulletin* 74 (1970):68–80; L. T. Farley and M. G. Newkirk, "Measuring Attitude Change in Political Science Courses," *Teaching Political Science* 4, 2 (January 1977):185–98; and R. J. Linn and J. A. Slinde, "The Determination of the Significance of Change Between Pre- and Post-Testing Periods," *Review of Educational Research* 47 (1977):121–50.

30. James J. Best and Thomas R. Hensley, "Causes and Consequences of Student Perceptions of Responsibility for the 1970 Kent State Shootings," *Heuristics* 8, 1 (Spring 1978):30–52.

31. Thomas R. Hensley and Deborah K. Sell, "A Study-Abroad Program: An Examination of Impacts on Student Attitudes," *Teaching Political Science* 6, 4 (July 1977):387–412.

32. Kirk, *Experimental Design.* We are assuming throughout this discussion that the reader has an understanding of the basic logic of analysis of variance.

33. See ibid., chapter 8 for a discussion of the split-plot or factorial design with block-treatment confounding.

34. The first independent variable is considered to be the before and after classifications.

35. Kerlinger, *Foundations of Behavioral Research,* p. 351.

36. We need to know this in order to determine if dissonance is created by the decision of the judicial structure. See the diagrams in Figure 4.1.

37. Kirk states that "the term interaction means that one treatment behaves differently under different levels of the other treatment" (Kirk, p. 177). For our study this means that the specific support scores for both the students who felt the Guard was responsible and the students who believed the Guard was not responsible will be significantly different in their before-and-after scores.

38. We also have significance scores for the two main effects, responsibility and time. Neither of these is significant at the .05 level.

39. See Kirk, *Experimental Design,* pp. 263–66 for a discussion of tests of simple main effects. The best discussion of the many alternatives for testing interactive effects is in S. G. Carmer and M. R. Swanson, "An Evaluation of Ten Multiple Comparison Procedures by Monte Carlo Methods," *Journal of the American Statistical Association* 68 (1973):66–74.

40. Fisher's least significant difference test is described in both Kirk, *Experimental Design*, pp. 87–88 and Carmer and Swanson, "An Evaluation of Ten Multiple Comparison Procedures," pp. 66–74.

41. In testing simple main interaction effects, we will use the .05 level throughout our analysis. In the example data we just analyzed, we needed a difference larger than 1.11 to achieve statistical significance.

42. Kirk, *Experimental Design*, p. 43.

43. Ibid., p. 245.

44. Ibid., p. 60.

45. Ibid.

46. Ibid.

47. Ibid., p. 62.

48. Ibid., p. 33.

49. *Akron Beacon Journal*, 30 March 1974, p. A6.

50. Ibid.

51. Ibid.

52. Ibid.

53. It is important to recognize that the number of subjects whom we can include in all aspects of the data analysis will be less than 141. This is because we must exclude from portions of the analysis any student for whom we have missing data because the respondent failed to answer one or more questions.

54. The responsibility matrix we utilized can be seen in each of the appendices. We chose this form for measuring responsibility because it corresponds with research undertaken by Stuart Taylor and his colleagues in the immediate aftermath of the May 4 shootings. They mailed questionnaires to all Kent State students in late May of 1970 and eventually received 7,000 responses. By utilizing similar measures of responsibility, we can meaningfully compare our results with those of Taylor. See Stuart Taylor et al., *Violence at Kent State: The Students' Perspective* (New York: College Notes and Texts, 1971).

55. Ibid.

56. The categories of students' perceptions of responsibility of the guardsmen were determined by combining those who felt the Guard-enlisted men were very or moderately responsible into one category—responsible—and those who felt the guardsmen were minimally or not responsible into a second category—not responsible.

57. Specific support scores were determined by adding students' responses to two questions, asked both before and after the grand jury's decision: (1) Do you think a federal grand jury is (was) necessary? and (2) Do you think that the federal grand jury will be (was) fair and unbiased? Students could respond yes, undecided, or no to each question, and these responses were assigned the values of 3, 2, and 1, respectively. Scores could thus range from a high of 6 to a low of 2.

58. Fisher's least-significant-difference test also established that none of the other changes was statistically significant.

59. *Akron Beacon Journal*, 28 August 1975, p. A1.

60. Ibid.

61. Cleveland (Ohio) *Plain Dealer*, 28 August 1975, p. 17A.

62. *Akron Beacon Journal,* 28 August 1975, p. A11.

63. Kent (Ohio) *Record-Courier,* 28 August 1975, p. 1.

64. As with the 1974 data, problems of missing data will reduce the number of students whom we can include in portions of our analysis.

65. Specific support scores for the federal district court were measured by asking students both before and after the trial (1) whether the federal district court is (was) an appropriate place to decide responsibility for the shootings and (2) whether the trial will be (was) fair and unbiased. Students could answer yes, undecided, and no to each question. These questions, which loaded together in a factor analysis we ran to test scale validity, were added together to give us a six-point scale of specific support, 6 being the highest score and 2 being the lowest score.

66. The classifications of Guard responsibility were created in the following manner. We assigned values from one through four to the rankings of not responsible through very responsible, respectively, for both the Guard officers and the enlisted men. For each student, we summed their scores of responsibility for both the officers and enlisted men. Students could thus have scores ranging from 2 (neither group was responsible) to 8 (both groups were very responsible). Students who had scores of 6, 7, or 8 were classified as considering the Guard responsible, while students who had scores of 5 or below were classified as viewing the Guard as not responsible.

67. Diffuse support scores for the American judicial system were measured through the use of three questions asked both before and after the 1975 trial: (1) "Ordinarily, the average person in America will get a just trial;" (2) "Most juries do just what the judge and prosecutor tell them to do;" and (3) "Wealthy and well-known people are less likely to be convicted than someone like me." Five-point scales from strongly disagree to strongly agree were used with each statement. Student scores on each of these statements, which loaded together on a factor analysis we ran to test scale validity, were added together to give a diffuse support scale which ranged from three (lowest support) to fifteen (highest support).

68. Tests of simple main interaction effects also were not significant. Technically, however, such tests are not appropriate, for they should only be undertaken when the overall interaction is significant or one has hypothesized a priori that specific simple main effects will be significant.

69. *The Cleveland Press,* 6 January 1979, p. B2. The story was written by Bob August.

70. For a detailed analysis of the 1977 controversy over the gymnasium addition, see Thomas R. Hensley, "Kent State 1977: The Struggle to Move the Gym," in Thomas R. Hensley and Jerry M. Lewis, eds., *Kent State and May 4th: A Social Science Perspective* (Dubuque, Ia.: Kendall/Hunt Publishing Co., 1978), pp. 121–43.

71. As in the 1975 study, we have excluded Ohio Governor James Rhodes from the analysis.

72. Responsibility scores were determined in the same manner as the 1975 study. We assigned values of 1 through 4 to the rankings of not responsible through very responsible, respectively, for both the Guard officers and the enlisted men. For each student's first-round responses we summed their scores of responsibility for both the

officers and enlisted men. Students could thus have scores ranging from 2 (neither group was responsible) to 8 (both groups were very responsible). Students who had scores of 6 and above were classified as considering the Guard responsible, while students who had scores of 5 or below were classified as viewing the Guard as not responsible.

73. We determined specific judicial support scores in the same manner as the previous studies. We used two questions asked both before and after the trial: (1) Is (was) the federal district court an appropriate place to decide responsibility for the shootings? and (2) Will the trial be (Was the trial) fair and unbiased? Students could answer yes, uncertain, or no to each question. These questions, which loaded significantly together on a factor analysis we ran to test scale validity, were added together to give us a six-point scale of specific support, 6 being the highest score and 2 being the lowest score.

74. Diffuse support scores were determined in the same way they were measured in the 1975 civil study. Students were given three statements both before and after the trial: (1) Ordinarily, the average person will get a just trial in America; (2) Most juries do just what the judge and prosecutor tell them to do; and (3) Wealthy and well-known people are less likely to be convicted than someone like me. Five-point scales from strongly agree to strongly disagree were used for each statement. Student scores on these statements, which loaded significantly together on a factor analysis we ran to test scale validity, were added together to give a diffuse support scale which ranged from 3 (lowest support) to 15 (highest support).

75. Technically, tests of simple main effects are not appropriate because we accepted our hypothesis of no significant overall interaction. The results of the tests give us even further confidence in our decision, however.

5
Conclusions

We have addressed a variety of issues and questions in this book. It is now possible to draw all the material together for the purpose of offering concluding observations about these issues and questions. First, we will examine the question whether the decisions of authoritative judicial structures can change people's attitudes. Second, attention will be given to the policy implications of the study. Third, we will examine the utility of cognitive consistency theory in studying judicial impact. Fourth, the value of an experimental approach in judicial impact research will be discussed. Our final concern will be the events and legal aftermath of May 4, specifically the most important questions which yet remain unanswered.

WHAT EFFECTS DO JUDICIAL DECISIONS HAVE UPON ATTITUDES?

We began this study by asking what impact judicial decisions have upon attitudes. The results of the preceding chapter provide some reasonably clear answers in regard to the May 4 trials. Kent State students' attitudes about responsibility for the shootings did not change to conform with the decisions of authoritative judicial structures. Attitude change was observed frequently for those students who were placed in a dissonant situation by a decision and who disagreed with the decision; the pattern for these students was a significant lowering of support for the judicial structure issuing the decision. No significant changes in diffuse support attitudes were found. Our results are thus quite different than those of William Muir,

who conducted a somewhat similar study in connection with the
Schempp case on school prayer. Muir concluded: "Can law change
deep-rooted attitudes? Of course it can. . . . Judiciously used, law can
and does manipulate our deep-rooted attitudes, our personalities."[1]
The results of our study, as well as a number of other studies on
attitudes and the judicial process, suggest that Muir's conclusions give
too much influence to the courts' abilities to change attitudes about
social issues. At least in the short run, the courts seem to have limited
influence on people's attitudes about controversial issues, and the
courts risk losing support in controversial cases.

POLICY IMPLICATIONS

What are the policy implications of these findings? While this study
was not undertaken for the purpose of answering questions directly
concerned with current public policy issues, nonetheless in chapter
one it was suggested that the results of the research could be brought
to bear on several issues involving the effectiveness of the American
judicial process. These concerns will now be examined.

One issue involves jury selection in a highly controversial and
publicized case. Our findings reveal that students' attitudes regarding
responsibility for the May 4 shootings did not change in response to
the decisions of the authoritative judicial structures, and this raises
serious questions about the possibilities of selecting an impartial jury
in a highly publicized case. Extraordinary efforts must be made by a
presiding judge to assure that individuals are selected who can attempt to make objective judgments in the case. Judge Thomas' in-
novative use of the "blind-strike" method of jury selection in the
1979 civil trial is a good example of the type of efforts that must be
made.[2] Carrying this issue further, it is possible to raise the question
of whether jury trials in certain civil cases are even desirable. If attitudes are deeply ingrained and not susceptible to change, then
perhaps lay juries should not be utilized in highly emotional, controversial cases. Perhaps panels of judges could be expected to render
more objective decisions in such cases.

Closely related to the issue of selecting impartial jurors is the
broader question of whether juries should be eliminated in long and
complex civil cases. This is an issue raised by Supreme Court Chief

Justice Warren Burger in a 1979 speech before a conference of state chief justices.[3] Without actually advocating such a policy, the Chief Justice cited numerous problems in jury trials in complex and lengthy civil cases: inordinate hardships on the jurors who are away from their jobs for long periods of time, the lack of community representativeness of juries, and the inability of the typical juror to understand the substantive and legal technicalities of a complex civil case.[4] Burger cited the British court system as one which has abolished juries in all civil suits except those involving libel and slander.[5] The May 4 federal civil trials are a classic example of the type of case about which Burger spoke. The task confronting the jury in the 1975 trial was overwhelming. They had to listen to over 100 witnesses testify during a three month period, testimony which resulted in a 13,000 page trial manuscript; they were confronted with a written charge from the judge which was over eighty pages of complex legal guidelines; and they had to make over 350 individual verdicts, because each plaintiff was suing each defendant. Clearly this made impossible demands upon a group of ordinary citizens. While a panel of experienced judges would have had difficulty reaching decisions in this case, it does seem preferable to have a group of legal experts making decisions in this type of case.

Another policy related question stemming from this study is whether the general public is more likely to accept an out-of-court settlement than a decision on the presence or absence of liability in a full trial. It was suggested in chapter one that public acceptance of an out-of-court settlement would be higher, because people could interpret such a settlement consistent with their own views of the issues. Such a process cannot occur when a full trial is held, for one side wins and one side loses. If this does occur, it suggests an important reason for the courts to seek out-of-court settlements.[6]

The results of the data analysis for the 1975 and 1979 trials reveal that public acceptance was higher for the 1979 out-of-court settlement than for the 1975 decision. Table 5.1 shows that 20 percent of the sample agreed with the 1975 verdict, while 64 percent disagreed and 16 percent were undecided. Reaction to the 1979 settlement was quite different. While only a slight increase can be noticed in those who agreed with the outcome (25 percent compared to 20 percent), the percentage of students who disagreed with the outcome

**Table 5.1: A COMPARISON OF STUDENTS' AGREEMENT WITH THE
OUTCOMES OF THE 1975 AND 1979 MAY 4 CIVIL TRIALS**

	Agreement/Disagreement with Outcome			
Trial	Agree	Undecided	Disagree	Totals
1975	20%	16%	64%	100% (N = 135)
1979	25%	38%	37%	100% (N = 184)

dropped dramatically from 64 percent in 1975 to 37 percent in 1979.
The undecideds increased from 16 percent in 1975 to 38 percent in
1979.

These results lend support to the argument that public acceptance
will be higher for out-of-court settlements in civil cases. While we did
not see strong increases in agreement between the 1975 and 1979
trials, the level of disagreement was much lower for the out-of-court
settlement in 1979. We thus have additional arguments for the advantages of out-of-court settlements in civil cases. Previous arguments have cited the mutual acceptability to the parties involved as
well as the benefits to the courts in terms of time and money. The
unique comparative data for the two Kent State civil trials suggest a
further argument; acceptance by the general public is likely to be
higher for out-of-court settlements because people can interpret the
results to be consistent with their views on the case.

A final policy-related consideration involves the ability of courts to
serve as agents of social change. The results of our analysis present a
pessimistic picture. In the three decisions we studied, students' attitudes did not change to conform to the decisions. We found no
significant change in the 1975 and 1979 civil trials, and we found
students changing opposite of the decision of the 1974 federal grand
jury. Also, we found a pattern of frequent lowering of support for the
judicial structure when its decision was opposed to students' views on
the shootings. Attitudes are an important determinant of behavior,
and hence our data suggest that courts can expect severe difficulties
in trying to change both attitudes and behaviors on controversial

social issues. Obviously courts cannot and should not avoid many controversial issues, but the results of our analysis lend support to arguments for the exercise of judicial self-restraint.

COGNITIVE CONSISTENCY THEORY AND JUDICIAL IMPACT

Turning now from policy-related issues to theoretical concerns, we need to evaluate the utility of cognitive consistency theory in this study as well as its general value in judicial impact research. Cognitive consistency theory, used in conjunction with theoretical and empirical research on judicial support, was useful in a number of ways in this study. It provided a way of organizing a variety of concepts and ideas, it led to the development of a series of hypothesized relationships which could be operationalized and tested, and it proved to be generally accurate in predicting patterns of attitude change. One cannot expect more from a social science theory.

Several limitations must also be recognized, however. First, it is important to acknowledge that we are only inferring that students who changed their specific support attitudes did so in order to reduce dissonance. We did not directly measure whether students were experiencing dissonance, and it will be remembered from our methodological discussion in chapter four that the lack of randomization means that confounding variables could be affecting the results of our data analysis. A second limitation involves those students who presumably experienced dissonance but did not undergo attitude changes as hypothesized. Did they not experience dissonance? Or is dissonance a condition which is acceptable to many people and hence not a condition which leads to attitude change? Social psychologists are in disagreement about these questions which must be resolved if the full potential of the theory is to be realized.[7] Finally, cognitive consistency theory as applied in this study has only been concerned with attitude change. While attitude change is an important subject, in the study of judicial impact we are most concerned with behavior and behavioral change. Presumably there is a close link between attitude change and behavior change, but the exact nature of the relationship has not been adequately examined, especially in the judicial impact research.[8] Must attitudes change before behavior can change? Will changes in behavior bring about corresponding changes in attitudes? Is there an interactive link between attitude change and behavior change? These are interesting theoretical questions, and they are also vitally important questions facing the courts involved in controversial areas of public policy. This is an important research focus for future studies on judicial impact.

THE EXPERIMENTAL APPROACH TO JUDICIAL IMPACT RESEARCH

The most unique contribution of this study to scholarship on the judicial process has been the utilization of an experimental approach. Scholars studying the judicial process in the coming years are likely to give a great deal of attention to the topic of judicial impact. The essence of this subject implies experimental research, for in the study of judicial impact one is interested in conditions before a particular event—the judicial decision—and then changes in those conditions which presumably were brought about by the event, the judicial decision.

The call for before-and-after studies which has characterized many discussions of judicial impact research is clearly an appeal which must be followed. But the mere call for before-and-after studies is insufficient. The explicit utilization of an experimental design approach in judicial impact studies is necessary to improve substantially the quality of research. By casting one's research in an experimental design framework, the researcher gains a clear awareness of both the strengths and weaknesses of the study. Especially if this is done in the planning stage of the study, the researcher may be alerted to various ways to strengthen the design of the study; for example, various control groups might be added, randomization might be achieved, or controls over important extraneous variables might be introduced. At a minimum, the researcher is alerted to the potential problems in the study and can adjust interpretations accordingly. It is also important to recognize some of the advantages of using analysis of variance. This statistical approach allows one to set forth and test hypotheses related directly to the conceptual ideas in the experimental design; the approach is based upon simple means which allow for a level of easy, intuitive analysis as well as sophisticated analysis based upon probability models; and the approach has great flexibility, allowing one to examine a wide variety of theoretical propositions.

We are thus making a strong call for increased attention to experimental design research in studying judicial impact. Most of the research will probably be quasi-experimental rather than true experimental research. In either case, however, this approach to political research promises substantial gains in methodological sophistication.

MAY 4: THE REMAINING QUESTIONS

A final area which must be addressed involves the important questions about the May 4 shootings which yet remain unanswered, despite the extensive amount of research which has been undertaken. The most critical of these seem to be 1) Were the events of May 1−4 spontaneous, or did the events result from the implementation of rather carefully planned strategies by individuals and groups seeking to cause trouble on the Kent State campus? and 2) Why did the guardsmen fire? Were they in fear of serious bodily injury and perhaps death at the moment they reached the crest of Blanket Hill, or did they conspire minutes before on the practice football field to punish the protestors who had been subjecting them to verbal and physical abuse?

In regard to the first question, most authors have viewed the events of May 1−4 as being basically spontaneous. Suggestions have arisen, however, that radical elements had developed plans to foment trouble on the Kent State campus as part of an overall strategy to create revolutionary conditions in the United States. Alternatively, a more recent, revisionist viewpoint is that the Nixon administration used federal agent provocateurs to seek confrontations on college campuses, including Kent State, in order to create conditions which could justify harsh suppression of the antiwar movement. In regard to the former thesis, it seems doubtful that radical elements played an important role in orchestrating the events of May 1−4, 1970. Hundreds of local, state, and federal officials spent thousands of hours exploring this possibility. Their efforts were unsuccessful. Further, it seems most unlikely that any new evidence will appear to establish that plans of radical elements were responsible for the disturbances of May 1–4. The latter thesis, focusing upon the role of the Nixon administration, has not yet been sufficiently explored. Some indirect evidence does exist which lends support to this interpretation, but the evidence is far from conclusive. The question deserves more attention; but even if the Nixon administration was involved in such efforts, the evidence to establish this has probably been altered or destroyed.

A second major question which has not yet been satisfactorily answered is why the guardsmen fired. The courts have provided one answer. Both criminal and civil trials have resulted in the guardsmen being exonerated of legal responsibility for the shootings. The question of whether the guardsmen conspired on the practice field to fire upon the protestors remains an open issue, however, for conspiracy is enormously difficult to establish in court. This too is an issue which may never be answered satisfactorily. What then will historians conclude about the thirteen seconds in May? The judgment of the Scranton Commission seems most likely to endure: "The indiscriminate firing of rifles into a crowd of students and the deaths that followed were unnecessary, unwarranted, and inexcusable."[9]

NOTES

1. William Muir, *Prayer in the Public Schools* (Chicago: University of Chicago Press, 1967), p. 138.

2. See Judge William K. Thomas, "Jury Selection in the Highly Publicized Case," *Columbus Bar Association Journal* 35, 5 (May 1979):3–4 ff.

3. *New York Times,* 6 August 1979, p. A 12.

4. Ibid.

5. Ibid.

6. Many other reasons exist, of course, for the courts to pursue out-of-court settlements. Among the most prominent are that the courts would become hopelessly clogged if all civil suits went to trial, and an out-of-court settlement also provides both sides with some degree of satisfaction.

7. A useful exchange of contrasting viewpoints can be found in Natalia P. Chapanis and Alphonse Chapanis, "Cognitive Dissonance: Five Years Later," and Irwin Silverman, "In Defense of Cognitive Theory: Reply to Chapanis and Chapanis," both in Peter Suedfeld, *Attitude Change: The Competing Views* (Chicago: Aldine/Atherton, Inc., 1971). A recent criticism of dissonance theory can be found in Jozef M. Nuttin, Jr., *The Illusion of Attitude Change: Toward a Response Contagion Theory of Persuasion* (London: Academic Press and Leuven University Press, 1975). A defense of

dissonance theory is Robert Wicklund and Jack Brehm, eds., *Perspectives on Cognitive Dissonance* (Hillsdale, N.J.: Halsted Press, 1976).

8. Sociologists and social psychologists have given considerable attention to this question. A review of scholarly debate on the relationship between attitudes and behavior is Steven J. Gross and C. Michael Minan, "Attitude-Behavior Consistency: A Review," *Public Opinion Quarterly* 39, 3 (Fall 1975):358–68. Scant attention has been given to this issue by students of the judicial process. Austin Sarat reports a significant relationship between supportive attitudes and compliance behavior: Sarat, "Support for the Legal System: An Analysis of Knowledge, Attitudes, and Behavior," *American Politics Quarterly* 3 (1975):3–24. No such relationship was found, however, by Harrell Rodgers and Edward Lewis, "Political Support and Compliance Attitudes," *American Politics Quarterly* 2 (1974):61–77.

9. The President's Commission on Campus Unrest, *The Kent State Tragedy* (Washington, D.C.: U.S. Government Printing Office, 1970), p. 87.

Appendices:
The Questionnaires

The 1974 Federal Grand Jury Questionnaire, Before

Interview No. ____

THE FIRST SERIES OF QUESTIONS CONCERN SOME GENERAL CHARACTERISTICS ABOUT YOURSELF.

1. In what year were you born? _____

2. What is your sex? M ____ F ____

3. What is your hometown? _____

4. What is the approximate population of your hometown? _____

5. What year in college are you? F ____ SO ____ J ____
   SN ____ MA ____ PHD ____

6. How long have you attended Kent State University? _____
   _____

7. What is your major? _____

8. Has any member of your immediate family ever attended classes at or worked for KSU?
   Yes ____ No ____

9. Into which of the following categories does the income of your family fall? Under $5000 ____ $5001-$10,000 ____
   $10,001-$20,000 ____ Over $20,000 ____

NOW WE WOULD LIKE TO THINK BACK TO THE EVENTS OF MAY 1-4, 1970 HERE IN KENT

10. Were you living in Kent during the period May 1-4, 1970?
    Yes ____ No ____

11. Were you a student at Kent State during the period May 1-4, 1970? Yes ____ No ____

12. Were you involved, either as a spectator or as a participant, in any of the events on campus or in town during that period? Yes ____ No ____

13. Do you remember if there was a state grand jury investigation of the shootings? Yes, there was an investigation ____
    No, there was no investigation ____ Don't remember ____

IF YOU ANSWERED "NO" OR DON'T REMEMBER TO QUESTION 13,
PLEASE SKIP QUESTIONS 14-19

14. Do you recall the results of the state grand jury's
     investigation? Yes _____ No _____ Don't remember _____

15. If you do recall, could you briefly describe these
     results?

     _____

     _____

16. What was your reaction to these results? Strongly
     agreed _____ Agreed _____ Undecided _____ Disagreed _____
     Strongly disagreed _____

17. How did you first become aware of the state grand
     jury's action? Magazines _____ Radio _____ Friend _____
     Newspapers _____ Television _____ Member of family _____
     Other _____ Don't remember _____

18. Do you recall ever asking someone to explain the state
     grand jury's action to you? Yes _____ No _____ Don't
     remember _____

19. Do you recall informing others of the state grand
     jury's action? Yes _____ No _____ Don't remember _____

NOW WE WOULD LIKE TO ASK YOU SOME QUESTIONS ABOUT THE CUR-
RENT INVESTIGATION.

20. Do you know who or what is currently investigating the
     Kent State shootings of 1970? Yes _____ No _____ Don't
     know for certain _____

IF YOU ANSWERED "NO" OR "DON'T KNOW FOR CERTAIN" TO QUES-
TION 20, PLEASE SKIP THE OTHER QUESTIONS ON THIS PAGE AND
GO ON TO THE NEXT PAGE. IF YOU ANSWERED "YES" TO QUESTION
20 AND ARE AWARE THAT THERE IS A FEDERAL GRAND JURY PROBE,
PLEASE ANSWER THE REST OF THE QUESTIONS ON THIS PAGE.

21. How much attention have you been paying to the federal
     grand jury investigation? A great deal _____ A mod-
     erate amount _____ A little _____ Paying no attention

     _____

22. How have you been keeping informed of the federal
    grand jury's activities? Friends, neighbors _____
    Magazines _____ Newspapers _____ Television _____
    Radio _____ Family member _____ Other _____ Have-
    n't been following it _____

23. Do you think a federal grand jury investigation is
    necessary? Yes _____ No _____ Don't know, depends
    _____

24. Do you think the federal grand jury investigation will
    be fair and unbiased? Yes _____ No _____ Don't know,
    depends _____

25. Is a federal grand jury the proper way to investigate
    what happened in 1970? Yes _____ No, some other agency
    _____ No investigation _____ Don't know _____

26. What issues do you think can be resolved by the fed-
    eral grand jury?
    1. _____

    2. _____

    3. _____

27. Referring back to question 26, how important to you is
    each of the issues which you identified?
    Issue 1: Very important _____ Moderately important
             _____ Not import. _____
    Issue 2: Very important _____ Moderately important
             _____ Not import. _____
    Issue 3: Very important _____ Moderately important
             _____ Not import. _____

28. How difficult do you think it will be for the grand
    jury to reach a decision? Very hard _____ Moderately
    hard _____ Not hard at all _____

THE FOLLOWING ARE A SERIES OF STATEMENTS ABOUT THE COMMUN-
ITY, POLITICS, AND LIFE IN GENERAL. THEY ARE STATEMENTS OF
OPINION AND THERE ARE NO RIGHT OR WRONG ANSWERS. AFTER
EACH STATEMENT CHECK THE DEGREE TO WHICH YOU AGREE OR DIS-
AGREE WITH THE STATEMENT.

1. News about the city of Kent is generally more inter-
   esting than national or international news.
   _____ Strongly agree   _____ Undecided   _____ Disagree
   _____ Agree   _____ Strongly disagree

2. I prefer the practical man anytime to the man of ideas.
    ____ Strongly agree   ____ Undecided   ____ Disagree
    ____ Agree   ____ Strongly disagree

3. The Kent Record-Courier is extremely important in order
    to know what's going on.
    ____ Strongly agree   ____ Undecided   ____ Disagree
    ____ Agree   ____ Strongly disagree

4. Sometimes politics and government seem so complicated
    that a person like me can't really understand what's
    going on.
    ____ Strongly agree   ____ Undecided   ____ Disagree
    ____ Agree   ____ Strongly disagree

5. A large number of city and county politicians are in-
    competent.
    ____ Strongly agree   ____ Undecided   ____ Disagree
    ____ Agree   ____ Strongly disagree

6. If something grows up after a long time there will al-
    ways be much wisdom to it.
    ____ Strongly agree   ____ Undecided   ____ Disagree
    ____ Agree   ____ Strongly disagree

7. The most rewarding organizations a person can belong
    to are local organizations serving local needs.
    ____ Strongly agree.   ____ Undecided   ____ Disagree
    ____ Agree   ____ Strongly disagree

8. Kent is one of the finest communities in the United
    States.
    ____ Strongly agree   ____ Undecided   ____ Disagree
    ____ Agree   ____ Strongly disagree

9. Money is an important factor influencing public pol-
    icies.
    ____ Strongly agree   ____ Undecided   ____ Disagree
    ____ Agree   ____ Strongly disagree

10. It's better to stick by what you have than to be try-
    ing new things you don't really know about.
    ____ Strongly agree   ____ Undecided   ____ Disagree
    ____ Agree   ____ Strongly disagree

11. People frequently are manipulated by politicians.
    ____ Strongly agree   ____ Undecided   ____ Disagree
    ____ Agree   ____ Strongly disagree

12. National and international happenings rarely seem as
    interesting and important as events that occur right
    in the local community in which I live.
    ____ Strongly agree   ____ Undecided   ____ Disagree
    ____ Agree   ____ Strongly disagree

13. If you start trying to change things very much you
    usually make them worse.
    ____ Strongly agree   ____ Undecided   ____ Disagree
    ____ Agree   ____ Strongly disagree

14. Politicians represent the general interest more fre-
    quently than they represent special interests.
    ____ Strongly agree   ____ Undecided   ____ Disagree
    ____ Agree   ____ Strongly disagree

15. I'd want to know that something would really work be-
    fore I'd be willing to take a chance on it.
    ____ Strongly agree   ____ Undecided   ____ Disagree
    ____ Agree   ____ Strongly disagree

16. National and international events are important large-
    ly because of the way they effect Kent as a community.
    ____ Strongly agree   ____ Undecided   ____ Disagree
    ____ Agree   ____ Strongly disagree

17. We must respect the work of our forefathers and not
    think that we know better than they did.
    ____ Strongly agree   ____ Undecided   ____ Disagree
    ____ Agree   ____ Strongly disagree

18. Politicians spend most of their time getting re-elected
    or reappointed.
    ____ Strongly agree   ____ Undecided   ____ Disagree
    ____ Agree   ____ Strongly disagree

19. A man doesn't have much wisdom until he is well along
    in years.
    ____ Strongly agree   ____ Undecided   ____ Disagree
    ____ Agree   ____ Strongly disagree

20. Big cities have their place, but when you get right
    down to it the local community is the backbone of Amer-
    ica.
    ____ Strongly agree   ____ Undecided   ____ Disagree
    ____ Agree   ____ Strongly disagree

21. Meeting and knowing many people is extremely important
     in establishing myself in the community.
     _____ Strongly agree   ____ Undecided   ____ Disagree
     _____ Agree   ____ Strongly disagree

22. Many   relationships and contacts with other
     people in the local community are essential in life to-
     day.
     _____ Strongly agree   ____Undecided   ____ Disagree
     _____ Agree   ____ Strongly disagree

THE FOLLOWING ARE A SERIES OF STATEMENTS ABOUT THE COURTS
AND THE JUDICIAL PROCESS. THEY ARE STATEMENTS OF OPINION
AND THERE ARE NO RIGHT OR WRONG ANSWERS. AFTER EACH STATE-
MENT CHECK THE DEGREE TO WHICH YOU AGREE OR DISAGREE.

1.   Agnew's sentence for income tax evasion was too light.
     _____ Strongly agree   ____ Undecided   ____ Disagree
     _____ Agree   ____ Strongly disagree

2.   Most grand juries just do what the judge and the pros-
     ecutor tell them to do.
     _____ Strongly agree   ____ Undecided   ____ Disagree
     _____ Agree   ____ Strongly disagree

3.   The courts are too harsh in sentencing people con-
     victed of breaking the law.
     _____ Strongly agree   ____ Undecided   ____ Disagree
     _____ Agree   ____ Strongly disagree

4.   If someone is brought to trial they're probably guilty.
     _____ Strongly agree   ____ Undecided   ____ Disagree
     _____ Agree   ____ Strongly disagree

5.   The federal grand jury will determine, once and for
     all, who was responsible for the shootings of May 4,
     1970.
     _____ Strongly agree   ____ Undecided   ____ Disagree
     _____ Agree   ____ Strongly disagree

6.   Wealthy and well-known people are less likely to be
     convicted in a trial than someone like me.
     _____ Strongly agree   ____ Undecided   ____ Disagree
     _____ Agree   ____ Strongly disagree

7. The law is so complex that it is difficult to convict
    someone even if they are guilty.
    ____ Strongly agree   ____ Undecided   ____Disagree
    ____ Agree   ____ Strongly disagree

8. Even if people don't like a jury's verdict they should
    accept it.
    ____ Strongly agree   ____ Undecided   ____Disagree
    ____ Agree   ____ Strongly disagree

9. Wealthy people and well-known people, if convicted of
    a crime, will get the same sentence as someone like me.
    ____ Strongly agree   ____ Undecided   ____ Disagree
    ____ Agree   ____ Strongly disagree

10. The state grand jury in 1970 did a good job of inves-
    tigating the shootings.
    ____ Strongly agree   ____ Undecided   ____ Disagree
    ____ Agree   ____ Strongly disagree

11. Most court cases are so long   it is difficult for a
    person like me to know who is guilty.
    ____ Strongly agree   ____Undecided   ____Disagree
    ____ Agree   ____ Strongly disagree

12. I don't know what a grand jury is supposed to do.
    ____ Strongly agree   ____ Undecided   ____ Disagree
    ____ Agree   ____ Strongly disagree

13. The law is mighty complicated so it's fortunate that
    we have well-trained judges to tell us what it means.
    ____ Strongly agree   ____ Undecided   ____ Disagree
    ____ Agree   ____ Strongly disagree

14. If chosen to serve on a jury I would willingly do so.
    ____ Strongly agree   ____ Undecided   ____ Disagree
    ____ Agree   ____ Strongly disagree

15. If you were charged with a crime would you want a
    trial by a judge alone or by a jury?
    ____ judge alone   ____ jury   ____ no difference

In the space below check the degree to which you believe
the _federal_ _grand_ _jury_ will find the following people responsible for the shootings of May 4th.

	Very Respon- sible	Moderately Respon- sible	Somewhat Respon- sible	Not Respon- sible
Governor Rhodes				
Non-radical students				
KSU President White				
Radical students				
Officers of the National Guard				
Non-student radicals				
Enlisted men of the National Guard				
Faculty at KSU				
President Nixon				
KSU administrators				
Vice-President Agnew				
Others (specify)				

In the space below check the degree to which you believe
the following people were responsible for the shootings on
May 4th.

	Very Respon- sible	Moderately Respon- sible	Somewhat Respon- sible	Not Respon- sible
Governor Rhodes				
Non-radical students				
KSU President White				
Radical students				
Officers of the National Guard				
Non-student radicals				
Enlisted men of the National Guard				
Faculty at KSU				
President Nixon				
KSU administrators				
Vice-President Agnew				
Other (specify)				

APPENDIX B: The 1974 Federal Grand Jury Questionnaire, After

Interview No. ____

WE WOULD LIKE TO THANK YOU FOR PARTICIPATING IN OUR EARLIER
PUBLIC OPINION POLL REGARDING THE FEDERAL GRAND JURY
INVESTIGATION OF THE EVENTS OF MAY 4, 1970. SINCE YOU FIRST
PARTICIPATED IN OUR STUDY THE FEDERAL GRAND JURY HAS CONCLUDED
ITS INVESTIGATION. WE ARE NO INTERESTED IN HOW PEOPLE LIKE
YOU FEEL ABOUT THE GRAND JURY'S ACTIONS.

WOULD YOU MIND ANSWERING A FEW QUESTIONS? THE QUESTIONNAIRE
WILL TAKE ONLY ABOUT TEN MINUTES TO COMPLETE AND YOU ANSWERS
WILL BE KEPT STRICTLY CONFIDENTIAL.

THANK YOU.

FIRST, WE'D LIKE TO GET SOME BACKGROUND INFORMATION.

1. Are you presently employed? ____full-time ____part-time
   ____not employed. If you are employed, what kind of work
   do you do? _____

2. Politically, do you consider yourself a Democrat, a
   Republican, an Independent, or something else?
   ____Democrat ____Republican ____Independent ____Other

3. In terms of where I stand on political issues I would
   classify myself as:
   ____Conservative   ____Moderate   ____Moderate liberal
   ____Moderate conservative   ____Liberal

4. Have you ever served with any branch of the U.S. Armed
   Services? ____Yes ____No

   If yes, were you: ____an officer ____an enlisted man

5. What are your feelings, overall, about:
   a. the townspeople in Kent
      ____Strongly favorable ____Lukewarm ____Unfavorable
      ____Favorable   ____Strongly unfavorable
   b. the students at Kent State University
      ____Strongly favorable ____Lukewarm ____Unfavorable
      ____Favorable   ____Strongly unfavorable

230

c. Kent State University
___Strongly favorable ___Lukewarm ___Unfavorable
___Favorable   ___Strongly Unfavorable

NOW I'D LIKE TO ASK YOU SOME QUESTIONS ABOUT THE RECENT FED-
ERAL GRAND JURY INVESTIGATION OF THE KENT STATE SHOOTINGS
OF 1970.

6. How well informed do you consider yourself about the
    federal grand jury and its actions?

    ___Very well informed   ___Not very well informed
    ___Moderately well informed ___Not informed at all

7. Do you know what actions were taken as the result of
    the federal grand jury investigation?
    ___Yes (What was it?) _____
    ___No
    ___Don't know
    (IF NO OR DON'T KNOW go on to Question 1 on the next
    page)
    (If YES) What is your reaction to the grand jury action?
    ___Strongly agree with it ___Undecided ___Disagree
    with it ___ Agree with it ___Strongly disagree
    with it

8. How did you first become aware of the federal grand
    jury's action?
    ___Magazine   ___Radio   ___Friend   ___Other
    ___Newspaper   ___Television ___Family member
    ___Don't remember

9. Did you get more information from other sources?

    ___Yes   ___No   ___Don't remember
    (IF YES) Which ones?
    ___Magazines   ___Radio   ___Friend   ___Other
    ___Newspapers   ___Television ___Family member
    ___Don't remember

10. Were the sources of your information in agreement or
    disagreement withe the grand jury action?
    ___Generally in agreement   ___Generally in disagree-
    ment ___Some agreed, some disagreed ___Took no posi-
    tion

11. Do you recall asking someone to explain the federal
    grand jury's action to you? ___Yes ___No ___Don't
    remember

12. Do you recall informing others of the federal grand
    jury's action?
    ____Yes ____No ____Don't remember

13. Do you think the federal grand jury investigation was
    necessary?
    ____Yes ____No ____Don't know

14. Do you think the federal grand jury investigation was
    fair and unbiased? ____Yes ____No ____Don't know

15. To what extent do you feel the federal grand jury's
    action answered important questions raised by the
    events of May 4, 1970?
    ____Answered all questions ____Answered some questions
    ____Answered few questions ____Answered most questions
    ____Answered no questions

16. Do you think the eight National Guardsmen indicted
    will be found guilty in a jury trial of violating the
    civil rights of KSU students?
    ____Yes ____No ____Don't know

17. Do most of your friends agree with your views about
    the grand jury indictments? ____Yes ____No ____Some
    do, some don't

THE FOLLOWING ARE A SERIES OF COMMENTS ABOUT THE COURTS AND
THE JUDICIAL PROCESS. THEY ARE STATEMENTS OF OPINION AND
THERE ARE NO RIGHT OR WRONG ANSWERS. AFTER EACH STATEMENT
CHECK THE DEGREE TO WHICH YOU AGREE OR DISAGREE.

1. Agnew's sentence for income tax evasion was too light.
   ____Strongly agree ____Undecided ____Disagree
   ____Agree ____Strongly disagree

2. Most grand juries just do what the judge and the pros-
   ecutor tell them to do.
   ____Strongly agree ____Undecided ____Disagree
   ____Agree ____Strongly disagree

3. The courts are too harsh in sentencing people convicted
   of breaking the law.
   ____Strongly agree ____Undecided ____Disagree
   ____Agree ____Strongly disagree

4. If someone is brought to trial they're probably guilty.
    ____Strongly agree   ____Undecided   ____Disagree
    ____Agree   ____Strongly disagree

5. The federal grand jury has determined, once and for
    all, who was responsible for the shootings of May 4,
    1970.
    ____Strongly agree   ____Undecided   ____Disagree
    ____Agree   ____Strongly disagree

6. Wealthy and well-known people are less likely to be
    convicted in a trial than someone like me.
    ____Strongly agree   ____Undecided   ____Disagree
    ____Agree   ____Strongly disagree

7. The law is so complex that it is difficult to convict
    someone even if they are guilty.
    ____Strongly agree   ____Undecided   ____Disagree
    ____Agree   ____Strongly disagree

8. Even if people don't like a jury's verdict they
    should accept it.
    ____Strongly agree   ____Undecided   ____Disagree
    ____Agree   ____Strongly disagree

9. Wealthy people and well-known people, if convicted of
    a crime, will get the same sentence as someone like
    me.
    ____Strongly agree   ____Undecided   ____Disagree
    ____Agree   ____Strongly disagree

10. The state grand jury in 1970 did a good job of inves-
    tigating the shootings.
    ____Strongly agree   ____Undecided   ____Disagree
    ____Agree   ____Strongly disagree

11. Most court cases are so long and involved it is diffi-
    cult for a person like me to know who is guilty.
    ____Strongly agree   ____Undecided   ____Disagree
    ____Agree   ____Strongly disagree

12. I don't know what a grand jury is supposed to do.
    ____Strongly agree   ____Undecided   ____Disagree
    ____Agree   ____Strongly disagree

13. The law is mighty complicated so it's fortunate that
    we have well-trained judges to tell us what it means.
    ____Strongly agree   ____Undecided   ____Disagree
    ____Agree   ____Strongly disagree

14. If chosen to serve on a jury I would willingly do so.
    ____Strongly agree   ____Undecided   ____Disagree
    ____Agree   ____Strongly disagree

15. The action of the federal grand jury investigating the
    KSU shootings has shaken my faith in the courts.
    ____Strongly agree   ____Undecided   ____Disagree
    ____Agree   ____Strongly disagree

16. The action of the federal grand jury investigating the
    Watergate affair has shaken my faith in the courts.
    ____Strongly agree   ____Undecided   ____Disagree
    ____Agree   ____Strongly disagree

17. The action of the county grand jury in clearing the
    MAT agent in the shooting death of Gary Sherman has
    shaken my faith in the courts.
    ____Strongly agree   ____Undecided   ____Disagree
    ____Agree   ____Strongly disagree

18. In the space below check the degree to which you be-
    lieve the following people were responsible for the
    shootings on May 4th.

	Very Respon- sible	Moder- ately Respon- sible	Some- what Respon- sible	Not Respon- sible
Governor Rhodes				
Non-radical students				
KSU President White				
Radical students				
Officers of the National Guard				
Non-student radicals				
Enlisted men of the National Guard				
Faculty at KSU				
President Nixon				

KSU administrators

Vice-President Agnew

Others

THE FOLLOWING STATEMENTS WERE MADE BY PEOPLE ABOUT THE FED-
ERAL GRAND JURY AND ITS ACTIONS. IT IS CLEAR THAT SOME
PEOPLE AGREED WITH THE GRAND JURY WHILE OTHERS DID NOT.
BEFORE STATEMENT PLACE THE NUMBER WHICH INDICATES THE EXTENT
TO WHICH YOU AGREE OR DISAGREE WITH THE STATEMENT:

+3	+2	+1	0	-1	-2	-3
Strongly Agree	Agree	Weakly Agree	Un-decided	Weakly Disagree	Dis-agree	Strongly Disagree

_____ 1. The Guardsmen were sold down the river in order to
protect Rhodes and some of the other officials.

_____ 2. The grand jurors acted independently and didn't
follow the recommendations of the Justice Department prosecutors.

_____ 3. The Guardsmen have civil rights, too. I'm wondering if anybody is looking after them.

_____ 4. Now we know there was a military riot committed
that day.

_____ 5. Although the shootings may have been wrong, blame
should not be placed on the young, inexperienced
men who faced rioting students.

_____ 6. The National Guard indictments should have happened three and a half years ago.

_____ 7. At least some semblance of justice is being meted
out, even if they didn't indict Rhodes and those
generals.

_____ 8. Justice works very, very slowly. But this shows
we still have a civilized country.

_____ 9. The students had a right to be out there protesting and demonstrating and they did not deserve to
be shot.

_____10. Morally, at least, people much higher than these
          Guardsmen have a responsibility for what happened.

_____11. Even if no one goes to jail I am satisfied that
          the story is set straight.

_____12. The investigation covered such a wide range of
          things and I have to assume there must be some real
          reason and justification for the indictments.

_____13. In the final analysis, the few triggermen must bear
          the blame for these deaths. At the same time, the
          blame must be shared equally by their superior of-
          ficers, former Governor Rhodes, and Richard Nixon.

_____14. It is enough to express the hope that the critics
          of our democratic system will find in this, care-
          ful and unfolding process grounds for encourage-
          ment whatever the final decision of the Court.

_____15. Kent state students and young people about town are
          pleased with the indictments. Their parents and
          older townspeople are not.

_____16. I'm glad to see justice done. This shows the rest
          of the country that those kids (the shooting vic-
          tims) didn't deserve what they got.

_____17. Those Guardsmen were only doing their job. It was
          just like Lt. Calley. They were only doing what
          they were told.

_____18. Justice is being served and that is what's impor-
          tant, even though it won't bring back the dead
          kids.

_____19. Why were there no indictments against National
          Guard officers? Why were no public officials
          named in indictments? Was there a threat to the
          lives of Guardsmen? What was revealed to this
          grand jury that was not told to the earlier grand
          jury in Portage County and to the Justice Depart-
          ment?

_____20. The kids asked for trouble. The Guardsmen didn't
          start it.

_____21. The grand jury decision makes it clear that former
          Governor Rhodes was not responsible for the shoot-
          ings.

_____22. Apparently the grand jury had some information
that wasn't known before.

_____23. The grand jury action makes it clear the students
had every right to be protesting and demonstrating and that it was Guardsmen who assaulted and
intimidated the students.

_____24. The students shot at by the Guard were hippy, radi-
cal Communists.

_____25. I don't think the Guardsmen had a right to shoot.
They should get at least five years in jail.

_____26. I am delighted to see the natural course of justice
taking place. It's not as important to me to see
Guardsmen convicted as to see the truth come out.

_____27. The length of time between the shootings and the
federal grand jury was excessive; the matter should
have been dropped.

_____28. My civil rights, 75% of the students' and the
people of Kent's civil rights were violated by
those rioting students.

_____29. I've almost lost confidence in the court system.

_____30. How can they get a fair trial? It's so long after,
and evidence is missing.

_____31. I feel the Justice Department has been selective
in its prosecution and I can't figure out how they
can indict 8 out of 28 men who fired that day.

_____32. My confidence in Kent State University and KSU
students has been restored.

The 1975 Civil Trial Questionnaire, Before

Interview No. _____

THE FIRST SERIES OF QUESTIONS CONCERN SOME GENERAL CHARACTER-
ISTICS ABOUT YOURSELF AND SOME OF YOUR OPINIONS

1. In what year were you born? _____

2. What is your sex? ____M ____F

3. What is your hometown? _____

4. What is the approximate population of your hometown? _____

5. What year of college are you? ____F ____So ____J ____S

    ____MA ____PhD

6. What is your major field? _____

7. Has any member of your immediate family ever attended

    classes at or worked for Kent State University? ____No ___Yes

8. What is the occupation of your father? _____

    What is the occupation of your mother? _____

9. Into which of the following categories does the income

    of your family fall? ____under $5,000 ____$5,000-$10,000

    ____$10,000-$20,000 ____over $20,000

10. Politically, do you consider yourself a Democrat, a

    Republican, an Independent, or something else?

    ____Democrat ____Republican ____Independent ____Other

11. In terms of where you stand on most political issues,

    would you classify yourself as:

    ____Conservative ____Moderate ____Moderate liberal
    ____Moderate Conservative ____Liberal

12. Have you ever served with any branch of the U. S. Armed

    Services? ____Yes ____No

13. What is your opinion, overall, about:

    a. the townspeople in Kent
       ___Strongly favorable ___No opinion ___Unfavorable
       ___Favorable   ___Very unfavorable

14. What is your general opinion of Governor James Rhodes?

    ___Very favorable ___Undecided ___Unfavorable
    ___Favorable   ___Very Unfavorable

NOW WE WOULD LIKE FOR YOU TO THINK BACK TO THE EVENTS WHICH
OCCURRED IN KENT ON MAY 1-4, 1970

15. Were you living in Kent during the period May 1-4, 1970?

    ___Yes ___No

16. Were you a student at Knet State during the period May

    1-4, 1970? ___Yes ___No

17. Were you involved, either as a spectator or as a participant,

    in any of the events on campus or in town during that period?

    ___Yes ___No

18. What is the extent of your current interest in the events

    of May 1-4, 1970 and the events which have subsequently

    occurred? ___High ___Moderate ___Low ___None

19. Have you attended any of the May 4 memorial services

    held on campus? ___Yes ___No

NEXT WE WOULD LIKE TO ASK YOU SOME QUESTIONS ABOUT THE CURRENT
TRIAL

20. Prior to receiving this questionnaire, were you aware of

    the trial going on now in federal district court?

    ___Yes ___No

21. How much interest do you have in the current trial?

    ___A great deal ___A moderate amount ___A little
    ___None

22. Do you think the federal district court is an appropriate
    place to decide responsibility for the May 4th shootings?

    ___Yes ___No ___Uncertain

23. Do you think the trial will be fair and unbiased?

    ___Yes ___No ___Uncertain

24. Even though there has not been much newspaper coverage
    of the trial thus far, do you have an opinion as to the
    verdict which you think the jury will reach in this case?

    ___Yes ___No

25. If you answered "yes" to question 24, would you please
    indicate what verdict you think the jury will reach?

THE FOLLOWING ARE A SERIES OF STATEMENTS ABOUT THE COMMUNITY,
POLITICS, AND LIFE IN GENERAL. THEY ARE STATEMENTS OF OPINION
AND THERE ARE NO RIGHT OR WRONG ANSWERS. AFTER EACH STATEMENT,
PLEASE CHECK THE DEGREE TO WHICH YOU AGREE OR DISAGREE WITH
THE STATEMENT.

1. Local community news is generally more interesting than
   national or international news.

   ___Strongly agree   ___Undecided   ___Disagree
   ___Agree   ___Strongly disagree

2. I prefer the practical man anytime to the man of ideas.

   ___Strongly agree   ___Undecided   ___Disagree
   ___Agree   ___Strongly disagree

3. My hometown newspaper is extremely important in order to
   know what's going on.

   ___Strongly agree   ___Disagree
   ___Agree   ___Undecided   ___Strongly disagree

4. Sometimes politics and government seem so complicated
   that a person like me can't really understand what's

going on.

___Strongly agree   ___Undecided   ___Disagree
___Agree   ___Strongly disagree

5. A large number of city and county politicians are incom-

petent.

___Strongly agree   ___Undecided   ___Disagree
___Agree   ___Strongly disagree

6. If something grows up after a long time there will

always be much wisdom to it.

___Strongly agree   ___Undecided   ___Disagree
___Agree   ___Strongly disagree

7. The most rewarding organizations a person can belong to

are local organizations serving local needs.

___Strongly agree   ___Undecided   ___Disagree
___Agree   ___Strongly disagree

8. Money is an important factor influencing public policies.

___Strongly agree   ___Undecided   ___Disagree
___Agree   ___Strongly disagree

9. It's better to stick by what you have than to be trying

new things you don't really know about.

___Strongly agree   ___Undecided   ___Disagree
___Agree   ___Strongly disagree

10. People are frequently manipulated by politicians.

___Strongly agree   ___Undecided   ___Disagree
___Agree   ___Strongly disagree

11. National and international happenings rarely seem as

interesting and important as events that occur right in

the local community in which I live.

___Strongly agree   ___Undecided   ___Disagree
___Agree   ___Strongly disagree

12. If you start trying to change things very much you
    usually make them worse.

    ___Strongly agree ___Undecided ___Disagree
    ___Agree   ___Strongly disagree

13. Politicians represent the general interest more fre-
    quently than they represent special interests.

    ___Strongly agree ___Undecided ___Disagree
    ___Agree   ___Strongly disagree

14. I'd want to know that something would really work before
    I'd be willing to take a chance on it.

    ___Strongly agree ___Undecided ___Disagree
    ___Agree   ___Strongly disagree

15. National and international events are largely important
    because of the way they affect my local community.

    ___Strongly agree ___Undecided ___Disagree
    ___Agree   ___Strongly disagree

16. We must respect the work of our forefathers and not
    think that we know better than they did.

    ___Strongly agree ___Undecided ___Disagree
    ___Agree   ___Strongly disagree

17. Politicians spend most of their time getting re-elected
    or reappointed.

    ___Strongly agree ___Undecided ___Disagree
    ___Agree   ___Strongly disagree

18. A man doesn't have much wisdom until he is well along in
    years.

    ___Strongly agree ___Undecided ___Disagree
    ___Agree   ___Strongly disagree

19. Big cities have their places, but when you get right down

to it the local community is the backbone of America.

____Strongly agree   ____Undecided   ____Disagree
____Agree   ____Strongly disagree

20. Meeting and knowing many people is extremely important

in establishing myself in the community.

____Strongly agree   ____Undecided   ____Disagree
____Agree   ____Strongly disagree

21. Many personal relationships and contacts with other

people in the local community are essential in life

today.

____Strongly agree   ____Undecided   ____Disagree
____Agree   ____Strongly disagree

THE FOLLOWING ARE A SERIES OF STATEMENTS ABOUT THE COURTS AND
THE JUDICIAL PROCESS. THEY ARE STATEMENTS OF OPINION AND THERE
ARE NO RIGHT OR WRONG ANSWERS. PLEASE CHECK THE DEGREE TO
WHICH YOU AGREE OR DISAGREE WITH EACH STATEMENT.

1. Ordinarily, the average person will get a just trial in

America.

____Strongly agree   ____Undecided   ____Disagree
____Agree   ____Strongly disagree

2. Most court cases are so long and involved it is difficult

for a person like me to know who is guilty.

____Strongly agree   ____Undecided   ____Disagree
____Agree   ____Strongly disagree

3. Most juries just do what the judge and the prosecutor

tell them to do.

____Strongly agree   ____Undecided   ____Disagree
____Agree   ____Strongly disagree

4. The courts are too harsh in sentencing people convicted
   of breaking the law.

   ___Strongly agree   ___Undecided   ___Disagree
   ___Agree   ___Strongly disagree

5. If someone is brought to trial, they're probably guilty.

   ___Strongly agree   ___Undecided   ___Disagree
   ___Agree   ___Strongly disagree

6. The federal district court will determine, once and for
   all, who was responsible for the shootings of May 4, 1970.

   ___Strongly agree   ___Undecided   ___Disagree
   ___Agree   ___Strongly disagree

7. Wealthy and well-known people are less likely to be
   convicted in a trial than someone like me.

   ___Strongly agree   ___Undecided   ___Disagree
   ___Agree   ___Strongly disagree

8. The law is so complex that it is difficult to convict
   someone even if they are guilty.

   ___Strongly agree   ___Undecided   ___Disagree
   ___Agree   ___Strongly disagree

9. Even if people don't like a court's verdict they should
   accept it.

   ___Strongly agree   ___Undecided   ___Disagree
   ___Agree   ___Strongly disagree

10. In regard to the shootings of May 4, 1970, justice has
    not yet been realized in the American courts.

    ___Strongly agree   ___Undecided   ___Disagree
    ___Agree   ___Strongly disagree

11. If chosen to serve on a jury, I would willingly do so.

    ____Strongly agree   ____Undecided   ____Disagree
    ____Agree   ____Strongly disagree

12. The sentences for the Watergate defendents were too light.

    ____Strongly agree   ____Undecided   ____Disagree
    ____Agree   ____Strongly disagree

13. The law is very complicated so it's fortunate that we have

well-trained judges to tell us what it means.

    ____Strongly agree   ____Undecided   ____Disagree
    ____Agree   ____Strongly disagree

14. If you were charged with a crime, would you want a trial

by a judge alone or by a jury?

    ____Judge alone   ____Jury   ____No difference

15. Despite its flaws, the American judicial system is pro-

bably the best one in the world.

    ____Strongly agree   ____Undecided   ____Disagree
    ____Agree   ____Strongly disagree

IN THE SPACE BELOW, PLEASE CHECK THE DEGREE TO WHICH YOU
BELIEVE THE FOLLOWING PEOPLE WERE RESPONSIBLE FOR THE SHOOTINGS
OF MAY 4, 1970.

	Very Responsible	Moderately Responsible	Minimally Responsible	Not Responsible
Governor Rhodes				
Non-radical students				
KSU President White				
Radical students				
Officers of the National Guard				
Non-student radicals				
Enlisted men of the National Guard				
Faculty at KSU				
President Nixon				
KSU Administrators				
Vice-President Agnew				
Others (specify)				

FIRST, WE WOULD LIKE TO ASK YOU SOME QUESTIONS ABOUT THE RE-
CENTLY CONCLUDED FEDERAL DISTRICT COURT TRIAL OF THE KENT
STATE SHOOTINGS OF 1970.

1. How well informed do you consider yourself about the case?

   ____Very well informed   ____Not very well informed
   ____Moderately well informed ____Not informed at all

2. Do you know what action was taken by the jury in this
   case?

   ____Yes   ____No

   (If you answered "No" to this question, do not complete
   the rest of the questionnaire)

3. Do you happen to remember the division of votes of the

   jury?

   ____Yes   ____No   ____Uncertain

   (If "yes") What was the division of the votes?

   __12-0 __11-1 __10-2 __9-3 __8-4

4. What is your general reaction to the jury's decision?

   ____Strongly agree with it ____Undecided ____Disagree
   ____Agree with it   ____Strongly
                                               Disagree
                                               with it

   If you would like to make some brief comments concerning
   your reaction, please feel free to do so.

5. How did you first become aware of the jury's decision?

   ____Magazine   ____Radio   ____Friend   ____Newspaper
   ____Television ____Family member   ____Other
   ____Don't remember

6. Did you get more information from other sources?

____Yes   ____No   ____Uncertain

(If "yes") Which other sources?

____Magazines   ____Radio   ____Friend   ____Newspaper
____Television   ____Family member   ____Other
____Don't remember

7. Were the sources of your information in agreement or

disagreement with the jury's dicision?

____Generally in agreement   ____Generally in dis-
                                         agreement
____Some agreed, some disagreed   ____Took no position

8. To what extent did you discuss the jury's decision with

other people?

____A great deal   ____Some   ____Little   ____None at all

9. Do you recall informing others of the jury's decision?

____Yes   ____No   ____Don't remember

10. Do most of your friends agree with your views about the

jury's decision?

____Yes   ____No   ____Some do, some don't
____Uncertain

11. How much interest did you have in this trial?

____A great deal   ____A moderate amount   ____A little
____None

12. To what extent was your interest in the current trial

heightened by your participation in this survey?

____A great deal   ____A moderate amount   ____A little
____None

13. How important to you in a personal, emotional sense was

the trial?

____Very important   ____Somewhat important
____Not very important ____Not important at all

14. Do you think the federal district court was an appro-

    priate place to decide responsibility for the May 4

    shootings?

    ____Yes   ____No   ____Don't know

15. Do you think the trial was fair and unbiased?

    ____Yes   ____No   ____Don't know

16. To what extent do you think the trial resolved important

    questions raised by the events of May 4, 1970?

    ____Resolved all questions   ____Resolved few questions
    ____Resolved most questions   ____Resolved no questions
    ____Resolved some questions

17. What are your present feelings, overall, about the towns-

    people of Kent?

    ____Strongly favorable   ____No opinion   ____Unfavorable
    ____Favorable   ____Strongly
                                                    Unfavorable

18. What are your present feelings, overall, about the

    students of Kent State University?

    ____Strongly favorable   ____No opinion   ____Unfavorable
    ____Favorable   ____Strongly
                                                    Unfavorable

19. What are your present feelings, overall, about Kent State

    University?

    ____Strongly favorable   ____No opinion   ____Unfavorable
    ____Favorable   ____Strongly
                                                    Unfavorable

20. What is your present opinion of Governor James Rhodes?

    ____Strongly favorable   ____Undecided   ____Unfavorable
    ____Favorable   ____Strongly
                                                   Unfavorable

21. Have your feelings about either the townspeople of

    Kent, Kent State students, Kent State University, or

    Governor Rhodes been affected by the recent trial?

    ____Yes   ____No   ____Uncertain

    (If "yes") Toward whom have your feelings changed?

    (check as many as apply)

    ____Kent townspeople   ____KSU students   ____KSU
    ____Governor Rhodes

THE FOLLOWING ARE A SERIES OF STATEMENTS ABOUT THE COURTS
AND THE JUDICIAL PROCESS. THEY ARE STATEMENTS OF OPINION AND
THERE ARE NO RIGHT OR WRONG ANSWERS. PLEASE CHECK THE DEGREE
TO WHICH YOU AGREE OR DISAGREE WITH EACH STATEMENT.

1. Ordinarily, the average person will get a just trial in

   America?

       ____Strongly agree   ____Undecided   ____Disagree
       ____Agree   ____Strongly disagree

2. Most court cases are so long and involved it is diffi-

   cult for a person like me to know who is guilty.

       ____Strongly agree   ____Undecided   ____Disagree
       ____Agree   ____Strongly disagree

3. Most juries just do what the judge and the prosecutor

   tell them to do.

       ____Strongly agree   ____Undecided   ____Disagree
       ____Agree   ____Strongly disagree

4. The courts are too harsh in sentencing people convicted

   of breaking the law.

       ____Strongly agree   ____Undecided   ____Disagree
       ____Agree   ____Strongly disagree

5. If someone is brought to trial, they're probably guilty.

       ____Strongly agree   ____Undecided   ____Disagree
       ____Agree   ____Strongly disagree

6. Wealthy and well-known people are less likely to be convicted in a trial than someone like me.

____Strongly agree   ____Undecided   ____Disagree
____Agree   ____Strongly disagree

7. The law is so complex that it is difficult to convict someone even if they are guilty.

____Strongly agree   ____Undecided   ____Disagree
____Agree   ____Strongly disagree

8. Even if people don't like a court's verdict they should accept it.

____Strongly agree   ____Undecided   ____Disagree
____Agree   ____Strongly disagree

9. If chosen to serve on a jury, I would willingly do so.

____Strongly agree   ____Undecided   ____Disagree
____Agree   ____Strongly disagree

10. The sentences for the Watergate defendants were too light.

____Strongly agree   ____Undecided   ____Disagree
____Agree   ____Strongly disagree

11. The law is very complicated so it's fortunate that we have well-trained judges to tell us what it means.

____Strongly agree   ____Undecided   ____Disagree
____Agree   ____Strongly disagree

12. If you were charged with a crime, would you want a trial by a judge or by a jury?

___Judge alone   ___Jury   ___No difference   ___It depends

13. Despite its flaws, the American judicial system is probably the best one in the world.

____Strongly agree   ____Undecided   ____Disagree
____Agree   ____Strongly disagree

IN THE SPACE BELOW PLEASE CHECK THE DEGREE TO WHICH YOU BE-
LIEVE THE FOLLOWING PEOPLE WERE RESPONSIBLE FOR THE SHOOTINGS
OF MAY 4, 1970.

	Very Respons-ible	Moderately Responsible	Minimally Responsible	Not Responsible
Governor Rhodes				
Non-radical students				
KSU President White				
Radical Students				
Officers of the National Guard				
Non-student radicals				
Enlisted men of the National Guard				
Faculty at KSU				
President Nixon				
KSU Administra-tors				
Vice-President Agnew				
Others (specify)				

Have your opinions concerning responsibility for the shootings
changed because of the trial?

____Yes   ____No   ____Uncertain

(If "yes") Toward whom have your opinions changed?

(check as many as apply)

____ Governor Rhodes   ____ Non-radical students
____ KSU President White   ____ Radical students
____ Officers of the National   ____ Non-student radicals
____ Guard
____ Enlisted men of the   ____ Faculty at KSU
____ National Guard
____ President Nixon   ____ KSU Administrators
____ Vice-President Agnew   ____ Others(please specify)

THE FOLLOWING STATEMENTS WERE MADE BY PEOPLE ABOUT THE RECENT
TRIAL. IT IS CLEAR THAT SOME PEOPLE AGREED WITH THE DECISION
WHILE OTHERS DID NOT. BEFORE EACH STATEMENT BELOW, PLEASE
PLACE THE NUMBER WHICH INDICATES THE EXTENT TO WHICH YOU AGREE
OR DISAGREE WITH THE STATEMENT.

+3	+2	+1	0	-1	-2	-3
Strongly Agree	Agree	Weakly Agree	Undecided	Weakly Disagree	Disagree	Strongly Disagree

____ 1. Blame should not be placed on the young, inexperienced
        guardsmen who faced a difficult situation.

____ 2. The verdict shows that our judicial system doesn't
        work.

____ 3. You almost have to take this case out of the state
        to the U. S. Supreme Court to get a fair trial
        because the people of Ohio elected Rhodes.

____ 4. The verdict did not reflect the overwhelming evidence
        in favor of the case presented for the dead and
        wounded students.

____ 5. The students had a right to be out there demon-
        strating and they did not deserve to be shot.

____ 6. The judge committed a number of errors which were
        detrimental to the students' case.

____ 7. Even if no one was found liable, I am satisfied that
        the story is set straight.

____ 8. The verdict supports the system of jurisprudence
        and law enforcement across the nation.

_____ 9. Thanks to the jury murder by the state is approved.

_____ 10. This country is based upon a system of justice; if the court said the defendents weren't guilty, then they simply aren't guilty.

_____ 11. Any other verdict would have opened the way to lawlessness and permissiveness.

_____ 12. Based on the evidence, I don't see how the trial could have turned out any other way.

_____ 13. The guardsmen didn't do anything wrong, because all they were doing was their duty.

_____ 14. The decision was just because the guardsmen were in danger.

_____ 15. The careful and unfolding process of our democratic system allowed all parties the opportunity to explore all avenues in open court.

_____ 16. I've almost lost confidence in the court system because of the decision in this case.

_____ 17. I think it was a just decison.

_____ 18. How can there be a fair trial when it is so long after and evidence is missing?

_____ 19. In regard to the shootings of May 4, 1970, justice has not yet been realized in the American courts.

_____ 20. As disgusting as the outcome of the trial was, we should not be too surprised. For, over the past years, we have learned through bitter experience what we can expect from the courts.

_____ 21. The federal district court in Cleveland has determined, once and for all, who was responsible for the shootings of May 4, 1970.

_____ 22. The trials have been nothing but a big show to whitewash what cannot be covered up. There are obviously guilty criminals in Rhodes and the higher ups in the National Guard.

_____ 23. The guardsmen have civil rights too. I wonder if anyone is looking after them.

____ 24. Billed as a trial that would bring forth the
         truth for the first time in more than five years,
         the lengthy courtroom proceedings saw conflicts in
         testimony in which "the truth" varied from witness
         to witness.

____ 25. No one will probably ever know who, if anyone, was
         really to blame for what happened.

____ 26. Kent State students and young people in Kent are
         displeased with the verdict. Their parents and
         older townspeople are not.

____ 27. The jury examined the facts presented to them and
         arrived at a verdict based upon those facts.

____ 28. If the jurors could have considered the liability
         of individual guardsmen rather than having to
         decide on the liability of all of them, there
         probably would have been some guardsmen found liable.

____ 29. The basis for the ruling seems clear to me.

____ 30. The jury's decision was clear.

THANK YOU VERY MUCH FOR COMPLETING THIS QUESTIONNAIRE!

____ Check here if you would like to receive a copy of the
     report we will prepare on this study.

APPENDIX E: The 1979 Civil Trial Questionnaire, Before

Interview No.____

THE FIRST SERIES OF QUESTIONS CONCERN SOME GENERAL CHARACTER-
ISTICS ABOUT YOURSELF AND SOME OF YOUR OPINIONS

1. In what year were you born? ____

2. What is your sex? ____F ____M

3. What is your hometown? _____

4. What is the approximate population of your hometown? ____

5. What year of college are you? ___F ___So ___J ___Se
    ____M.A. ___Ph.D

6. What is your major field? _____

7. Has any member of your immediate family even attended

    classes at or worked for Kent State University? ___Yes ___No

8. What is the occupation of your father? _____

    What is the occupation of your mother? _____

9. Into which of the following categories does the income

    of your family fall? ____under $5,000 ____$5,000-10,000

    ____$10,001-15,000 ____$15,001-$20,000 ____$20,001-$30,000

    ____over $30,000

10. Politically, do you consider yourself a Democrat , a Re-

    publican, an Independent, or something else: ____Democrat

    ____Republican ____Independent ____Other

11. In terms of where you stand on most political issues,

    would you classify yourself as:

    ____Conservative   ____Moderate   ____Moderate liberal
    ____Moderate conservative   ____Liberal

12. Have you ever served with any branch of the U. S. Armed

    Services? ____Yes ____No

    If you answered yes, were you: ____an officer ____an en-
                                                  listed man

13. What is your opinion, overall, about:

    a. The townspeople in Kent

        ____Strongly favorable ___No opinion ___Unfavorable
        ____Favorable   ___Very unfavorable

    b. the students at Kent State University

        ____Strongly favorable ___No opinion ___Unfavorable
        ____Favorable   ___Strongly
                                                 unfavorable

    c. Kent State University

        ____Strongly favorable ___No opinion ___Unfavorable
        ____Favorable   ___Strongly
                                                 unfavorable

14. What is your general opinion of Governor James Rhodes?

    ____Very favorable ____Undecided ___Unfavorable
    ____Favorable   ___Strongly unfavorable

NOW WE WOULD LIKE FOR YOU TO THINK BACK TO THE EVENTS WHICH
OCCURRED IN KENT ON MAY 1-4, 1970.

15. Were you living in Kent during the period May 1-4, 1970?

    ____Yes ____No

16. Were you a student at Kent State during the period May

    1-4, 1970? ____Yes ____No

17. Were you involved, either as a spectator or as a parti-

    cipant, in any of the events on campus or in town during

    that period? ___Yes ____No

18. What is the extent of your current interest in the
    events of May 1-4, 1970 and the events which have sub-
    sequently occurred?

    ___High ___Moderate ___Low ___None

19. Have you attended any of the May 4 memorial services
    held on campus? ___Yes ___No

20. Were you involved in any of the activities relating to
    the recent controversy over the building at the gymnasium
    annex? ___Yes ___No

21. If you answered yes to question 20, would you please
    indicate briefly the nature of your activities?

22. Prior to receiving this questionnaire, were you aware
    of the trial in the federal district court? ___Yes ___No

23. How much interest do you have in the current trial:

    ___A great deal ___A moderate amount ___A little ___None

24. Do you think the federal district court is an appropriate
    place to decide responsibility for the May 4th shootings?

    ___Yes ___No ___Uncertain

25. Do you think the trial will be fair and unbiased?

    ___Yes ___No ___Uncertain

26. Even though there has not been much newspaper coverage
    of the trial thus far, do you have an opinion as to the
    verdict which you think the jury will reach in this case?

    ___Yes ___No

27. If you answered "yes" to question 24, would you please

indicate what verdict you think the jury will reach?

THE FOLLOWING ARE A SERIES OF STATEMENTS ABOUT THE COURTS AND
THE JUDICIAL PROCESS. THEY ARE STATEMENTS OF OPINION AND THERE
ARE NO RIGHT OR WRONG ANSWERS. PLEASE CHECK THE DEGREE TO
WHICH YOU AGREE OR DISAGREE WITH EACH STATEMENT.

1. Ordinarily, the average person will get a just trial in

America.

___Strongly Agree   ___Undecided   ___Disagree
___Agree   ___Strongly disagree

2. Most court cases are so long and involved it is difficult

for a person like me to know who is guilty.

___Strongly Agree   ___Undecided   ___Disagree
___Agree   ___Strongly disagree

3. Most juries just do what the judge and the prosecutor

tell them to do.

___Strongly agree   ___Undecided   ___Disagree
___Agree   ___Strongly disagree

4. The courts are too harsh in sentencing people convicted

of breaking the law.

___Strongly agree   ___Undecided   ___Disagree
___Agree   ___Strongly disagree

5. If someone is brought to trial, they're probably guilty.

___Strongly agree   ___Undecided   ___Disagree
___Agree   ___Strongly disagree

6. The federal district court will determine, once and for

all, who was responsible for the shootings of May 4, 1970.

___Strongly Agree   ___Undecided   ___Disagree
___Agree   ___Strongly disagree

7. Wealthy and well-known people are less likely to be

   convicted in a trial than someone like me.

   ___Strongly Agree   ___Undecided   ___Disagree
   ___Agree   ___Strongly disagree

8. The law is so complex that it is difficult to convict

   someone even if they are guilty.

   ___Strongly Agree   ___Undecided   ___Disagree
   ___Agree   ___Strongly disagree

9. Even if people don't like a court's verdict they should

   accept it.

   ___Strongly Agree   ___Undecided   ___Disagree
   ___Agree   ___Strongly disagree

10. In regard to the shootings of May 4, 1970, justice has

    not yet been realized in the American courts.

    ___Strongly Agree   ___Undecided   ___Disagree
    ___Agree   ___Strongly disagree

11. If chosen to serve on a jury, I would willingly do so.

    ___Strongly Agree   ___Undecided   ___Disagree
    ___Agree   ___Strongly disagree

12. The law is very complicated so it's fortunate that we

    have well-trained judges to tell us what it means.

    ___Strongly Agree   ___Undecided   ___Disagree
    ___Agree   ___Strongly disagree

13. If you were charged with a crime, would you want a trial

    by a judge alone or by a jury?

    ___Judge alone   ___Jury   ___No Difference

14. Despite its flaws, the American judicial system is

    probably the best one in the world.

    ___Strongly Agree   ___Undecided   ___Disagree
    ___Agree   ___Strongly disagree

15. Most court cases are so long and involved it is difficult

for a person like me to know who is guilty.

___Strongly Agree   ___Undecided   ___Disagree
___Agree   ___Strongly disagree

IN THE SPACE BELOW PLEASE CHECK THE DEGREE TO WHICH YOU BE-
LIEVE THE FOLLOWING PEOPLE WERE RESPONSIBLE FOR THE SHOOTINGS
OF MAY 4, 1970.

	Very Responsible	Moderately Responsible	Minimally Responsible	Not Responsible
Governor Rhodes				
Non-Radical students				
KSU President White				
Radical Students				
Officers of the National Guard				
Non-student radicals				
Enlisted men of the National Guard				
Faculty at KSU				
President Nixon				
KSU Administrators				
Vice-President Agnew				
Others (specify)				

APPENDIX F: The 1979 Civil Trial Questionnaire, After

FIRST WE WOULD LIKE TO ASK YOU SOME QUESTIONS ABOUT THE
RECENTLY CONCLUDED FEDERAL DISTRICT COURT TRIAL OF THE KENT
STATE SHOOTINGS OF MAY 1970.

1. How well informed do you consider yourself about the

   case?

   ___Very well informed   ___Not very well informed
   ___Moderately well informed ___Not informed at all

2. Are you aware that there was an out-of-court settlement?

   ___Yes ___No

   (If you answered "No" to this question, then go to question
   24.)

3. Are you aware of the basic terms of the settlement?

   ___Yes ___No ___Uncertain

   (If yes or uncertain) What do you think are the most
   important terms of the settlement?

   _____

   _____

   _____

4. Do you happen to remember the total dollar amount that

   was involved in the resolution of the case?

   ___Yes ___No

5. In regard to the monetary settlement, do you think that

   the plaintiffs

   ___Should have received more money
   ___Received about the right amount of money
   ___Should have received less money
   ___Undecided
   ___Don't know how much money was awarded

6. Have you read or heard about the statement written
   by the defendants--Governor Rhodes and the National
   Guardsmen--as part of the settlement?
   ___Yes ___No ___Not Sure
   (If "Yes") In your own words what did the statement say?

   _____

   _____

   _____

7. If you remember the statement, do you think that the
   statement by the defendants was an admission of responsibilty
   for the shootings?
   ___Yes ___No ___Uncertain ___Don't remember statement

8. What is your general reaction to the overall settlement?
   ___ Very satisfied   ___Undecided   ___Moderately
   ___ Moderately satisfied   dissatisfied
                                                ___Very dissatisfied

9. Based on the out-of-court settlement who do you think
   "won" the court case--the plaintiffs (the parents and
   wounded students) or the defendants (Governor Rhodes
   and the National Guardsmen)?
   ___Plaintiffs ___Defendants ___Both won ___Neither won

10. From what sources did you learn about the settlement in
    the case? (Check as many as apply)
    ___Magazine ___Radio ___Friend ___Newspaper ___Television
    ___Family member ___Other ___Don't know

11. What was your primary source of information?

    _____

12. To what extent did you read about the settlement in the
    following newspapers?

	Great deal	Some	Little	None
Daily Kent Stater				
Akron Beacon Journal				
Record Courier				
Other_____				

13. Were the media you used for information in agreement or
    disagreement with the settlement?

    ___Generally in agreement   ___Generally in disagreement
    ___Some agreed, some disagreed ___Took no position

14. Have you talked to others about the settlement?

    ___Yes ___No

    (If "Yes") Did they agree with your evaluation of the
    settlement?
    ___Yes ___Some did, some didn't ___No

    When talking to others about the settlement did you
    (check those answers which apply)

    ___Give information about the settlement
    ___Receive information about the settlement
    ___Give your opinion about the settlement
    ___Listen to others' opinions about the settlement

15. How much interest did you have in this trial?

    ___A great deal ___A moderate amount ___A little ___None

16. To what extent was your interest in the current trial
    heightened by your participation in this survey?

    ___A great deal ___A moderate amount ___A little ___None

17. How important to you in a personal, emotional sense was
    the trial?

    ___Very important   ___Not very important
    ___Somewhat important   ___Not important at all

18. Do you think the federal district court was an appropriate place to decide responsibility for the May 4 shootings?

____Yes ____No ____Uncertain

19. Do you think the process of settling the civil suit out-of-court was fair and unbiased?

____Yes ____No ____Uncertain

20. Do you think the federal district judge was instrumental in getting the parties to agree to terms?

____Yes ____No ____Uncertain

21. To what extent do you think the settlement resolved important questions raised by the events of May 4, 1970?

____Resolved all questions   ____Resolved a few questions
____Resolved most questions   ____Resolved no questions
____Resolved some questions

22. In your own words, why do you think an out-of-court se settlement was reached?

_____

_____

_____

23. Do you believe an out-of-court settlement is a legitimate way to resolve a lawsuti?

____Yes ____No ____Uncertain

THE FOLLOWING ARE A SERIES OF STATEMENTS ABOUT THE COURTS AND THE JUDICIAL PROCESS. THEY ARE STATEMENTS OF OPINION AND THERE ARE NO RIGHT OR WRONG ANSWERS. PLEASE CHECK THE DEGREE TO WHICH YOU AGREE OR DISAGREE WITH EACH STATEMENT.

24. Ordinarily, the average person will get a just trial in America.

_____Strongly Agree _____Undecided _____Disagree
_____Agree   _____Strongly disagree

25. Most court cases are so long and involved it is diff-

icult for a person like me to know who is guilty.

_____Strongly agree _____Undecided _____Disagree
_____Agree   _____Strongly disagree

26. Most juries just do what the judge and the prosecutor

tell them to do.

_____Strongly agree _____Undecided _____Disagree
_____Agree   _____Strongly disagree

27. The courts are too harsh in sentencing people convicted

of breaking the law.

_____Strongly agree _____Undecided _____Disagree
_____Agree   _____Strongly disagree

28. If someone is brought to trial, they're probably guilty.

_____Strongly agree _____Undecided _____Disagree
_____Agree   _____Strongly disagree

29. The out-of-court settlement resolves, once and for all,

who was responsible for the 1970 shootings.

_____Strongly agree _____Undecided _____Disagree
_____Agree   _____Strongly disagree

30. Wealthy and well-known people are less likely to be

convicted in a trial than someone like me.

_____Strongly agree _____Undecided _____Disagree
_____Agree   _____Strongly disagree

31. The law is so complex that it is difficult to convict

someone even if they are guilty.

_____Strongly agree _____Undecided _____Disagree
_____Agree   _____Strongly disagree

32. Even if people don't like a court's verdict they should
    accept it.

    ____Strongly agree   ____Undecided   ____Disagree
    ____Agree   ____Strongly disagree

33. If chosen to serve on a jury, I would willingly do so.

    ____Strongly agree   ____Undecided   ____Disagree
    ____Agree   ____Strongly disagree

34. In regard to the shootings of May 4, 1970, justice has
    not yet been realized.

    ____Strongly agree   ____Undecided   ____Disagree
    ____Agree   ____Strongly disagree

35. The law is very complicated so it's fortunate that we
    have well-trained judges to tell us what it means.

    ____Strongly agree   ____Undecided   ____Disagree
    ____Agree   ____Strongly disagree

36. Despite its flaws, the American judicial system is
    probably the best one in the world.

    ____Strongly agree   ____Undecided   ____Disagree
    ____Agree   ____Strongly disagree

37. I am relieved that the settlement finally ends the liti-
    gation stemming from the May 4th shootings.

    ____Strongly agree   ____Undecided   ____Disagree
    ____Agree   ____Strongly disagree

IN THE SPACE BELOW PLEASE CHECK THE DEGREE TO WHICH YOU BE-
LIEVE THE FOLLOWING PEOPLE WERE RESPONSIBLE FOR THE SHOOTINGS
OF MAY 4, 1970.

	Very Responsible	Moderately Responsible	Minimally Responsible	Not responsible
Governor Rhodes				
Non-radical students				
KSU President White				
Radical students				
Officers of the National Guard				
Non-student radicals				
Enlisted men of the National Guard				
Faculty at KSU				
President Nixon				
KSU administrators				
Vice-President Agnew				
Others (specify)				

THE FOLLOWING STATEMENTS WERE MADE BY PEOPLE ABOUT THE RECENT
TRIAL. IT IS CLEAR THAT PEOPLE HAD WIDELY VARYING REACTIONS TO
THE SETTLEMENT. BEFORE EACH STATEMENT BELOW, PLEASE PLACE THE
NUMBER WHICH BEST INDICATES THE EXTENT TO WHICH YOU AGREE OR
DISAGREE WITH THE STATEMENT.

3	2	1	0	-1	-2	-3
Strongly Agree	Weakly	Undecided	Weakly	Disagree	Strongly
agree		Agree		Disagree		Disagree

_____I don't read the statement by the defendants as an apology
but as an expression of grievance.

_____I'm glad the trials are finally over.

_____When justice seemed attainable, the plaintiffs settled for
money instead.

_____It has never been easy or simple--or perhaps possible--
to fix the blame for the events that occurred on the Kent
campus May 4th 1970. So it is only right that the settlement does not forever place the blame with the students or
the guardsmen or the governor who ordered them onto campus.

_____The defendants' statement is an admission of moral respon-
sibility and the compensation is an acknowledgement of
legal liability.

_____Our judicial system is in trouble when plaintiffs and their
families are rewarded for civil disturbances.

_____This is something I think everybody in America would like
to forget.

_____The taxpayers get hit with the bill. If the governor and
the guardsmen were liable, then they should have been made
to pay for it out of their own pockets.

_____This means the court will not investigate the situation to
find out what happened and why, and that is a real shame.

_____Although there was no admission of guilt from the defendants
the settlement itself implies that those who acted for the
state bore some responsibility for the tragedy.

_____This settlement is a great bargain for the state. Without
it the costs are likely to be millions before this thing is
finished.

____This case has reaffirmed my sense of democracy and my feelings that the system really does work.

____The settlement will help the tarnished image of KSU.

____I am stunned at the utterly inadequate amount of money that has been paid.

____The terms of the settlement perhaps came as close to justice as any neutral observer could hope for.

____The settlement accomplished to the greatest extent possible under present law the objectives toward which the families have struggled during the past eight years.

____The defendants expressed sorrow and regret for what happened. But this is no admission of liability.

____No outcome could have undone what happened, and none could have altogether satisfied those who most sharply disagree on the subject. But this one seems at least reasonable and humane.

____The statement of regret can only be seen as an apology by someone who desperately wants to do so.

____It is time to look ahead, to learn from the mistakes of the past, and turn the bitterness into more constructive emotions and ventures.

____We would have liked to have seen a real admission of guilt from a legal standpoint, but it seems realistically as much as we could have hoped for.

____I think it is an outrage and an insult to the vast majority of Americans that any money is being paid to the students or families involved at Kent.

THANK YOU VERY MUCH FOR COMPLETING THIS QUESTIONNAIRE!

____Check here if you would like to receive a copy of the report we will prepare on this study.

Bibliography

BOOKS

Abelson, Robert, et al., eds. *Theories of Cognitive Consistency: A Sourcebook.* Chicago: Rand McNally and Co., 1968.

Abraham, Henry, J. *The Judicial Process,* 3rd ed. New York: Oxford University Press, 1975.

Becker, Theodore and Feeley, Malcolm, eds. *The Impact of Supreme Court Decisions,* 2nd ed. New York: Oxford University Press, 1972.

Casale, Ottavio and Paskoff, Louis, eds. *The Kent State Affair: Documents and Interpretations.* Boston: Houghton Mifflin, 1971.

Campbell, Donald T. and Stanley, Julian C. *Experimental and Quasi-Experimental Designs for Research.* Chicago: Rand McNally and Co., 1963.

Davies, Peter, *The Truth About Kent State: A Challenge to the American Conscience.* New York: Farrar, Straus & Giroux, 1973.

Easton, David. *A Systems Analysis of Political Life.* New York: John Wiley and Sons, 1965.

Eszterhas, Joe and Roberts, Michael. *Thirteen Seconds: Confrontation at Kent State.* New York: Dodd, Mead, 1970.

Goldman, Sheldon and Jahnige, Thomas P. *The Federal Courts as a Political System,* 2nd ed. New York: Harper & Row, 1976.

Goldman, Sheldon and Sarat, Austin, eds. *American Court Systems.* San Francisco: W. W. Freeman and Co., 1978.

Grant, Edward, and Hill, Michael. *I Was There: What Really Went on at Kent State.* Lima, Oh.: C. S. S. Publishing Co., 1974.

Hensley, Thomas R. and Lewis, Jerry M., eds. *Kent State and May 4th: A Social Science Perspective.* Dubuque, Ia.: Kendall/Hunt, 1978.

Johnson, Richard. *The Dynamics of Compliance: Supreme Court Decision-Making from a New Perspective.* Evanston, Ill.: Northwestern University Press, 1967.

Kelner, Joseph and Munves, James. *The Kent State Coverup.* New York: Harper & Row, 1980.

Kerlinger, Fred N. *Foundations of Behavioral Research,* 2nd ed. New York: Holt, Rinehart, & Winston, Inc., 1973.

Kirk, Roger E. *Experimental Designs: Procedures for the Behavioral Sciences.* Belmont, California: Brooks Cole Publishing Co., 1968.
Krislov, Samuel, et al., eds. *Compliance and the Law: A Multidisciplinary Approach.* Beverly Hills: Sage Publishing Co., 1972.
Manheim, Jarol B. *The Politics Within: A Primer in Political Attitudes and Behavior.* Englewood Cliffs, N.J.: Prentice-Hall, 1975.
McConnell, James V. *Understanding Human Behavior.* New York: Holt, Rinehart & Winston, Inc., 1974.
McLauchlan, William P. *American Legal Processes.* New York: John Wiley & Sons, 1977.
Michener, James. *Kent State: What Happened and Why.* New York: Random House, 1971.
Muir, William. *Prayer in the Public Schools: Law and Attitude Change.* Chicago: University of Chicago Press, 1967.
Murphy, Walter F. and Pritchett, Herman C., eds. *Courts, Judges, and Politics,* 3rd ed. New York: Random House, 1979.
Murphy, Walter, Tanenhaus, Joseph, and Kastner, Daniel. *Public Evaluations of Constitutional Courts: Alternative Explanations.* Beverly Hills: Sage Publications, 1973.
O'Neill, Robert M., Morris, John P. and Mack, Raymond. *No Heroes, No Villains.* Washington: Jossey-Bass, 1972.
Peterson, Richard E. and Bilowsky, John A. *May 1970: The Campus Aftermath of Cambodia and Kent State.* Berkeley, Calif.: Carnegie Commission on Higher Education, 1971.
Rosenau, James. *Public Opinion and Foreign Policy.* New York: Random House, 1961.
Sheldon, Charles H. *The American Judicial Process: Models and Approaches.* New York: Dodd, Mead & Co., 1974.
Shriver, Philip R. *The Years of Youth.* Kent, Ohio: Kent State University Press, 1960.
Stone, Isidor F. *The Killings at Kent State University: How Murder Went Unpunished.* New York: A New York Review Book, 1971.
Taylor, Stuart, et al. *Violence at Kent State, May 1 –4, 1970: The Students' Perspective.* New York: College Notes and Texts, 1971.
Tompkins, Phillip K. and Anderson, Elaine Vanden Bout. *Communication Crisis at Kent State: A Case Study.* New York: Gordon and Breach, 1971.
Warren, Bill. *The Middle of the Country: The Events of May 4th as Seen by Students and Faculty at Kent State University.* New York: Avon, 1970.
Wasby, Stephen. *The Impact of the United States Supreme Court.* Homewood, Ill.: Dorsey Press, 1970.
Wasby, Stephen. *Small Town Police and the Supreme Court: Hearing the Word.* Lexington, Mass.: Lexington Books, 1976.
Wasby, Stephen. *The Supreme Court in the Federal Judicial System.* New York: Holt, Rinehart & Winston, 1978.

ARTICLES

Adams, John P. "Kent State: Justice and Morality," *Cleveland State Law Review* 22, 1 (Winter 1973): 26–47.

Adamek, Raymond J. and Lewis, Jerry M. "Social Control Violence and Radicalization: Behavioral Data," *Social Problems* 22, 5 (June 1975): 663–74.

Adamek, Raymond J. and Lewis, Jerry M. "Social Control Violence and Radicalization: The Kent State Case," *Social Forces* 51 (March 1973): 341–47.

Baum, Lawrence. "Implementation of Judicial Decisions: An Organizational Analysis," *American Politics Quarterly* 4, 1 (January 1976): 86–114.

Bennett, Stephen Earl. "Consistency Among the Public's Social Welfare Policy Attitudes in the 1960's," *American Journal of Political Science* 17, 3 (August 1973): 544–70.

Best, James J. and Hensley, Thomas R. "Causes and Consequences of Student Perceptions of Responsibility for the 1970 Kent State Shootings," *Heuristics* 8, 11 (Spring 1978): 30–52.

Brown, Steven. "The Resistance to Reason: KSU 1969–1970," *Political Science Discussion Papers* 3, 1 (Spring 1971): 17–54.

Bullock, Charles S. and Rodgers, Harrell. "Coercion to Compliance: Southern School Districts and School Desegregation Guidelines," *Journal of Politics* 38, 4 (November 1976): 987–1011.

Carlson, James M. "Politics and Interpersonal Attraction," *American Politics Quarterly* 7, 1 (January 1979): 12–26.

Casey, Gregory. "Popular Perceptions of Supreme Court Rulings," *American Politics Quarterly*, 4, 1 (January 1976): 3–46.

Cronbach, L. J. and Furby, L. "How We Should Measure 'Change'—Or Should We?" *Psychological Bulletin* 74 (1970): 68–80.

Easton, David. "A Re-Assessment of the Concept of Political Support," *British Journal of Political Science* 5, 4 (October 1975): 435–58.

Easton, David. "An Approach to the Analysis of Political Systems," *World Politics* 9 (1957): 383–400.

Easton, David. "Theoretical Approaches to Political Support," *Canadian Journal of Political Science* 9, 3 (September 1976): 431–38.

Easton, David. "The New Revolution in Political Science," *American Political Science Review* 63 (December 1969): 1051–61.

Engdahl, David E. "Immunity and Accountability for Positive Governmental Wrongs," *University of Colorado Law Review* 44, 1 (1972).

Engdahl, David E. "Soldiers, Riots and Revolution: The Law and History of Military Troops in Civil Disorders," *Iowa Law Review* 57, 1 (October, 1971).

Engdahl, David E. "The Legal Background and Aftermath of the Kent State Tragedy," *Cleveland State Law Review* 22, 1 (Winter 1973): 3–25.

Engdahl, David E. "The Legislative History of the Law Revision Center: A Comprehensive Study of the Use of Military Troops in Civil Disorders, with Proposals for Legislative Reform," *University of Colorado Law Review* 42, (1972).

Engstrom, R. and Giles, M. "Expectations and Images: A Note on Diffuse Support for Legal Institutions," *Law and Society Review* 6, 4 (May 1972): 631–36.

Eszterhas, Joe and Roberts, Michael D. "James Michener's Kent State: A Study in Distortion," *The Progressive* 35 (September 1971): 35–40.

Farley, L. T. and Newkirk, M. G. "Measuring Attitude Change in Political Science Courses," *Teaching Political Science* 4, 2 (January 1977): 185–98.

Furlong, William. "The Guardsmen's View of the Tragedy at Kent State," *New York Times Magazine,* (June 1970).

Gatlin, Douglas S., Giles, Michael, and Cataldo, Everett, F. "Policy Support within a Target Group: The Case of School Desegregation," *American Political Science Review* 72, 3 (September 1978): 985–95.

Gross, Steven J. and Neman, Michael C. "Attitude-Behavior Consistency: A Review," *Public Opinion Quarterly* 39, 3 (Fall 1975): 358–68.

Hensley, Thomas R. and Sell, Deborah K. "A Study-Abroad Program: An Evaluation of Impacts on Student Attitudes," *Teaching Political Science* 6, 4 (July 1979): 387–412.

Hensley, Thomas. "The Impact of Judicial Decisions on Attitudes of an Attentive Public: The Kent State Trials, *Sociological Focus* 13, 3 (August 1980): 273–92.

Keller, Gordon. "Middle America Against the University: The Kent State Grand Jury," *The Humanist* 31 (March/April 1973): 28–29.

LaPiere, R. T. "Attitudes Versus Actions," *Social Forces* 13 (1934): 230–37.

Lehne, Richard and Reynolds, John. "The Impact of Judicial Activism on Public Opinion," *American Journal of Political Science* 22, 4 (November 1978): 896–904.

Lempert, Richard. "Strategies of Research Design in the Legal Impact Study: The Control of Plausible Rival Hypotheses," *Law and Society Review* 1 (November 1966): 111–32.

Levine, James P. "Methodological Concerns in Studying Judicial Efficacy," *Law and Society Review* 4 (1970): 583–611.

Lewis, Jerry M. "The Moods of May 4, 1970: The Students' View," *Political Science Discussion Papers* 3, 1 (Spring 1971): 1–15.

Lewis, Jerry M. "A Study of the Kent State Incident Using Smelser's Theory of Collective Behavior," *Sociological Inquiry* 42, 2 (1972): 87–96.

Linn, R. J. and Slinde, J. A. "The Determination of the Significance of Change Between Pre- and Post-Testing Periods," *Review of Educational Research* 47 (1977): 121–50.

Manning, W. H. and Dubois, P. H. "Correlational Methods in Research on Human Learning," *Perceptual and Motor Skills* 15 (1962): 287–321.

Merelman, Richard M. "On Social Psychology Handy Work: An Interpretive Review of *The Handbook of Social Psychology,* Second Edition," *American Political Science Review* 71, 3 (September 1977): 1109–20.

Miller, A. S. and Scheflin, A. W. "The Power of the Supreme Court in the Age of the Positive State: A Preliminary Excursus," *Duke Law Journal* (April 1967): 273–320.

Rodgers, Harrell R., Jr. "Law as an Instrument of Public Policy," *American Journal of Political Science* 17, 3 (August 1973): 638–47.

Rodgers, Harrell R., Jr. and Hanson, Roger. "The Rule of Law and Legal Efficacy: Private Values vs. General Standards," *Western Political Quarterly* 27 (1974): 387–94.

Rodgers, Harrell and Lewis, Edward. "Political Support and Compliance Attitudes," *American Politics Quarterly* 2 (1974): 61–77.

Sarat, Austin. "Support for the Legal System: An Analysis of Knowledge, Attitudes, and Behavior," *American Politics Quarterly* 3 (1975): 3–24.

Silverson, Randolph. "A Research Note on Cognitive Balance and International Conflict: Egypt and Israel in the Suez Crisis," *Western Political Quarterly* 27, 2 (1974): 387–94.

Sindell, Steven A. "Sovereign Immunity—An Argument Con," *Cleveland State Law Review* 22, 1 (Winter 1973): 55–71.

Spears, David, Hensler, Carl P., and Spear, Leslie K. "White's Opposition to 'Busing': Self-interest or Symbolic Politics?" *American Political Science Review* 73, 2 (June 1979): 369–84.

Stover, Robert V. and Brown, Don. "Understanding Compliance and Noncompliance with Law: The Contributions of Utility Theory," *Social Science Quarterly* 56 (1975): 363–75.

Thomas, Charles. "The Kent State Massacre: Blood on Whose Hands?" *Gallery* 7, 5 (April 1977): 39 ff.

Thomas, Judge William K. "Jury Selection in the Highly Publicized Case," *Columbus Bar Association Journal* 35, 5 (May 1979): 3–4 ff.

Wald, Kenneth D. and Lupfer, Michael B. "The Presidential Debate as a Civics Lesson," *Public Opinion Quarterly* 42, 3 (Fall 1978): 342–53.

Wasby, Stephen. "The Study of Supreme Court Impacts: A Round-Up," *Policy Studies Journal* 2, 2 (Winter 1973): 136–40.

Watts, Meredith M. and Sumi, David. "Studies in the Physiological Component of Aggression-Related Social Attitudes," *American Journal of Political Science* 23, 3 (August 1979): 528–58.

Zajonc, Robert. "The Concepts of Balance, Congruity, and Dissonance," *Public Opinion Quarterly* 24 (Summer 1960): 280–96.

PAPERS DELIVERED

Goldenson, Dennis R. "The Measurement of Attitude Intensity." Paper presented at the 1979 meeting of the Midwest Association for Public Opinion Research.

Hensley, Thomas R., Best, James J., and Heller, Marlyn. "The Impact of the 1975 Kent State Civil Trial on Student Attitudes: An Application of Dissonance Theory." Paper presented at the 1978 meeting of the Midwest Association for Public Opinion Research.

Hensley, Thomas R., Best, James J., and Heller, Marlyn. "The Impact of the 1974 'Kent State Grand Jury' on Student Attitudes Toward Guard Responsibility and

Judicial Support." Paper presented at the 1977 meeting of the Midwest Political Science Association.
Hensley, Thomas R. and Griffin, Glen. "The Kent State University Board of Trustees
and the 1977 Gymnasium Controversy: Victims of Groupthink?" Paper presented at the 1978 meeting of the Midwest Political Science Association.

DOCUMENTS AND OTHER RESOURCES

Akron Beacon Journal. *Kent State University Disorder: May 2, 1970 through April 29,
1971.* Wooster, Ohio: Bell and Howell Micro Photo Division, 1972.
Cuyahoga County Public Library. *Kent State Post-Mortem, An Index to Articles on
KSU Incident Appearing in The Cleveland Press and the Plain Dealer,
May–November 1970.* Cuyahoga County Public Library: Publication #22,
1971.
"Excerpts from Summary of F.B.I. Report on Kent State University Disorders Last
May." *The New York Times,* 30 October 1970.
"Kent State: The Search for Understanding," *Akron Beacon Journal,* 24 May 1970,
pp. 17–24.
Kent State University. *Commission on K.S.U. Violence.* Kent, Ohio. 1972 4 vols.
Knight Newspapers, Inc. *Reporting the Kent State Incident.* New York: American
Newspaper Publishers Association Foundation, 1971.
Krause v. Rhodes, Trial Transcript, 390 F. Supp. 1072 (N.D. Ohio, 1975).
Krause v. Rhodes, Brief for Appellants, 390 F. Supp. 1072 (N.D. Ohio, 1975), on
appeal.
Portage County, Ohio, Special Grand Jury. *Report of the Special Grand Jury.*
Ravenna, Ohio, Special Grand Jury, October 16, 1970.
U.S. Congress. House. Representative John Sieberling's Insertion of the Justice De-
partment's Summary of the F.B.I. Report. *Congressional Record,* January 15,
1973, pp. E207–E213.
U.S. Department of Commerce. *County and City Data Book: 1972.* U.S. Govern-
ment Printing Office, 1973.
U.S. President's Commission on Campus Unrest. *The Kent State Tragedy: Special
Report.* Washington, D.C.: U.S. Government Printing Office, 1970.
U.S. President's Commission on Campus Unrest. *Report.* Washington, D.C.: U.S.
Government Printing Office, 1970.

Index

277

About the Author

THOMAS R. HENSLEY is Associate Professor of Political Science at Kent State University. He is the co-author of *UNSIM: United Nations Security Council Simulation* and *Kent State and May 4th: A Social Science Perspective.*